The Reverend Dr Thomas Sedgwick Whalley and the Queen of Bath

A True Story of Georgian England at the Time of Jane Austen

**The Reverend Dr Thomas Sedgwick Whalley
and the Queen of Bath**
- 2014 -

Text © Christopher Stephens 2014
Edited by Will Rees
Cover by Bryn Lloyd
Layout by Steve Upham & Will Rees

Published by
Candy Jar Books, 113-116 Bute Street, Cardiff, CF10 5EQ
www.candy-jar.co.uk

A catalogue record of this book is
available from the British Library

ISBN: 978-0-9928607-6-9

Printed and bound in the UK by
CPI Group (UK) Ltd, Croydon, CR0 4YY

To my dear granddaughters, Charlotte and Abigail, in the hope that when they grow up they will derive as much enjoyment from studying the past as I have.

CONTENTS

ACKNOWLEDGEMENTS

Many people have been of great assistance in the collection of material for this book.

First, I suppose I should give thanks posthumously to the Reverend Dawe Hill Wickham for documenting and then publishing the selected correspondence of his great uncle. Second, to Brian Pike, very much alive, through whose contacts I was able to acquire these treasured volumes.

Then there are the members of the Langford History Group, particularly Alex Kolombos and John Gowar, Jo Fryer, Stan Croker and Pat Wilson, for their help and encouragement. Sheila Johnson of the Blagdon History Society provided many pieces of information from Langford and Blagdon, of which I was completely unaware, and Maria Forbes was my source of knowledge regarding the history of Winscombe.

It was my good fortune to make internet contact with Madeleine Gill and Jan Walsh, through which I gained access to the portrait miniatures of Richard Chaple Whalley and his wife. Through the same medium the discovery of Rick Crune's two papers on the Penningtons in America led to numerous email exchanges with the author and put me in contact with Michael Pascoe and his earlier work on the history of William Pennington.

Moira Bonnington, a national authority on "the Macaronis", gave me great assistance in unravelling the histories of General Horneck, the Military Macaroni, and his first wife, later to become Mrs Horneck Whalley. More recently, Kathryn Byrnell's diligent research led to the discovery of who the mysterious Robert Boyle (O') Sullivan really was.

Contact with the Chippenham/La Flèche Twinning Group and its members on both sides of the Channel, in particular Richard and Karin Meek in England and Monique and Guy Massé in France, led to the publication of a short article in 'Cahier Fléchois' and the discovery of Frances Sullivan's house in La Fléche and details of its purchase and later sale.

I am sure there must be others whom I have omitted to mention. My only excuse is that during 10 years of research I have not been so highly organised as I should have been.

ABBREVIATIONS TO MAJOR REFERENCES

JCTSW   Wickham, H.D., *Journals and correspondence of Thomas Sedgewick Whalley DD,* Vols 1-2, Richard Bentley, London, 1863

TPL   Bloom, E.A., Bloom, L.D., *The Piozzi Letters,* Vols I-VI, Associated University Presses, London, 1999

TIL   Knapp, O.G., *The intimate letters of Hester Piozzi and Penelope Pennington 1788-1821,* John Lane, The Bodley Head, London, 1913

ABBREVIATIONS TO MAJOR REFERENCES

INTRODUCTION

Disinterested intellectual curiosity is the life blood
of real civilization.

G. M. Trevelyan, *English Social History* (1942)

After I retired I was able to spend more time working as a volunteer for the Woodland Trust and improving my dry stone walling skills. One day, these two interests came together, and I was asked if I would assist the Trust in putting together a bid for Heritage Lottery funding to enable them to restore the perimeter wall of their Dolebury Warren Wood property in North Somerset. This had become dangerous and needed urgent attention as it bordered a public right of way. By this time I had become Deputy Chairman of the Dry Stone Walling Association of Great Britain and with a few colleagues had founded the SW England Branch of the DSWA. We were already running courses of basic instruction for the general public, and the possibility of assisting the Woodland Trust in the rebuilding of these dry stone walls seemed a mutually beneficial enterprise.

A grant application was to be submitted by the Trust under the Heritage Lottery Fund's "Local Heritage Initiative Scheme", and so there was a need to describe the contribution we would be making to local heritage and the community. A few hours spent in the local library and on the internet showed that we would have no difficulty at all in this respect, as the walls we were intending to rebuild had formed part of the estate which surrounded an Italianate house built in the late 18th century by the unusual Reverend Dr Thomas Sedgwick Whalley. After three years the walls have been successfully restored. Since then I have given many talks on Dr Whalley, including one to the Langford Local History Group, whose members have subsequently been a constant source of encouragement to undertake further investigation into his life and those of his friends.

The time has now come to set this all down. A starting point in my researches was the book published in two volumes by Whalley's great nephew the Reverend Dawe Hill Wickham; but this kindly and often sanitized collection of his great uncle's letters does not tell the whole story. A much wider perspective can be gained from the published letters of his friends Mrs Piozzi, Hannah More and Anna Seward, and various contemporary newspaper announcements and articles. Other writers, such as Thomas De Quincey, have penned cruel distortions of small parts of Thomas Sedgwick Whalley's long and eventful life. In this book I have tried to retell his life in a way which does it justice. This is a far from complete account, and I hope it will encourage others to fill its many gaps as well as correct any misconceptions I may have held.

The tragedy is that Mendip Lodge was demolished in the 1950s, something which would never be allowed to happen today, and since then its site and adjacent buildings have been almost completely levelled; yet the magic of the place endures for anyone to enjoy.

CHAPTER 1
The Times of Dr Whalley

It is not easy at a distance of 200 years to get oneself into the mindset of the Reverend Dr Whalley and his contemporaries, but at least one should try to be aware of the social context. The span of his long life (1746-1828) was a period of great social, political and cultural change in England.

The period just before Thomas Sedgwick Whalley's birth had seen the beginnings of the changes which would lead to the industrial revolution. At that time France still had a king and Britain still had American colonies. By the time of Whalley's death, Britain had become the workshop of the world, Napoleon Bonaparte had been dead for seven years and John Quincey Adams was the fifth President of an independent United States of America. It is not possible in a few words to give a complete history of the late 18th century, and those requiring this should seek elsewhere. What is given below is a brief background of some of the key issues which affected the lives of characters described in this West Country history.

Agriculture and Industry

The Industrial Revolution was preceded by the equally important but much slower Agricultural Revolution, which is thought to have embraced three major changes: the selective breeding of livestock; the removal of common property rights to land; and new systems of cropping. Charles "Turnip" Townshend, who died in 1738, had put in hand the crop rotation involving turnips and clover in a four field system, rather than the traditional and inefficient three field system in which one field was left to lie fallow each year. The means to make more effective use of land in this way was by the enclosure of arable land, waste and common, by private Acts of Parliament, which became commonplace from 1750 onwards. Increases in agricultural output and improvements in the efficiency of agricultural labour went hand in hand with changes in the social relationships between those involved in farming. Thus, the yeoman farmer and more especially the late 18th century landowner prospered and introduced further improvements in farming methods. But for the peasant it spelt disaster. Fewer agricultural workers were needed, and many moved to the towns to become the impoverished and often hungry workforce for the infant industrial revolution. At this time a large part of the country's wealth still came from the export of woollen cloth produced by a cottage industry, though cotton cloth was beginning to challenge its pre-eminence. In 1733 John Kay had invented the flying shuttle. This and other earlier inventions were initially popular with the cottage weavers and spinners. Later inventions, such as Hargreaves' spinning jenny (1764), Arkwright's water frame (1769) and the use of water power, were soon to revolutionise the manufacture of cloth. Joshia Wedgwood (1730-1795) brought about industrial changes to the manufacture of pottery, and three generations of the Derby family in Coalbrookdale developed the process of coke-smelted cast iron, which went into steam engines, bridges and many of the inventions of the 19th century.

To support increasing industrial output as well as to feed a rising and increasingly urbanised population, a better inland transport infrastructure was required. In the mid 17th century goods travelled either by road or river. Although some of the major rivers had already been canalised by the mid 1600s, the first *Act to enable the Most Noble Francis Duke of Bridgewater, to make a navigable Cut or Canal...* was passed in April 1737. Road transport, too, was improving, through the establishment of toll roads (turnpikes). Between 1700 and 1750 four hundred Turnpike Trusts had been agreed by parliament, a figure which was to be quadrupled in the next 50 years. However, while stage coaches on turnpike roads provided relatively rapid travel between the major cities, bulky goods still relied on the use of pack horses, and in rural areas roads were little more than rutted tracks and bridle paths. For example, in 1766 hundreds of tons of pottery were still taken from Stoke on Trent to the Severn ports of Bridgnorth and Bewdley by packhorse, and this was the means by which cotton goods from Lancashire reached these towns on their journey to Bristol and overseas.

Education and the Arts

In the 18th century, for those who could afford it, public schools were seen as the natural place to develop boys' masculinity, while private education at home was thought to be the proper setting to nurture girls' feminine identity. Not all agreed with this, and William Pitt the elder (later to become Lord Chatham) was so appalled by his experiences of education at Eton that all his sons, including William Pitt the younger, were educated by a tutor at home. Non-conformist schools were beginning to appear, as were Sunday schools established by philanthropists in the larger towns, but for the villages of Mendip there was no education for the poor until Whalley's close friends the playwright and educationist Hannah More (1745-1833) and the philanthropist William Wilberforce (1759-1833) resolved to establish rural Anglican schools, following a visit to Cheddar in 1789.

University education was limited to Oxford, Cambridge, Edinburgh or Dublin and was a rarity. In the 18th century University served as a meeting place for the able sons of the rich, as entry required both wealth and ability. If a potential pupil showed a great promise, the usual fees became more flexible, but the bulk of those studying at universities were wealthy and aristocratic. Most attended from the age of 18 years, but a few outstandingly able boys, like Pitt the younger, from as young as 14 years. Universities were not open to Roman Catholics and indeed served as a seminary for the Anglican Church; over half of those graduating went into the Church. Courses were general and included classical literature – taught in Greek and Latin – moral and political philosophy, theology, medicine and mathematics. Science (natural philosophy) was regarded as a hobby for the rich. Degrees were taken by examination, conducted orally and in Latin, but at this time the sons of the nobility were entitled to purchase a Master's degree.

The term 'Grand Tour' was introduced by Richard Lessels in his 1670 book *Voyage to Italy*. By the mid 17th century it was regarded as the means by which those young men who were not obliged to work completed their education between school or University and the inheritance of family wealth. Sometimes these young men were accompanied by their tutor; more often, they were not. Rome was initially the most southerly point in their travels, but when excavations began of Herculaneum (1738) and Pompeii (1748) these two sites became major destinations.

In 1795 Edward Gibbon, who was himself a "grand tourist", was told that 40,000 English, including masters and servants, were then touring or resident on the continent. Certainly, the upsurge of interest in archaeology and classical art and architecture by those able to patronise the arts was in no small measure

9

attributable to "The Tour". Sir John Vanbrugh published his work *The Country House* in 1698, and Lancelot "Capability" Brown was soon to be at work landscaping the gardens of the rich to complement their newly completed great houses, such as Chatsworth and Blenheim. Sir James Thornhill (1675-1734), a Dorset man, was the doyen of English decorative history painters in his day and the first to make a fortune from painting. His grand house Thornhill was built from the profits of his works at Greenwich, St Paul's Cathedral, Chatsworth and Hampton Court. Joshua Reynolds, Gainsborough, Romney and Zoffany also prospered, leading to the establishment of the Royal Academy under Royal patronage in 1768.

Perhaps because George III, unlike his father and grandfather, spoke and wrote in English, there was a flowering of English poets, essayists and writers from this time onward. The writings of Gray, Goldsmith, Cowper, Johnson, Burke and Blake were all a reflection of the age. Private libraries increased in number, and the first circulating libraries for the public had started by 1740 and were well known in London and Bath. It soon seemed as if every educated woman was writing a novel based on their experiences and those of their friends at the spas. Likewise, characters in the plays of Richard Brinsley Sheridan and others were drawn from life.

Public Morality and Public Conscience

The new Enlightenment, led on the continent by Voltaire and Rousseau and driven by powerful critics of the contemporary mores at home, such as Hogarth, Fielding and Smollet, slowly affected political thought. Non-conformist challenges made on the basis of rational argument slowly had a significant impact on accepted religious dogmas. Evangelism and non-conformist teaching became the driving force behind the anti-slavery movement. Dr Johnson, who published his dictionary in 1755, was already objecting to slavery on moral grounds. The sea change in public opinion on this issue was to find fruition in the hands of Whalley's lifelong friend William Wilberforce.

Drunkeness was already acknowledged as the national vice of England at this time. Cheap gin during the period 1720-1750 produced much early death, especially in the cities. The combination of the Act of 1751, which taxed spirits and limited their points of sale, and the introduction of vaccination did much to reduce the death rate, which for a short time exceeded baptisms in London. Gambling was universal in all classes of society and was socially quite acceptable for men and women. Prostitution was rife, duelling was still commonplace. Among the gentry there was the view that marriage was a convenient way of acquiring an income. The bride in these transactions was often not consulted. At a time when there was no income tax or inheritance tax, such opportunities for generating huge fortunes among the already wealthy only served to intensify class distinctions. Although it had been many years since a witch was burned at the stake (the Witchcraft Act was not finally repealed until 1736), public hanging was commonplace. Social justice was not generally available to those without money. Debtors' prisons were filled to bursting, while punishments for trivial crimes committed by the starving poor could be death or transportation for life. On the other hand, public conscience, at least among those who could afford it, was expressing itself. Between 1720 and 1745 Guys, The Westminster, St Georges and the London and Middlesex Hospitals had all been established in the capital by charitable acts, joining the medieval St Bartholomew's and St Thomas's hospitals in catering for the needs of the sick. Captain Coram opened his Foundling Hospital in Lamb's Conduit Fields in 1745. He had been moved to do so because he was distressed to see babies dying in the gutters and their bodies rotting in the dung-heaps of London. William Hogarth and George Frederick Handel, who gave fundraising concerts in the Hospital Chapel, were early supporters of this charity.

Science and Religion

The Royal Society had been founded by Charles II in 1665, and science became a laudable hobby of the rich. One of the most cultured of monarchs, George III started a new royal collection of books (65,000 of his books were later given to the British Museum as the nucleus of a national library) and opened his library to scholars. Thereafter, science, which was not taught at university at this time, was seen to be an appropriate occupation for the intelligent rich[1]. When Voltaire visited England between 1726 and 1729, he commented favourably on the English nobility as patrons of letters and science.

During the Commonwealth (1649–1660) Article 37 of the Instrument of Government had provided greater freedom of worship for Protestants. Radical ideas found expression in sects such as the Ranters and Diggers, who favoured an approach to worship more akin to modern street preachers. These very extreme Protestants would eventually prove unpalatable to the post-Civil War regime because of their implied rejection of state control. Other lesser forms of non-conformism were soon to take root: in May 1652 George Fox had climbed to the top of Pendle Hill and had a vision which lead to the establishment of the Quaker movement. With the restoration of the monarchy,

---

[1] George III was the first king to study science as part of his education. He had his own astronomical observatory, and examples of his collection of scientific instruments can now be seen in the Science Museum.

Charles II used the 1662 Oath of Allegiance as one of the methods by which to restore the dominance of the established Anglican Church. Then Henry Osland, Joseph Odley and Francis Holcroft, who were Cambridge-trained clergymen, refused to take the oath and were imprisoned in Cambridge Castle to become pioneers of non-conformism in England. The Toleration Act of 1689 later exempted protestant subjects who dissented from the Church of England rule from the earlier penalties, and non-conformism no longer was a hazard to citizenship.[2]

By the middle of the 18th century, many Church of England ministers had non-conformist leanings, and public concern about corruption within the Church of England was equally widespread. Nepotism had effectively made the established Church a branch of the aristocracy, where the acquisition of lucrative livings had become the main concern of a majority of the clergy. The holding of several parishes was commonplace, as was the practice of a Rector placing a curate within each to obviate the need to preach there themselves. This only served to increase the anger of the general population, which supported the clergy through their tithe payments. Methodism arose in reaction to this decline in the morals of the established church. John Wesley, who was a priest in the Church of England, started preaching to the poor in the open air in Bristol in 1739 and rapidly acquired a huge following in the West of England.

The Place of Women

Although it is difficult to generalise about the role of women in

---

[2] For Roman Catholics, such freedoms were not yet available. While the 1778 Catholic Relief Act allowed Catholics to own property and inherit land, it was not until the Roman Catholic Relief Act of 1829 that Catholic emancipation was achieved throughout Britain.

polite society at this time, women's lives were limited by both education and the laws of inheritance. Household management, needlework, music, painting and even languages were thought to be suitable areas of study for a girl. Even enlightened and educated fathers restricted what their able daughters could study. When the eight-year-old Hannah More, the evangelical philanthropist, was taught mathematics and Latin by her father, she progressed so rapidly that he took fright and the lessons were abandoned.[3]

"Bluestockings" who engaged in political discussion and literary and intellectual pursuits were regarded as being unfeminine and frumpy, and their fathers feared they might never marry. When a gentleman's daughter did marry, her father's dowry immediately became the property of her husband. The one area in which 18th-century women had authority was in running their household, and once they had provided the necessary heir, many were able to recover an element of control in their domestic lives.

Most of the women in the Rev Thomas Sedgwick Whalley circle were highly educated, of independent means and unmarried. A few, such as the actress Sarah Siddons, were not. But even for those who became wealthy after marriage, the importance of having control over their household was paramount. As we shall see in the case of Thomas Sedgwick's niece, the failure to obtain this led to the breakdown of her marriage.

Europe and Beyond

The greater part of Whalley's life was to take place against a background of European wars. Hardly was Frederick II (The Great) on the throne of Prussia before he launched into the war

---

[3] Stott, A., *Hannah More: the first Victorian,* Oxford University Press, Oxford, 2003, p.6

of Austrian Succession. From 1740-1748 England was allied with Austria while France sided with Prussia.[4] Exhaustion on both sides brought the War of the Austrian Succession to a close with the peace of Aix-la-Chapelle in 1748. There was only an interval of 8 years before England, this time allied with Prussia, entered into the Seven Years War against France and Austria (1756-1763). French colonial interests also made it necessary for Britain to wage war at a distance in India and Canada. French and Dutch interests had been defeated in India by 1760, and in the same year Canada changed hands, following Wolfe's victory over the French at Quebec. The end of the European war in 1763 still left Britain in dispute with the American colonies. This was to become the War of Independence of 1776-1781. Then, in 1793 Britain was drawn in to the first of the wars with post-revolutionary France, which were to last until 1815.

At the turn of the century, the greatest effect of these wars was the decline in trade, with the consequent shortages of food made worse by violent price fluctuations and low wages. This reduced the poor to near starvation, and there were fears of revolution in England. The first of the Corn Laws of 1804 only added to the underlying problem. These measures were introduced when the landowners who dominated Parliament sought to protect their profits by imposing a duty on imported corn. The Corn Laws led to an expansion of British wheat farming but also high bread prices which increased the wealth of the landed gentry but penalized the poor. When the war with France came to an end in 1815, the import of foreign corn lowered prices and the price of corn fell from 126s.6d a quarter to 65s.7d. This brought relief to the English poor but was disastrous for Ireland, which had enjoyed considerable economic prosperity during

---

[4] In the course of this conflict, the Young Pretender's abortive Jacobite revolution was an additional concern.

the war.

Britain eventually bowed to pressure in Ireland and in 1782 reluctantly granted her an independent Parliament. This had little real power; Ireland was still ruled from Westminster, and Irish land remained for the most part in the hands of English Protestants. Encouraged by Wolfe Tone, the United Irish leader, a French expeditionary force of 15,000 troops arrived off Bantry Bay in December 1796 but failed to land. Two years later, rebellion had broken out in the southeast of Ireland, only to be cruelly put down by the British with an estimated loss of 30,000 lives. Despite this Irish Anglicans remained largely untroubled by such matters, and trade and social exchange between Bristol and Dublin continued to prosper. By 1814 the Irish mail was arriving daily in Bristol, with many Anglo Irish regarding Bath as their second home.

One can only be astonished at the extent to which the 18th-century landed English gentleman, and especially those who held holy orders, appear to have been totally unconcerned with the plight of the poor. The majority of the clergy seemed quite prepared to live on tithes and rents while actively opposing any attempts to educate the agricultural labourers who provided them. Against this background the Reverend Thomas Sedgwick Whalley was one of the more enlightened members of the Church of England.

Further Reading

Churchill, W.S., *A History of the English Speaking Peoples*, Volumes III and IV. Cassell and Co., London, 1937

Edwards, R.E., *An Atlas of Irish history* (2nd Ed.), Methuen and Co., New York, 1981

Grant, A.J., *Outlines of European History*, Longmans Green and Co., London, 1947

Hague, W., *William Pitt the Younger*, Harper Perennial, London, 2005

Trevelyan, G.M., *English Social History* (2nd Ed.), Longmans Green and Co, London, 1946

Vickery, A., *Behind closed doors. At home in Georgian England*, Yale University Press, London, 2009

Vickery, A., *The gentleman's daughter*, Yale University Press, London, 1998

CHAPTER 2
The Whalley Family

The Whalley family claimed to be descended from Wyamarus Whaley, the standard bearer of William the Conqueror at the Battle of Hastings.[1] There is some evidence that as a result of this role Wyamarus Whaley was granted the lordship of Whaley in Lancashire in 1067.[2] By 1296 an abbot and twenty monks had arrived to create a church which later became an abbey. Whalley Abbey still exists as a Church of England retreat and conference centre belonging to the Diocese of Blackburn. Thomas Sedgwick Whalley (1746-1828) referred to Welbeck Abbey in 1808 as his 'old family seat'.[3] The estate was originally settled by the Conqueror on the de Flemmaugh family, however at the dissolution of the monasteries it was bought by Richard Whalley of Shelford.[4] The family coat of arms can only be traced back to John Whalley, who was presented to the living of Cosgrove, Northamptonshire, in 1601. It would seem that the Herald at the time (William Camden, 1551-1623) had a sense of humour, since three whale heads were included as a major feature. The Whalley coat of arms is still faintly discernable on the almshouses built by

---

[1] JCTSW I p.1

[2] Whaley, S., *The English Record of the Whaley family and its branches in America*, Andrus and Church, Ithaca, New York, 1901. p.13

[3] JCTSW I p.288

[4] 'House of Premonstratensian canons: The Abbey of Welbeck', in *A History of the County of Nottingham* (Page, W., ed.) Nottingham, 1910, Vol. II, pp.129-138

John Whalley, whose grave is in the chancel of Cosgrove parish church.[5]

Mirabilis in profundis

2.1 The Whalley Coat of Arms

Arms: Argent, three whale heads hauriant sable, a canton of the second, charged with a mascle of the first.

Crest: A whale's head hauriant sable, charged with a mascle argent.

Motto: *Mirabilis in profundis* (Marvel in the profound).[6]

Thomas Sedgwick Whalley, the subject of this book, was descended though this line of the family:

5 Gill, L., Personal communication, 2009

6 Burke, J. A., *Genealogical and heraldic history of the common of Great Britain and Ireland*, Henry Colburn, London, 1838, Vol. IV

John Whalley BD (1555-1647)
Rector of Cosgrove (Northants)

|

Arthur Whalley (- 1692)

|

Roger Whalley (- 1727)

|

John Whalley (- 1739)
Rector of Riddlesworth (Norfolk)

|

John Whalley MA DD (1698-1748)
Master of Peterhouse
Regius Professor of Divinity, Cambridge University

Thomas Sedgwick's father was Professor John (Johannes) Whalley of Cambridge University, a very able and notably absent-minded man.[7] His wife Mary was the only daughter of Francis Squire, a Canon and Chancellor of Wells Cathedral. Her family included several clergy based in Devon and Wiltshire.[8] How the two families met is unknown. Francis Squire obtained his MA from St John's, Cambridge in 1715; John Whalley went to Pembroke Hall in 1715, so they could have met then, but it is unlikely. More probably, John Whalley used the Wells cathedral library, which was well known at the time, in connection with his research for a doctorate and met Francis and his family while he was there. By this time Francis Squire was Warminster Prebend of Wells, an appointment which he held until his death in 1750.

---

7 JCTSW I pp.1-2 (Footnote)

8 Another distant relation may have been Samuel Squire FRS (1714-1766), Fellow of St Johns (1735) and Canon of Wells; later Bishop of St Davids (1761)

At the time of their marriage in about 1734, John Whalley had become one of the King's Chaplains in Ordinary and was already Master of Peterhouse, having become a Fellow of Pembroke in 1721 and a Doctor of Divinity in 1737. Five years later, he succeeded Dr Bentley as Regius Professor of Divinity. Thomas Gray, the poet, became a Fellow of Peterhouse during the time that John Whalley was Master. While John Whalley is not noted as a contemporary poet, he did write poetry, and his rustic elegy for Queen Caroline, based on Edmund Spencer's 'November' and entitled 'Thenot and Cuddy', received praise.[9] It has been described more recently as as 'an academician's successful poetic exercise in reproducing Spencer's archaisims, syntax and pretty lamentation'.[10] Spencer had been a graduate of Peterhouse, and there is some suggestion that Whalley was preparing a book on his works at the time of his death.

Although the family lived in Cambridge, it is clear that Mrs Whalley maintained her links with Wells. Her first child, Frances, was born in 1735 but was buried with a younger sister, Sarah, in Wells Cathedral on December 12th, 1742. As Sarah had been baptised in Wells on December 23rd, 1740, one can perhaps deduce from these two dates that it was customary for the family to visit there at Christmas, when their grandfather would have played a prominent role in the Christmas services.

Professor Whalley died suddenly in St John's College garden on December 17th 1748.[11] This was only seven days after his youngest son Richard Chaple Whalley had been baptised. Mrs Whalley then took her young family to Wells. This itself was no mean undertaking. Twenty five years later, the fourteen-year-old

---

9 Told, H.J., ed. *Edmund Spenser in eight volumes* Vol. 1, London, 1805, p.183

10 Wasserman, E.R.. *Elizabethan Poetry in the 18th Century.* University of Illinois Press, Urbana , 1947, p.145

11 JCTSW I pp.1-2

William Pitt and his tutor took five days to travel from Cambridge to Burton Pynsent, near Curry Rivel in Somerset.[12] Mrs Whalley must have been a remarkable lady, as she then set about bringing up her seven children, which she did with great success. One glimpses her character and abilities from letters written many years later to her son Thomas Sedgwick and his friends. For example, Mrs Piozzi, the "blue stocking" and friend of Dr Samuel Johnson and Thomas Sedgwick (see Appendix 1), wrote in 1791:

> Am glad Mr. Whalley has so much comfort from his Mother, for whom he always seemed to have so great a share of Regard... How happy it is tho' to possess one's Faculties at such an advanced Age as the Lady at Longford [sic] Cottage.[13]

Ten days earlier, Sophia Weston, who had by this time become Thomas Sedgwick's cousin by marriage (see Appendix 1), had written to her friend Mrs Piozzi:

> At near 90 (she) is beautiful well bred, clear in her intellect... and animated and entertaining to a very uncommon degree in Conversation and Society, which She greatly enjoys. - She has still many resources of amusement within herself and 'tis quite delightful to see her sit down to the Piano Forte and divert herself for an hour together in as good Time and Task as most people- Indeed she is in every way a phenomenon.[14]

---

12 Taylor, W.S., and Pringle, J.H., eds., *Correspondence of William Pitt Earl of Chatham*, Vol IV, John Murray, London, 1840, pp.288-9

13 TPL I pp.272-3

14 *Papers of Hester Lynch Thrale-Piozzi née Salusbury*, John Rylands Library,

Mrs Whalley's income at this time is unknown but must have been considerable. Initially, she and her seven surviving children probably lived with her father, Dean and Chancellor of Wells Cathedral. Later, she occupied the Tower House in St Andrew's Street.[15] This was large enough to comfortably accommodate all her family. Eventually, Mrs Whalley moved thirteen miles away to live with her eldest surviving son, Francis, and his family at Winscombe Court.[16] One assumes that this was after the last of her children had left home,[17] but she certainly moved there after 1773, as her daughter Elizabeth was still visiting her at Wells in August of that year.[18] She lived until the remarkable age of 96 years. There is a memorial tablet to her in the church of St James the Great, Winscombe, high up on the south wall of the tower. Very strangely, this contains a number of errors; these are underlined, and suggested corrections are in bold and enclosed in square brackets:

> Sacred to the Remains of MARY WHALLEY/ The only Child of FRANCIS WHALLEY ESQUIRE AM [**FRANCIS SQUIRE MA**] Rector of Exford and Canon and Chancellor/ of the Cathedral Church of Wells/ And Relict of JOHN WHALLEY DD/ Head [**Master**] of St Peters College [**Peterhouse Hall**] and Regis Professor [**of Divinity**]/ in the University of Cambridge/ She

University of Manchester. Ref 566.16

15 Bailey, S., *Canonical Houses of Wells*, Gloucester, 1982, pp.132-3

16 Francis Whalley had leased this property from the Wells Chapter in 1771 but bought the leasehold from them in 1788.

17 Thomas Sedgwick moved to Langford Court in 1774, and Richard Chapel to his wife's house on Cathedral Green in 1775.

18 JCTSW I p.272

died on the 14th Day of September, 1803./ In the
<u>ninetieth year</u> [**97**th year] of her Age.

As Thomas was responsible for three other flawless memorial
tablets in Burrington Church and was very particular about all
such matters, one must assume he did not supervise the work on
this occasion. The explanation may be that as he had only recently
remarried, and because his mother had died at Winscombe Court,
he left the funeral and memorial arrangements to his elder brother
Francis. The 31 line poem which follows the inscription comes
from a longer epitaph written by Thomas Sedgwick Whalley in
memory of his mother.[19]

Mary Whalley's Children
It is clear that this was a very close and mutually supportive
family. It would seem that when their father died the eldest
daughter, the then nine-year-old Susan (Susannah), became her
mother's right hand, remaining at home for the next thirty years.
This may account for her later marriage. This female environ-
ment might also account for Thomas Sedgwick's unusually
enlightened attitude to women.

Frances (1735-1742) and Sarah (1740-42)
Mrs Whalley's first daughter did not survive beyond six years of
age. She and two-year-old younger sister Sarah died in the same
month while in Wells and were buried there. Formerly, there was
a monument recording these sad deaths in the Cathedral.[20]

---

[19] JCTSW I pp.258-9
[20] Jewers, A.J., *Wells Cathedral – its monumental inscriptions and heraldry,* Mitchel
and Hughes, London, 1848, pp.173-4

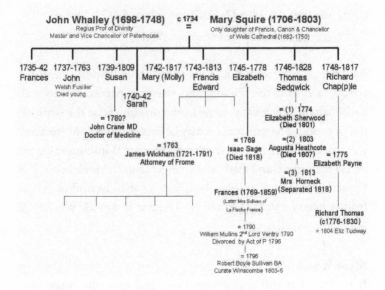

John Whalley (1698-1748)
Regius Prof of Divinity
Master and Vice Chancellor of Peterhouse

c 1734
=

Mary Squire (1706-1803)
Only daughter of Francis, Canon & Chancellor
of Wells Cathedral (1682-1750)

1735-42 Frances

1737-1763 John
Welsh Fusilier
Died young

1739-1809 Susan
= 1780?
John Crane MD
Doctor of Medicine

1740-42 Sarah

1742-1817 Mary (Molly)
= 1763
James Wickham (1721-1791)
Attorney of Frome

1743-1813 Francis Edward

1745-1778 Elizabeth
= 1769
Isaac Sage
(Died 1818)

Frances (1769-1859)
(Later Mrs Sullivan of
La Fleche France)
= 1790
William Mullins 2nd Lord Ventry 1790
Divorced by Act of P 1796
= 1796
Robert Boyle Sullivan BA
Curate Winscombe 1803-5

1746-1828 Thomas Sedgwick
= (1) 1774
Elizabeth Sherwood
(Died 1801)
=(2) 1803
Augusta Heathcote
(Died 1807)
=(3) 1813
Mrs Horneck
(Separated 1818)

1748-1817 Richard Chap(p)le
= 1775
Elizabeth Payne

Richard Thomas
(c1776-1830)
= 1804 Eliz Tudway

2.2 The Whalley family tree

John (1737-1763)

Her eldest son, John (born 1737), was educated at Charterhouse and entered his father's College, Peterhouse, in 1754 as a pensioner. He matriculated in 1756, and his mother purchased for him a commission in the 23rd Regiment of the Welsh Fusiliers, but he died on the homeward passage from India in 1763. It is curious that his younger sister Elizabeth was later to suffer an almost identical fate. The only other information which Hill Wickham provides is that 'he was a young man of great promise'.[21]

---

[21] JCTSW I p.2

Susan (Susannah) (1739 - 1809)

Of Mrs Whalley's three other daughters, least is known about Susan, her eldest surviving daughter. Though the eldest, she was the last to marry. It was usual at that time for the least marriageable daughter to remain at home to support aging parents, and Susan was described by Thomas in a poem as 'plump'.[22] She married John Crane MD of Bristol, a physician, probably after 1775. Maybe Dr John Crane was related to the Reverend Francis Crane Parsons (1731- 1798), vicar of Yeovil, whose family seems to have owned significant property. Like Thomas Sedgwick, Parsons was also a prebendary of Wells, as had been Susan and Thomas's maternal grandfather, Francis Squire.

There is no surviving correspondence of Susan, and indeed Thomas Sedgwick rarely mentions her in any of his many letters to other correspondents. The only suggestion as to her character and appearance occurs in the poem mentioned above (see Appendix 2). It is clear that Susan was on very good terms with her younger sister Elizabeth. In 1775 she had offered to accompany Elizabeth to India (see Chapter 4), indicating she was a kindly and caring soul. Elizabeth decided against it on the grounds that it would give their mother additional worry and expense.[23] This confirms that Susan was still unmarried at this time.

According to the Hill Wickham footnote, she died at Henstridge, near Bath, and was buried there.[24] The date is confirmed as August 1809 in newspaper reports: 'Last week at Henstridge near Bath, Mrs. Crane, wife of Dr. Crane Physician. elder daughter of John Whalley.'[25]

---

[22] JCTSW I p.251

[23] ibid I p.283

[24] ibid I p.283 (Footnote)

[25] *York Herald*, Sept. 2nd, 1809

An examination of the churchyard has revealed no head-stones with the name of Crane. At Henstridge she was only a very few miles from Horsington, where her youngest brother, Richard Whalley, had been Rector for 11 years and where the Wickhams, their relatives by marriage, had been rectors for many generations.

Later, her daughter Frances Elizabeth Crane (1781-1812) married a Mr John Luther Yeates of Brecon (1766-1839), with Thomas Sedgwick officiating. This was in St Stephen's church, Bristol in May 1807.[26] This suggests that Bristol was where the Crane family was then living, but there is no record of a John Crane practising in Bristol at that time.[27] Following his wife's death, John Crane rewrote his Will, leaving everything to his executor Thomas Sedgwick Whalley, his heirs and assigns to be held in Trust for his only daughter, Frances Elizabeth,[28] and her child 'separate and apart from any present or future husband'. The Will was dated 2nd August 1810, and Dr Crane died the following year. Since Thomas Sedgwick was already 61 years old, the choice of executor suggests that Dr Crane trusted the Whalley and Wickham families to keep his daughter's inheritance out of the hands of his son-in-law. It is highly likely that he already knew that James A. Wickham, Attorney of Frome, would be the executor of Thomas Sedgwick in the event that the latter prede-ceased his daughter.

26 *Hereford Journal*, June 10th, 1807

27 Matthews, W., *Matthews New Bristol Directory 1793/4*, Bristol

28 National Archives Online Document, PROB 11/1520

Mary (Molly) (1742-1814)

Mary, known as Molly, married the attorney James Wickham of Frome.[29] Thereafter, the affairs of the Wickham and Whalley families were entwined for next 100 years. Thomas Sedgwick visited the family at Frome frequently and spent some months living with them in his old age. As already indicated, their eldest son, James Anthony Wickham, was on very good terms with Thomas and became his executor. One of their sons, Thomas's great nephew the Reverend Hill Dawe Wickham, was a favourite of Thomas's and became the author of what amounted to a biography of his great uncle, which was published in 1863.

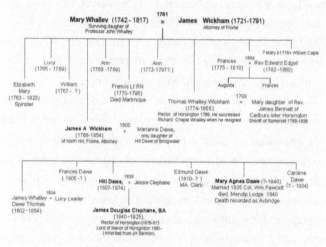

2.3 The Wickham family Tree

---

[29] Although James Wickham was an attorney, the family had been clergy for many generations. His father, John, had been a much loved Rector of Horsingham. James and Mary's youngest son, Thomas, who married a daughter of the Rev James Bennett, succeeded his uncle Richard Chaple Whalley as Rector of Horsington, the latter incumbent having resigned in his favour. This living ultimately passed to Mary's nephew the Rev James Douglas Clephane, better known as JDC Wickham, the author of *Records by Spade and Terrier,* an early source of Somerset history.

Francis Edward (1743-1813)

Nothing is known of the early life of Mrs Whalley's second son, Francis Edward. It seems that when his elder brother died in 1763 the 21 year old took over the role as head of the family. He too probably entered the army, since he married late and eventually became the Lieutenant Colonel and Commander of the West Mendip Volunteer Regiment. Francis was the "fixer" of the family and was prominent in local affairs. He became a JP and was a commissioner for several enclosure Acts. In September 1787 he married Bridget Maria Salmon, the daughter of Thomas Salmon of Stratton on the Fosse. Her mother was Mary, daughter of James Tooker Esquire of Norton Hall, Somerset, whose property eventually passed to Colonel Whalley's son Hyde Salmon Whalley (1790-1836). Because whale heads appeared on the Whalley coat of arms, there was apparently much merriment at that time about the union being between a Whale and a Salmon.[30]

Francis played a major role in the enclosure of North Somerset. In 1774 he was one of the two arbitrators in the matter of the enclosure of Wedmore.[31] In 1797 he was one of the two commissioners for the enclosure of Kings Sedgmoor and Chewton Mendip[32,33] and one of the three commissioners for the enclosure of Banwell and Churchill. The latter was to be of great advantage to his younger brother Thomas Sedgwick, who by the process of "exchanges" was able to greatly increase his estate (see Chapter 6). Each of these appointments would have carried a fee of perhaps £60, equivalent to a curate's annual pay at the time.

Francis was a shareholder in the Somerset Coal Canal and also one of the proponents of the West Harptree Turnpike Act

---

[30] JCTSW II p.15 (Footnote)

[31] Somerset Heritage Centre, DD\SE/69/1

[32] ibid DD\AHW/1/4/13

[33] ibid DD\SAS\H70\12\8

29

of 1793. The latter was greatly to the advantage of the Whalley family in general, as it provided a much needed route between Langford, Chelwood, Bath, Wells and Winscombe, where the various members of the family lived and worked.

When in 1793 Britain feared civil unrest and Napoleonic invasion, a loyalist meeting of Justices, clergy and gentlemen took place in Langford Inn, chaired by Francis Whalley JP, at which the following resolutions were passed unanimously:

> 1. Fidelity to the King and attachment to the Constitution;
> 2. To suppress sedition;
> 3. To thank the elected County representatives;
> 4. To thank the Chairman.

Francis eventually bought Winscombe Court, then known as 'The Parsonage House of Winscombe', on a leasehold from the Chapter of Wells in 1788.[34] He and his family lived there with his mother until she died in 1803 at the age of 96 years. Francis himself died there on 5th May 1813.[35]

Very surprisingly, there is no correspondence between Thomas Sedgwick and Francis included in Hill Wickham's book. This is maybe because for the greater part of their lives they lived close enough to each other to make correspondence unnecessary, but one suspects there was no close relationship between them. The only mention made of Francis by Hill Wickham is in his introduction, and this is concerned with the role each brother played in the "Blagdon controversy" (see Chapter 9). Here Hill Wickham quotes a description of Francis by his younger brother Richard, which, according to Hill

---

[34] Somerset Heritage Centre DD\CC/B/111105

[35] JCTSW II p.361 (Footnote)

Wickham, appeared in a letter from Richard to his niece Frances
Sullivan (née Sage), dated June 11th, 1800:

> In your Uncle Whalley, (who as a natural man, is
> the best tempered creature that lives and one whom
> I dearly love as a brother) you will meet with the
> decided enemy of all serious religion – so entirely
> ignorant of himself, and perfectly wrapped up in his
> own sufficiency for understanding, willing and
> doing, that he treats the Gospel as trash when it
> crosses his own conceits and opinions. His character
> helps to confirm me, more than any other person I
> have met with, in my opinion of the deceitfulness
> of the human heart, and how easy it is for a man to
> think himself a Christian, without the least
> foundation of faith in the word of Christ. [36]

It would seem from this that Francis, unlike his two younger
brothers, regarded the Anglican religion as merely an attribute of
social acceptability. He, in common with the great majority of
landowners at the time, regarded the 'increase of evangelical
religion' with distaste if not alarm, as it undermined the position
of the gentry. His two ordained younger brothers were more
informed and thoughtful on such matters and were not entirely
unsympathetic to evangelical teachings, particularly when it came
to educating the young. This diversity of opinion was how the
"Blagdon controversy" arose and why Thomas Sedgwick and
Francis took opposite sides in this prolonged public argument.

---

[36] JCTSW I p.25

Elizabeth (1745-1778)

Thomas Sedgwick's favourite sister, Elizabeth, was only a year his senior. He adored her and had commissioned at least two paintings of her, one of which he kept with him all his life. None of these, he maintained, did her beauty justice.[37] Only a few months before his death in March 1827, he was writing to his favourite nephew, asking him to arrange to pack up the picture so that the frame could be re-gilded.[38] She was closest to him in age and, one suspects, temperament. Elizabeth married Isaac Sage, who had returned a rich man from service in the East India Company. This was in the Whalley family church of St Cuthbert's, Wells in May 1769, not 1768 as stated in Hill Wickham's book – for reasons which are explained in Chapter 4. On Elizabeth's death, aged only 33, Thomas transferred all his affection to her only surviving daughter, Frances, whom he continued to support throughout his life.

Thomas Sedg(e)wick (1746-1828)

The main character in this story was born on September 20th, 1746 in Cambridge, the third son and sixth child of the marriage. Having no memory of his father, the greatest influences on his life were his mother and eldest sister, who remained at home long after Thomas was married. His life is covered fully in subsequent chapters.

Richard Chap(p)le (1748-1817)

Mrs Whalley's youngest son, Richard Chaple, was baptised at St Mary the Less, Cambridge on 10 December 1748, just two days before the sudden death of his father. Richard had a very colour-

---

[37] JCTSW I p.6

[38] ibid II pp.504-5

ful life. Initially, he aspired to be an historical artist.[39] In those days a well-connected and able artist could earn a good living, as Sir James Thornhill had shown. Richard was educated at Charterhouse but did not attend a university. His passion was for the arts, and at 24 years of age he left England to study art in Rome, remaining there two years. According to Thomas Banks, as quoted by Ingamells, he was in Rome from 1772. He seems to have been well funded, probably by his mother, since the following year he presented letters of credit to Barazzi and Byres in Rome.[40] However, by this time he had decided that 'he was incapable of sustaining the requisite application for acquiring eminence as an artist', and he gave up the idea. Despite this a surviving etching of the Bishops Palace and Wells Cathedral, and two miniatures, show he had considerable artistic talent.

2.4 Richard Chaple Whalley's drawing of the Bishops Palace and Wells Cathedral

---

[39] JCTSW I p.263

[40] Ingamells, J., *A dictionary of British and Irish travellers in Italy 1701-1800*, Yale University Press, London, 1997, p.994

By September 1773 he was missing Frances Paine, whom he hoped to marry very greatly, and this as much as anything else might have contributed to him giving up the idea of becoming an artist. In a letter to Thomas Sedgwick from Rome, he says,

> If I am persuaded that the deprivation of such a treasure as my Fanny, ought incessantly to be deplored, I am for that very reason capable of every effort to obtain it; and I am convinced of this by the ease with which I have passed from a life of dissipation to a life of study and by my great contempt for such things as were once the objects of my attention.[41]

This revealing letter suggests that Richard had not spent his time wisely in his early years and may explain his rather curious career.

2.5 Francis Chaple Whalley – a self portrait for a miniature

---

41 JCTSW I p.265

2.6 Frances Paine, later to become the wife of Reverend
Richard Chaple Whalley

The inscription reads:

Wells – October 1772

A Modest, humble, generous & innocent Girl – with
too much Beauty for a Woman of Sense, and too
much Sense to Value herself on her Beauty. Sincere
enough to declare her Feelings and constant enough
to maintain them – So very unambitious as to place
all her Hopes of Happiness in the Society and
Friendship of one who has nothing to bestow on
her but his Affections and whose best endowments
are that he is sensible of hers. The Features and
Character of Elizabeth Frances Paine Drawn by her
faithful Friend Richard Chaple Whalley who is
about to encounter a long, perhaps everlasting
separation from her – But tho' he is so uncertain

35

whether it will ever be permitted him to make her
happy he is certain that there remains to him no
other possible means of being so Himself.

Richard returned to England sometime after September
1773, and in 1775 he and Frances Paine were married. This was
the year after the Reverend Paine died. For some reason 7
Cathedral Green, where they lived, was sublet by Frances Elizabeth Paine to a Richard Chaple Whalley in 1775.[42] Quite why this
should be is not clear. Perhaps by this time she had inherited the
property from her father but the couple had not yet married.[43]

2.7 7 Cathedral Green Wells today

Richard's later life is revealed in considerable detail in the *memoire*
completed by his friend John Scandrett Harford (1787-1866),
who was the son of a wealthy banker and Quaker of the same
name (1754 –1815), himself the builder of Blaise Castle House,

---

[42] Somerset Heritage Centre, DD/CC 13202

[43] Frances was a wealthy heiress. Her father Canon John Paine had inherited
Midsomer Norton properties from his uncle the Reverend Richard Healy. Wells
and Bishops Lydeard estates were acquired either by John Paine, or from his
father John Paine senior.

now a museum in Bristol. According to John Harford junior, the memoir was intended to be written by Richard Chaple's son, the Rev R.T. Whalley, Rector of Yeovilton, but the latter died before completing the work.[44] Harford knew Richard well; they had been born in the same year and both shared a love of art and had travelled on the continent and studied in Rome. Harford was later baptised an Anglican at Chelwood, perhaps by Richard Chapel himself. According to Harford, in his early life on the continent Richard had been much influenced by Voltaire and if not actually an atheist was certainly a sceptic at this time.

> Mr. Whalley at length returned to his native country, with opinions, tastes, and habits uncongenial with those of the friends and associates among whom he was to live. He missed the exciting objects of art in which he had taken such delight, and happily he found among his countrymen few admirers of the French philosophy. The elegance of his manners, his refined taste, and his familiarity with foreign scenes and objects, naturally made his company sought after; but there was a hauteur and reserve about him which was justly deemed repulsive.[45]

Despite this Richard spent the next ten years in domestic bliss, presumably living off his wife's fortune, during which time he acquired two children. John Harford again takes up the story:

> In the year 1786, Mr. Whalley again visited the continent, accompanied by his wife and children.

---

[44] Harford, J.S., *Memoir of the Revd Richard Chapple Whalley BD*, James Nisbet and Co, London, 1866
[45] ibid p. xii

> He spent many months in the South of France, more especially at Tours, and amused his leisure by drawing and studying from nature. During his stay there, it was proposed to him to take orders, and to hold the living of Horsington, in Somersetshire, for his nephew, as yet a minor.[46]

It seems possible that this suggestion came from his elder brother the Reverend Thomas Sedgwick Whalley, who was also touring the continent with his wife at this time. Though Tours is not mentioned in his itinerary (see Chapter 5),who else would have known of his family circumstances to this extent, the Wickham's having held this living for several generations? It also confirms that Thomas, as many others at the time, saw the Church as a convenient way to make a comfortable living, rather than a calling based on one's personal religious beliefs.

Leaving his family in Tours, Richard returned to England in May 1787 and was ordained deacon in June the same year. The following year he was installed as Rector of Horsington, which was in the gift of his brother-in-law James Wickham.[47] Fortunately, the previous incumbent, John Wickham, had died in August 1787.[48] It seems that the Bishop of Bath & Wells had recommended Richard to the Bishop of Litchfield as being of sufficient academic standing to be ordained as a deacon even though he had no degree. Then, a few months later, the Bishop ordained him priest!

---

[46] Harford, J.S., *Memoir of the Revd Richard Chapple Whalley BD*, James Nisbet and Co, London, 1866, p. xvii

[47] JCTSW I p.264

[48] *Clergy of the Church of England Database*
(http://www.theclergydatabase.org.uk/index.html)

Almost immediately, in July of that year, he entered Jesus College, Cambridge as a "Sizar".[49] One might ask how he was able to pursue a degree while at the same time discharging his responsibilities as Rector of Horsington. Normally, four years full-time study would be required after matriculation to achieve a BA and a further four years thereafter to obtain a BD. Fortunately, the statutes of the University of Cambridge at the time gave flexibility to the usual requirement that students should spend their time in residence.[50] It must have helped that his relative Richard Beadon, who would go on the become Bishop of Gloucester in 1787, happened to be Master of Jesus at this time. 'Statute Elizabeth 9' permitted the award of the BD degree to someone with no other degrees who had been registered at the college for ten years. This period only required residence for a number of terms. But although 11 years passed between Richard joining Jesus College and graduating BD (Stat Eliz), the date of his matriculation, which would normally be required before starting his degree, is given as the same date as he achieved his degree.

According to Harford, the death of Richard's youngest son in 1793, followed by that of his wife in 1795, caused him to become a changed man:

> He lived, but so closely had his heart been bound
> up with her who was now gone for ever, that
> existence became to him a dreary blank, a profound
> vacuity. Fain would he have flown from himself and

---

[49] A student originally financing his studies by undertaking more or less menial tasks within his college and, as time went on, increasingly likely to receive small grants from the college without being 'on the foundation' (see http://janus.lib.cam.ac.uk/db/)

[50] Kleine, T.E.D., *Ceremonies of Cambridge University,* Cambridge, 1828, p.179

his own thoughts, but they haunted him with images of grief and distraction. This affliction, according to his own deliberate judgment, found him in a state of religious ignorance… Under these circumstances he could no longer endure the solitude of his house, nor the associations of his parish. He therefore made arrangements for quitting home, and trying what change of place and absence from the scene of his sorrows could effect. His sole companion on this mournful occasion was his Bible. He travelled with it from place to place; he read it seriously and diligently, convinced that it was capable of yielding him divine consolation.[51]

But in due course he overcame his despair to become an exemplary clergyman. His elder brother Thomas Sedgwick described him to a mutual friend as follows:

If you are well acquainted, I believe, with my brother Richard; but unless you can compare him, as I can, with his former self, you can scarcely imagine what religion has done for him. I well remember him as one of the proudest and most fastidious of human beings. He was, in fact, the proudest man I ever knew.[52]

He was thereafter much admired by Hannah More, who used to say 'she had known many persons who appeared to live near

[51] Harford, J.S., *Memoire of the Rev Richard Chapple Whalley BD*, James Nisbet and Co., London, 1866, p. XX
[52] JCTSW I pp.263-4

heaven but only Mr [Richard] Whalley who seemed to live in heaven'.[53]

In 1798 he obtained his degree and immediately became Prebend of Wells Cathedral. In the same year he preached to the King in the Chapel Royal.[54] In 1800 he resigned the living at Horsington in favour of his great nephew Thomas Whalley Wickham (1794-1856), the third son of James A. Wickham, as had always been the intention. Just over a year later, Bishop Bleadon, another relative who was now Bishop of Bath and Wells, presented Richard Chaple to the living of Chelwood, which he held until his death in 1817.[55] All in all, a fine 18th-century example of keeping it in the family!

---

53 JCTSW.I p.2

54 Somerset Heritage Centre, DD\GIL/18

55 *Clergy of the Church of England Database* (http://www.theclergydatabase.org.uk/index.html)

CHAPTER 3
Thomas Sedgwick Whalley's Early Life

Thomas was born in 1746, but by the time he was two years old, his father had died, and Mrs Whalley took her young family of seven to live in Wells. It was logical for her to do so, as her father was Chancellor of the Cathedral there. Quite where they lived is not clear. It could have initially been in the Chancellor's house, which is now the museum. Another report suggests it was the Tower House to the rear of this building.[1]

3.1 The Chancellors House on the Cathedral Green at Wells

---

[1] See Pevsner, N., *The buildings of England - North Somerset and Bristol*, Penguin Books, Middlesex, 1958, p.326

Hill Wickham states that Thomas was probably sent to Charterhouse, as his younger brother Richard Chaple had been.[2] However, this is probably incorrect. The Clergy of the Church of England Database gives no school for Richard but for Thomas Sedgwick states 'Ilminster (Mr. Davis)',[3] and Ilminster is confirmed in the Annals Cantab.[4] The Ilminster Free School had been founded in 1440, the same year in which Henry VI founded Eton College and other free schools,[5] but there is no clear record of a 'Mr. Davis' being there at the time when Thomas would have been a pupil, either as an incumbent in the parish or as a teacher at the school. However, Henry White, Vicar of East Coker and schoolmaster at Ilminster, had died in 1755, and the next recorded schoolmaster is Thomas Tomkins in 1804. The Annals Cantab also has a cryptic entry for Thomas Davis of 'Perhaps V[icar]. of Ilminster, Somerset, till 1768', so this would seem to fit.

Thomas Sedgwick entered St John's, Cambridge at 18 years of age in April 1763 and matriculated in Michaelmas the same year, which would indicate that his earlier schooling had been well spent. It is perhaps curious that he did not enter Pembroke Hall, where his father had been Professor and Vice Chancellor, particularly when the College had a tradition of encouraging poetry, which was to prove to be a lifelong passion for Thomas. It is perhaps relevant to his choice of St John's that the college had the best library at the time, [6] but perhaps more importantly,

[2] JCTSW I p.3

[3] *Clergy of the Church of England Database,*

(http://www.theclergydatabase.org.uk/jsp/persons/index.jsp)

[4] Venn, J.A., *Alumni Cantabrigienses*, Part II volume VI, Cambridge University Press, Cambridge, 1954

[5] See Gillard D, *Education in England: a brief history*, 2011

(http://www.educationengland.org.uk/history)

[6] Another ancestor, Thomas Whalley (died 1637), had donated three volumes

his cousin Richard Beadon was a fellow and a tutor there and about to become the Orator for the University. Perhaps also Thomas Sedgwick's mother took advice from her cousin, the Reverend Samuel Squire, who was an old St John's man and must have been a source of local advice when he was the newly appointed Vicar of Winscombe (1746-1750).

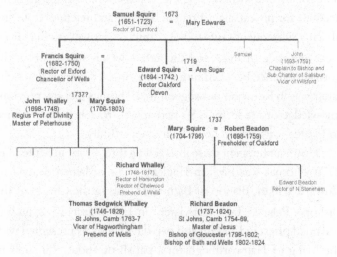

3.2 The Squire family tree and its relationship to Thomas Sedgwick Whalley

Thomas was clearly both able and diligent in his scholarship. He is reported as having retained until his latest days the custom of rising early and reading scripture, either in the Septuagint version (an ancient Greek translation of the Old Testament) or in the Greek new testament. He was well acquainted with the French and Italian languages. The latter was not surprising, since

of Boissard's *Topographia Romana Urbis* (1597) to the College library; they are still there today. The book's previous owner had been King James I, but the reason for their presentation to Thomas's namesake is unknown.

until 1792 degree examinations in Cambridge were conducted orally and in Latin. In later life Thomas was virtually bilingual in French, though, we are told, with a very poor accent.

He obtained his degree at Cambridge in 1767 but did not take holy orders for another three years, and perhaps this time was spent on a Grand Tour, which was very fashionable at that time for anyone with the wherewithal to do so. It would certainly account for his excellent French, his later architectural taste and also his subsequent visits to the continent. However, there is no clear evidence of this,[7] and the letters which survive from the correspondence between him and his brother Francis when the latter was in Rome do not suggest that Thomas had any previous knowledge of life in Italy. So perhaps his travels were confined to France, with which he had a lifelong affinity.

However he spent these intervening three years, in September 1770 Thomas was back in England to be ordained deacon by Edward Wilkes, Bishop of Bath and Wells in the Chapel of the Bishop's Palace.[8] Two years later, on 15th March 1772, he was ordained priest in London and two days later was presented with the living of Hagworthingham, a parish of about 300 souls in Lincolnshire.[9] It would seem that this was under the patronage of the Bishop of Ely, who had held Professor John Whalley in high regard. This would have been Bishop Edmund Keene, who, although a graduate of Caius, became a Fellow of Peterhouse and obtained his Doctorate there in the time of Whalley's father, whom he greatly admired. Thomas Sedgwick's living had a

[7] Ingamells J, *A dictionary of British and Irish travellers in Italy 1701-1800*, Yale University Press, Newhaven, 1997

[8] Clergy of the Church of England Database
http://www.theclergydatabase.org.uk/ Entry 40820

[9] The Clergy of the Church of England Database
(http://www.theclergydatabase.org.uk/)

singular provision from Bishop Keene: that he was never to reside there since the air of the fens was fatal to anyone but a native.[10] Thomas immediately hired a curate to represent him, and while he was obviously grateful for this living, he was perhaps also a little guilty about it. Three years before his death he arranged for a new parsonage to be built there at his own expense. Also, when he died in 1828, he bequeathed £300 to generate interest to support a Sunday School there, but the money was never paid from his estate for reasons which will become clearer later.

3.3 Thomas Sedgwick Whalley aged 25 years. Miniature by John Taylor, dated 1771. © Trustees of the British Museum

---

[10] JCTSW I p.3

3.4 Holy Trinity Hagworthingham

In a letter of June 10th, 1773 from his brother Richard, at that time in Rome studying to be a historical painter,[11] we learn that Thomas has 'departed for Wales'. This letter was addressed to the Reverend Warrington at Little Acton, Wrexham, where it seems Thomas was based. Both George Warrington (1744-1830) and Thomas had matriculated from St John's, Cambridge in the same year and were to be lifelong friends (see Appendix 1). The last letter between them is dated October 30th, 1827, within a year of Thomas Sedgwick's death, in which George addresses Thomas as 'My Dear Old Friend'.[12] However, apart from one other letter from George, dated October 1774, there is no other correspondence recorded between them in the two Hill Wickham volumes.

By 1773 George had been ordained deacon in Chester and had become Cannon of St Asaph's, in whose diocese Wrexham lay. Quite whether Thomas Sedgwick lived at Little Acton and

11 JCTSW I pp.263-4
12 ibid II p.503

was ever employed at the magnificent church of St Giles has yet to be discovered, but there is no doubt that he preached while he was there, perhaps to gain a little experience in such matters. According to his brother, during this time Thomas experienced life in a cottage and the happiness to be found in it.[13]

On August 21st 1773 Thomas's favourite sister, Elizabeth, replied promptly to his letter of the previous day, expressing her pleasure at the news that he would soon be leaving Wales. He was still living at George Warrrington's house at this time, and it is clear that his sister, now married for four years to Isaac Sage, was already well acquainted with George and his wife. In the same letter she includes a paragraph which suggests marriage was also on Thomas's mind. Perhaps the happy circumstances of George Warrington's state had influenced him.

> I hear of your leaving Wales with pleasure; I have been somewhat jealous of their detaining you there so long already. I shall look on the hopes you give me of spending a few days with us in town, as a promise, and if you should exceed that time we shall not show you the door. A pretty gentleman you are to talk of days , when you visit a sister whom you have not seen for this, I do not know how long; it appears to me as an age, as I measure the time by my affection . If you are in the widow's good graces, you should not boast of her favours; at least defer your information till we are tête à tête. In truth, I shall begin to harbour some suspicions if you stay at Acton much longer. The first wish of my heart is to see my dear favourite brother well settled; no one

13 JCTSW I .p.275

is more formed for domestic happiness, and I trust
the good Bishop will, ere it is long, enable you to
offer your hand and heart to some woman who is
worthy of you, if among women there is such to be
found. [14]

This must refer to Thomas obtaining a suitable living, which is
odd since he had already been appointed as Rector of
Hagworthingham. Maybe he had not revealed this to her while
he gained some experience in preaching well away from his own
parish; but who was the widow? It could be that his intentions
to marry Mrs Elizabeth Sherwood, who had been widowed in
1770, were already well advanced. On the other hand, it is difficult
to see how he would have progressed this while living in N.
Wales, and Elizabeth Sage adds a footnote: 'My best respects to
Mr. Warrington's family, particularly Mrs. Simpson'. So was this
his 'widow', and did Thomas subsequently change his affections
on returning to Somerset?

In a later letter, merely dated autumn 1773, Elizabeth Sage,
now in London, reports that their mutual friends the Warringtons
are also there. It is clear from this and from the previous letter
from their brother Richard that the Warringtons were close
friends of all the Whalley family. She goes on:

Pray present my compliments to the amiable widow
of your [unknown!] friend; I feel for her in the
absence of a husband... Pack up your all and
begone from Little Acton, I am sure your friends
must be heartily tired of you by this time. We long
to be so plagued in our turn.[15]

[14] JCTSW I pp.270-1
[15] ibid I pp.278-9

So one presumes the same widow was still at Little Acton in Denbighshire, but who was his friend? It is clear from a subsequent letter from Elizabeth that Thomas intended to preach a Christmas sermon in Wales before departing for England, but it is not certain that he did so.[16]

His sister's next recorded letter is from Lovell Hill and dated Boxing Day 1773. Thomas is already back in Wells from Wales; this is confirmed by the fact that Elizabeth refers to him sleeping in his own chamber. A footnote tells of a recent fall he has had from his horse, perhaps while on his way back from Wales. More relevant to Thomas's pursuit of a suitable wife, she also asks: 'I hope by this you have had a good account of dear Mrs. Sherwood'.[17]

From this it would seem that as far as Elizabeth was aware Thomas had not yet made up his mind to marry, but he soon did. A later footnote refers to the poem which Thomas wrote a year later on the first anniversary of his marriage to Mrs Sherwood, in which he describes in gushing terms how it had been her kind ministrations to him at Wells after his fall which convinced him of her merits as a wife[18] (see also Appendix Two).

But was this really the case, or was the whole incident part of a cunning strategy? One has to remember that in August he appears to be pursuing a widow in N. Wales, but only three months later he has transferred his affections to another widow. Even more remarkable is that a prenuptial legal document dated December 31st 1773 / January 1st 1774 contains details of the arrangements for transferring the ownership of the Langford Estate to Thomas, in anticipation of his forthcoming marriage

16 JCTSW I p.275

17 ibid I p.280

18 ibid I p.231

to Mrs Sherwood.[19] She was a great granddaughter of the wealthy Cadwallader Jones (1630-1692), whose family also had estates in America.[20] The marriage took place only 5 days later, on January 6th 1774, in St Marylebone Church, Westminster and was conducted by Bishop Edmund Keene of Ely, who had provided Thomas with his living at Hagworthingham two years earlier. Others in attendance included his sister Elizabeth and her husband Isaac Sage, who signed the register, as did Thomas's cousin Dr Richard Beadon, who was a prebend of St Pauls at the time and would become Bishop of Bath and Wells.

3.5 Wedding at St Marylebone church, Westminster

In 1774 Thomas Sedgwick obtained his MA. It could be that this was how he came into contact with George Pretyman-Tomline, who by this time was a very young fellow of Pembroke Hall and an outstanding mathematician. He was later to become a Member of Parliament and a tutor to William Pitt the younger.

---

[19] *Abstract of Title to the Langford Inn* (then the White Hart), Somerset Heritage Centre, Taunton DD\SOG/151

[20] It is just possible that the two widows were in fact one and the same, and that Mrs Sherwood (née Jones), who came from a wealthy Welsh family, had been staying in N. Wales, perhaps as another guest of the Warringtons.

More importantly for Thomas Sedgwick, Pretyman-Tomline was in due course ordained, later becoming Bishop of Lincoln and thus technically responsible for Thomas's parish of Hagworthingham. It was as a theologian that Bishop Sir George Pretyman-Tomline was to have greatest influence on Whalley. In 1799 Tomline had published his two volume *Elements of Christian Theology*, a work dedicated to Pitt and designed for Anglican ordinands. Its lucidity and accessibility earned it considerable popularity, and Whalley was greatly influenced by this until his final years.[21]

Early Married Life

Elizabeth Sherwood was the only daughter, and thus heiress, of Edward Jones of Langford Court. When she married Thomas Sedgwick on 6th January 1774, she was aged 34 and he just 28 years. Surprisingly, they were married in Marylebone, Middlesex, though neither appear to have been living in London at the time.[22] We know nothing of Mrs Sherwood's education and early life. There was a Mrs Sherwood who during 1768-9 was a player in the Bath/Bristol Theatre Company.[23] If this was the same person, it would fit with the suggestion that her first husband fell ill sometime in 1769, necessitating her leaving the theatre to nurse him until his death in August 1770. While this is pure speculation, it would give Elizabeth a shared interest with the would-be playwright Thomas Sedgwick. It is also perhaps of relevance that, when snowed in shortly after their marriage, a play was written

21 JCTSW I p.41

22 Courtney, W.P., *Whalley, Thomas Sedgwick (1746–1828)*, revised. Rebecca Mills, Oxford Dictionary of National Biography, Oxford University Press, 2004

23 *Theatre Royal Bath A calendar of performances at the Orchard Street Theatre 1750-1805*, (Hare, A., Ed), Kingsmead Press, Bath, 1977, p.29

by Thomas and performed at Langford Court by those detained there (see below).

The marriage brought Thomas great wealth. According to the Will of Edward Jones, Elizabeth Jones was only to have a life interest in the family estate, but it seems that her first husband John Withers Sherwood, a lawyer, had started legal proceedings to break entail, in anticipation that he would have children to inherit the Jones estate. Thomas seems to have taken advantage of this and progressed matters further, though he does seem to have had something of a conscience about this. After their marriage Elizabeth and Thomas lived at Langford Court, where Thomas was responsible for adding bays and a west wing to the original 17th century house.[24]

3.6 Langford Court. The west wing was added by Thomas Sedgwick Whalley

Thomas Sedgwick's great nephew credits him with being the first

[24] Marsden-Smedley, C., *Burrington Church and Village – a short history*, Burrington, 1991, p.21

to plant trees on what had been the northern slope of the bare Mendip hillside.[25] Hill Wickham suggests that this was part of the later building of Mendip Lodge. However, Thomas Sedgwick may well have undertaken this planting while still at Langford. A plaintive paragraph written by Mrs Miller on November 1780, calling his attention to the 'first day of the opening of the vase at Bath-Easton',[26] that is to say the first of her poetry meetings for that season, states:

> We had hoped we should have seen you and Mrs.
> Whalley before now in Bath, but suppose you are
> planting clumps etc at that elegant retreat
> Langford Court.[27]

In an earlier account of 1788, in what would become the publication of the Bath and West Society, a Somerset correspondent identified only as 'R.E.' urged members to consider planting trees on barren land as had already been undertake on the Mendips

> On the north slope of the Mendip Hills in particular
> (a situation as unfavourable as most, on account of
> its being a bed of rocks exposed to the bleak North
> and East winds) we see beautiful woods of large
> extent hanging over the parishes of Compton-
> Martin, Ubley, Blagdon, Hutton and Churchill. In
> these woods although the timber is not large, the
> growth of the pollarded trees and copse wood must
> every twelve years bring in considerable sums to the

---

25 JCTSW I p.21

26 Often written this way at the time, now known as Batheaston

27 JCTSW I p.315

owners.[28]

This was before Whalley's work began on Mendip Lodge and suggests the trees were already established above Churchill, although not yet big enough to coppice. Thus, the planting must have been undertaken even earlier. However, not all this area belonged to the Langford estate, so it was perhaps a general move to arboriculture at this time.

His changed circumstance also allowed him to move into a more gracious style of living, and he become renowned for lavish entertainment. Hill Wickham records a notable occasion:

> One party was remembered by all present. A company of neighbours came to dinner on a winter's evening in 1776, and during their stay, which in those days was protracted, far beyond the limits of modern fashion [the author, Hill Wickham, was writing this in 1863], the snow fell so fast that when the carriages were ordered it was impossible to leave, and some of the more distant neighbours were detained, not unwilling prisoners for several days. For animal cheer, the sheepfold, close at hand, supplied good mutton in abundance; and the cellar, famous since the days of an old Somersetshire toast "A bumper Squire Jones!" was well calculated to keep the blood in active circulation. To prevent ennui a play was written and performed, and various pieces of poetry composed and recited.[29]

---

[28] *Letter and papers selected from the correspondence book of the Society, Instituted at Bath for the Encouragement of Agriculture, the Arts, Manufactures and Commerce,* Vol.. II, 1788, p.352

[29] JCTSW I p.4

Quite where Thomas's interest in poetry came from is not clear. It is likely that while in Cambridge he was in contact with the poets of Pembroke, where Thomas Gray still held court. This would certainly account for his later friendship with Wilberforce and his support for the politics of William Pitt, both of whom graduated later from Pembroke Hall. At that time the College had a tradition of encouraging the study of oratory and poetry, and Wilberforce and Pitt became notable parliamentary orators (see William Hague's biographies on these two).

One of the poems composed and recited by Thomas Sedgwick on this occasion has been preserved. Hill Wickham says that Miss Luders, a Bath resident and the sister of Theodore von Luders, who later would accompany the Whalleys on their continental tour, made a pen for Dr Whalley and insisted on him writing a copy for her. This was subsequently lost, but the 200 lines which Hill Wickham reproduces was recalled from memory by Mrs Torriano (née La Fausille), who had also been present.[30] (See Appendix 2.)

From the poem we can deduce that those present on this occasion included Mrs G Anstey, Miss La Fausille, Susan Whalley (who would marry Dr John Crane), Mary Wickham née Whalley and her husband James Wickham, Mrs Knollis (this is likely to be the widow of the Reverend Charles Knollis, 5th Earl of Banbury), Mrs Rodd, Miss Luders and Monsieur Zenovief (was this perhaps Zinovieff?), who appears to be the Russian ambassador. One thing this tells us is that as early as 1776 Thomas was already keenly writing poetry and plays, and it was not long before this that it became a major part of his social activities.

Hill Wickham states that 'within a year or two of his marriage Thomas had bought the centre house in the Crescent at Bath'. [31]

---

30 JCTSW I pp.246-252
31 ibid I p.4

In fact it seems that the house may have been bought for her husband by Elizabeth Sherwood in 1775, the same year as her marriage to Thomas Sedgwick. Lowndes, quoting Philip Gosse,[32] says that number nine was the first house to be completed and had been bought in 1768 by Philip Thicknesse, an ambitious and ill tempered soldier of fortune.[33] Thicknesse lived there with his third wife until 1774, whereupon he sold it to a 'lady of quality' for £2000. This was almost certainly the new Mrs Whalley. Ison identifies number nine, later renumbered as twenty, as being occupied by the Rev Thomas Sedgwick Whalley in 1778.[34] William Lowndes is quite definite in stating that Thomas Sedgwick bought the house currently numbered twenty.[35] While by current numbering the centre house would be number fifteen or sixteen, it is likely that Hill Wickham never visited the house of his great uncle in Bath.

Work on the Royal Crescent had started early in 1767 and was completed in 1775. Its designer, Wood the Younger, put out the building of each of the 30 houses in the now famous terrace to contract. We know from the contract for number seven, one of the last to be completed in 1771, that Mrs Tyndall paid the builder Mr Hemmings £1700.[36]

By this time Thomas's career in the church had advanced significantly. In 1777, on the death of Samuel Hood, he was appointed Prebend of Combe XIII at Wells, an appointment he held until shortly before his death.

[32] Gosse, P., *Dr Viper, the querulous life of Philip Thicknesse,* Cassell and Company Ltd, London, 1952

[33] Lowndes, W., *The Royal Crescent in Bath*, Redcliffe Press Ltd., Bristol, 1981, p.43

[34] Ison, W., *The Georgian Buildings of Bath*, 1730-1830, Kingsmead Press, 1980

[35] Lowndes, W., *The Royal Crescent in Bath*, Redcliffe Press Ltd., Bristol, 1981, p.48

[36] ibid p.88

3.7 The seat of Prebend Combe XIII in the Wells Chapter
House

Neighbours in Royal Crescent

Having acquired their house in Bath, it became the Whalleys'
custom to spend the season from October until April there, and
the summer months at Langford Court. Quite what literary and
social contacts Thomas Sedgwick had in Bath before owning a
house in Royal Crescent can only be guessed at, but his new
neighbours opened many doors.

3.8 Royal Crescent today

According to Ison,[32] other occupants of Royal Crescent in 1778 were:

No. 1: Mr Henry Sanford-Princess de Lamballe lived here 1786 and 1791, the Duke of York in 1796

No. 2: Mrs Elesha Macartney

No. 3: Mr George Burgis

No. 4: Mr Christopher Anstey – moved to smaller Marlborough Buildings in 1792

No. 5: Mr John Bathoe

No. 6: Mr Winthrop Baldwin

No. 7:. Mrs Elizabeth Tyndale -who had bought her house in 1771

No. 8: Mr John Bennett

No. 9: Rev Mr. Whalley (The house was later renumbered as No. 20 – see above).

No. 10: Mr John Riddle
No. 11: Capt John Martin
No. 12: Dr Edward Cooper
No. 14: Mr John Charnock
No. 14: Hon Charles Hamilton
No. 15: Mr McGillchrist
No. 16: Dr Claud Champion de Crespigny
No. 17: Mrs Victory Kynaston
No. 18: Mr Edward Hoare
No. 19: Mr John Jefferys
No. 20: Lady Hester Malpas
No. 21: Lady Stepney
No. 22: Dean of Ossory
No. 23: Dr William Watson
No. 24: Lady Isabella Stanley
No. 25: Col John Stibbert
No. 26: Mrs Mary Cunliffe
No. 27: Lady Mary Stanley
No. 28: Philip Thicknesse – now living here with the third Mrs
Thicknesse née Ford
No. 29: Col Champion
No. 30: Hon Henry Greville

Philip Thicknesse has already been mentioned; more respectable,
though only slightly so, was Christopher Anstey at No. Four,
whose portrait by William Hoarse now hangs in the Bath
Guildhall and shows him as he must have been when he and
Whalley first met. Anstey had been born in 1724 in
Cambridgeshire, the son of the Vicar of Brinkley, also named
Christopher Anstey. The latter would have known Thomas
Sedgwick's father; not only were they were subject to the same
Bishop, but John Whalley had been born only three miles from

where Christopher Anstey senior was to become Rector. Christopher Anstey junior become a Fellow of King's in 1745 and would have known Professor Whalley as the Master of Peterhouse during his time at Cambridge.

In 1756 Anstey junior had married the daughter of a wealthy brewer and settled down to manage the estate his father in law had bequeathed him. After a 'bilious fever' he visited Bath to take the waters and on his return to Cambridgeshire had written the *New Bath Guide*. This hugely popular work was a satirical review of Bath's fashionable society in verse. It was first published in 1766 and was the author's only work of any consequence. The book eventually ran to 40 editions and was said to be an influence on the form adopted by WS Gilbert in his *Bab Ballards*. *The New Bath Guide* gained him praise at the time from those not noted for such generosity, including Hugh Walpole and Thomas Gray. Perhaps because of its success, the family moved to Bath in 1770, where Anstey's new neighbour in Royal Crescent, Philip Thicknesse, was moved to attempt a more serious account of Bath in his *New Prose Bath Guide*, but this was not a success.

3.9 20 Royal Crescent today – the second door from the left

Having moved to Bath, Anstey gained the friendship of the actor and manager David Garrick, the playwright Richard Brinsley Sheridan and Sir John and Lady Miller, whose poetry gatherings were a feature of the Bath season. Two poems by Anstey, 'Envy' and 'Winter Musements' appear in volume four of Lady Miller's *Poetical Amusements at a Villa near Bath*.

The history behind these poetical occasions is as follows: Mr and Mrs Miller had returned to Batheaston from Italy in 1759 with an Etruscan vase which had been dug up at Frascati. This was incorporated into a Temple of Apollo at their new home. Sometime after this Mrs Miller started her poetical gatherings at Batheaston, which were certainly established by 1774. These were based initially on the "Bouts Rimés" poetry fashion brought by Lady Miller from France. From December to May within the Bath season, Mrs, later Lady, Miller would issue a general invitation to ladies and gentleman of fashion to attend a fortnightly poetry festival at her house. Here, the would-be poets found the Etruscan vase set up on a modern altar in the bay window of the Batheaston villa. Each gentleman and lady was required to submit their poetical offering to it. The assembly having all contributed, Mr Miller selected a lady who would draw these out one at a time at random to be read aloud by a gentleman. After this a small committee of six retired to an adjacent room to determine the four best submissions while food was served. The four chosen then identified themselves by their coded signatures and were crowned with myrtle by Mrs Miller. Initially, this event was held on Friday but because of a clash with the Bath ball was later held on a Thursday afternoon. Winners were expected to display their wreaths or sprigs of myrtle at the Ball the following day.[37] In 1775 the first selection of these poems

---

[37] Sturge, M., *Lady Miller and her Poetical Assemblies at Batheaston 1774-1781*. Proceedings of the Bath Royal Literary and Scientific Association, 2012; 10:

was published and proved extremely popular. This and three later volumes were sold in aid of the Millers' charity, the Bath Casualty Hospital, which, with the Bath City Dispensary and Infirmary, later became Royal United Hospital Bath. These assemblies continued until shortly before Lady Miller's death in 1781.

3.10 Lady Miller's Etruscan Vase

It was probably through Anstey that Thomas Sedgewick became a regular contributor to Lady Miller's gatherings. Hill Wickham includes a letter from Lady Miller to him, dated November 3rd 1780, urging him to be available to attend the first day of the winter season on 21st December.[38] It is clear that by this time Anstey and Whalley were on very good terms. In a letter from Bath, dated 3rd August 1779, Anstey writes to thank Thomas and his wife for providing his son with a 'continued [sic] round of pleasure and entertainment'.[39] This was almost certainly Arthur

47-49 10, pp.47-49 2009 (http://www.bath.ac.uk/lmf/fileinfo/37757)
[38] JCTSW I p.315
[39] ibid I pp.311-2

Anstey (also known in Hill Wickham's book as Mr Anstey Calvert, by adding his mother's maiden name), who became an Attorney and Thomas Sedgwick Whalley's legal adviser.[40] This entertainment presumably took place at Langford Court, since after their marriage it was the custom of the Whalleys to spend from May to October there. Christopher Anstey also asks to be remembered to Thomas Sedgwick's mother, referring to her as 'my old and respected friend'. This rather confirms that the two families were known to each other long before Thomas acquired his house in Bath – maybe from their Cambridge days; like Thomas Sedgwick, Christopher Anstey was a Cambridge scholar with an interest in poetry. In 1790 Thomas Sedgwick officiated the marriage of Anstey's third daughter, Caroline, to another friend, Henry Bosanquet, a barrister of Lincoln's Inn, who would later rent Langford Court from him.[41]

Fanny Burney, who later became Madame D'Arblay, was already the successful novelist of *Evelina* when she met Thomas Sedgwick in 1780 at Lady Miller's literary circle. Though she was a near contemporary, she was never a close friend of Whalley. Nonetheless, she was invited to join one of the many soirees at Royal Crescent run by Thomas Sedgwick, whom she described as 'immensely tall, thin and handsome, but affected delicate and sentimentally pathetic'. This description seems to be been borne out by both his portrait and other written accounts. Her account of a typical gathering at Royal Crescent, in May 1780, paints a very vivid picture of these occasions.

> In the Afternoon we all went to the Whalleys, where we found a large & high Dressed Company:- at the

---

[40] It is curious that although Hill Wickham refers to him as 'Mr. Anstey Calvert' Thomas Sedgwick only ever calls him Arthur Anstey.

[41] Bath Chronicle and Weekly Gazette, May 6th, 1790

Head of which sat Lady Miller. Among the rest, were Mr. Anstey, his lady & 2 Daughters, Miss Weston, Mrs. Aubrey, the thin quaker like woman I saw first at Mrs. Laws's - Mrs. Lambart, & various others, male & female, that I knew not.

Miss Weston instantly made up to me, to express her delight at my return to Bath, & to beg she might sit by me,- Mrs. Whalley, however, placed me upon a sofa next herself & that meagre fright Mrs. Aubrey - which, however, I did not repine at, for the extreme delicacy of Miss Weston makes it prodigiously fatiguing to converse with her, as it is no little difficulty to keep pace with her refinement in order to avoid shocking her by too obvious an inferiority in daintihood & ton.

Mr. Whalley, to my great astonishment, so far broke through his delicacy, as to call to me across the Room to ask me divers questions concerning my London Journey:- during all which Mr. Anstey, who sat next to him, earnestly fixed his Eyes in my Face, & both then, & for the rest of the Evening, examined me with a look of most keen penetration. As soon as my discourse was over with Mr. Whalley, during which, as he called me by my Name, every body turned towards me, - which was not very agreeable ,- Lady Miller arose, & went to Mrs. Thrale, & whispered something to her. Mrs. Thrale then rose too, & said 'If your Ladyship will give me leave. I will first introduce my Daughter to you,- making Miss. Thrale, who was next her mother, make her reverences, -'And now, she continued, Miss. Burney, Lady Miller desires to be introduced

65

to you,' - Up I jumped, & walked forward, - Lady Miller, very civilly, more than met me half way, & said very polite things of her wish to know me, & regret that she had not sooner met me,-& then we both returned to our seats.

Do you know now that notwithstanding Bath Easton is so much Laughed at in London, nothing here is more tonish than to visit Lady Miller, who is extremely curious in her Company, admitting few people who are not of Rank or of Fame, & excluding of those all who are not people of character very unblemished.

Some Time after. Lady Miller took a seat next mine on the sofa, to play at Cards,- & was excessively civil indeed, - scolded Mrs. Thrale for not sooner making us acquainted, & had the politeness to offer to take me to the Balls, herself, as she heard Mr. & Mrs. Thrale did not chuse to go.

After all this, it is hardly fair to tell you what I think of her,- however, the truth is I always, to the best of my intentions, speak honestly what I think of the folks I see, without being biased either by their civilities or neglect, - & that, you will allow, is being a very faithful Historian.

Well then, -Lady Miller is a round, plump, course [sic] looking Dame of about 40, - &, while all her aim is to appear an elegant Woman of Fashion, all her success is to seem an ordinary Woman in very common Life with fine Cloaths on. Her manners are bustling, her Air is mock-important. & her Language very inelegant.

So much for the Lady of Bath Easton .- who,

however, seems extremely good natured, & who is, I am sure, extremely civil.

The Card Party was soon after broken up, as Lady Miller was engaged to Lady Dorothy English. & then I moved to seat myself by Mrs. Lambart. I was presently followed by Miss Weston ,- & she was pursued by Mr. Bouchier, a man of Fortune who is in the Army, or the militia, & who was tormenting Miss Weston, en badinage, about some expedition upon the River Avon to which he had been witness. He seemed a mighty ratling, har'em scar'em Gentleman, but talked so fluently that I had no trouble in contributing my mite towards keeping up the conversation, as he talked enough for 4, - & this I was prodigiously pleased at, as I was in an indolent mood, & not disposed to bear my share. I fancy, when he pleases, & thinks it worth while, he can be sensible & agreeable; - but all his desire then was to alarm Miss Weston, & persuade the Company she had been guilty of a thousand misdemeanours. [42]

The Theatre and Mrs Siddons

It is clear that Thomas Sedgwick was already writing plays in the early years of his marriage and would have attended the theatre at Bath during the season. Hill Wickham states that Thomas Sedgwick's house in Bath brought him into contact with Mrs Siddons,[43] who at this time was still a struggling actress touring the country with her actor husband. The couple had arrived in

[42] 'The Streatham Years, Part II 1780-1781' in *Early Journals and Letters of Fanny Burney* Volume IV (Rizzo, B., Ed.) Oxford University Press, 2003, pp.126-9
[43] JCTSW I p.6

Bath in 1778 and were members of the Bristol / Bath Company from 1778 until 1782.[44] Her first recorded performance as leading lady in Bath was on Saturday October 24th, 1778, in *The provoked Husband* by Vanbrugh, a popular play there.[45,46] It is doubtful if Thomas Sedgwick met her on this occasion, as his sister was probably already back in Bath by this time and died there only 6 weeks later (see Chapter 4). This loss greatly affected him, and the following year he published anonymously his tragic poem *Edwy and Edilda*. This brought him into contact with Anna Seward, who regarded herself as patroness of the poetic muse and was to prove to be a lifelong friend. Her father was a minor Canon of Litchfield Cathedral, and it was her influence which encouraged Whalley to republish the same poem under his own name.

He may well have met Mrs Siddons the following May (1779), when Hannah More's play *The Fatal Falsehood* was performed for the first time. It was by this time that Mr Samuel Jackson Pratt had ingratiated himself into Bath Society. Pratt, the son of a brewer, had been ordained into the Church of England but in 1772 had eloped with a girl he never married to try a career on the stage as "Courtney Melmoth".[47] This he did with less success than "Mrs Melmoth", and they parted company, he to turn to writing. He arrived in Bath in 1779 and soon found friends in the influential Bath Literary Society, whose secretary Edmund Rack considered him to be the 'Addison of his age... his pen truly the most classical of any we have in the kingdom'.[48]

---

[44] *Theatre Royal Bath A calendar of performances at the Orchard Street Theatre 1750-1805,* (Hare, A., ed), Kingsmead Press, Bath, 1977

[45] ibid p.63

[46] The first performance in Bristol had been on 15th March, 1778 (see Barker, K., *The Theatre Royal Bristol,* The Historical Assn, Bristol, 1969, p.8)

[47] See the Oxford Dictionary of National Biography.

However, this colourful character was not to everyone's liking. Despite warnings from Charles Layland, both Thomas Sedgwick and Anna Seward were soon favourably disposed towards him, and he was soon lodging with the Whalleys. Later, Pratt would insult both Mrs Siddons[49] and Anna Seward,[50] and finally Whalley was persuaded to discontinue his association with him.

During the next three years Mrs Siddons made a sufficient name for herself among London visitors to Bath to be invited by Garrick to join the Drury Lane Company. By the time of her Bath benefit performance on June 17th 1782, she and the Whalleys were firm, if not close, friends.[51,52] Thomas's play *The Castle of Montval* had been written in 1781, and he clearly hoped it might be performed at Bath.[53] He wrote a poem, 'Verses Addressed to Mrs. Siddons on being engaged at Drury Lane'. Her return to London was announced late in 1781, in an advertisement doubtless inserted by himself. This mentions that 'The Reverend Mr. Whalley was also the author of Edwy and Edilda, The Fatal Kiss etc. etc.'[54] By October 1781 Thomas Sedgwick had unsuccessfully sought the support of Mrs Siddons and others to get the play performed by the company at Bath, which was pleased to support local authors at this time[55]. According to the

---

48 Rack E. *A Disultory Journal of Events &c at Bath*, transcribed and edited by Trevor Fawcett, Bath City Library, (MS1111)

49 Seward, A., *Letters of Anna Seward, Written Between the Years 1784 and 1807, Vol II*, George Ramsay and Co., Edinburgh, 1811, p.361

50 JCTSW II p.28

51 *Theatre Royal Bath A calendar of performances at the Orchard Street Theatre 1750-1805*, (Hare, A. Ed), Kingsmead Press, Bath, 1977, p 84

52 JCTSW I pp.370-1

53 ibid I p.338-9

54 ibid I p.339

55 ibid I p.338

Dictionary of National Biography, Courtney and Charlotte Melmoth performed at Bath during 1778-9, although they are not listed as members of the company. However, this may explain why Mr Pratt's two act farce *The Fair Circassian*, written in the same year, was performed eleven times at Bath between January and May 1782 and had a continuous run of twenty six nights at Drury Lane. It is very likely that Mr Pratt's previous experience as an actor had served him well as a playwright, and perhaps it was for his advice that Thomas Sedgwick had accommodated him at Langford Court for so many months.

The Castle of Montval was finally put on at Drury Lane in July 1799. Thomas Sedgwick was living at Hampton Court at the time; it seems that he and a number of his titled friends were able to rent accommodation at Hampton Court. (George III, from the moment of his accession, never set foot in the palace, as he associated the state apartments with a humiliating scene when his grandfather had once struck him, following an innocent remark.)[56] According to his brother, the Reverend Richard Chaple Whalley, Thomas Sedgwick was in high anxiety about this production for many weeks. Richard always disapproved of someone in Thomas's position in life ever having written such a play. In a letter to Frances Sullivan (née Sage), he says

> Your uncle Sedgwick, I suppose you know, has been in the neighbourhood of London for some time, staking his reputation on the reception of a play. T' was a sad losing game, for, whatever the fate of the play, his reception with all good and wise people was sure to suffer; but our vanities and our views blind us to a degree that

---

56 Williams, N., *Royal Homes*, Lutterworth Press, London, 1971, p.54

is hardly credible or conceivable.[57]

There seems to have been some doubt as to whether the play would ever appear. Mr Siddons wrote to Thomas Sedgwick on December 15th, 1797, describing a rival version of the play by Matthew (Monk) Lewis, which appeared under the title of *The Castle Spectre*. Siddons gave it a favourable review and noted that the audience had received the ghost scene with great enthusiasm. In a period when very few plays reached ten performances in a season, this rival was staged forty-seven times before the theatre closed for the summer of 1797. The play also had a long run in the following year and toured the provincial theatres. From 1798 to 1803 it went to eleven printed editions and was sufficiently popular to remain in the repertoire until the late 1820s. Even now it remains on the reading list of many Universities as the archetypical Gothic play!

In the same letter William also reported that his wife, the anticipated leading lady, had withdrawn from the theatre again, on account of the failure of *Tereus*. However, he also speaks of a promise which the Drury Lane theatre had clearly given to Thomas Sedgwick to stage the play, which Mr Siddons expected they would keep.[58] In the event, when the play did finally appear eighteen months later, despite efforts by Anna Seward to ensure all the appropriate influential members of Society were present[59] and despite having Mrs Siddons in the leading role as had been planned, the critics were not favourably impressed. The play was only given nine performances and was never put on again. This must have been particularly galling for Thomas Sedgwick, since

---

[57] JCTSW I p.22

[58] ibid II p.109

[59] ibid II pp.119-120

the young author of its rival *The Castle Spectre* had only graduated from Oxford three years before. Anna Seward's predictable glowing letter of congratulation to Thomas, in which she discounted the newspaper criticisms, can have been of little comfort to him.[60] He would have been further distressed to learn that by 1855 his one time friend Samuel Jackson Pratt is still recorded as 'a versatile genius' by the Bath Literary Club; Thomas Sedgwick Whalley has no mention at all![61]

3.11 Thomas Sedgwick Whalley in 1781, aged 32 years with Sappho

[60] JCTSW II p.12

[61] Monkland, G., *Supplement to the Literature and Literati of Bath*, J.H.Parker, London, 1855, p.12

CHAPTER 4
Thomas's Adored Sister 1745-1778

It is appropriate at this point to provide the background to those events which would have a profound influence on the rest of Thomas Sedgwick's long life. As mentioned in Chapter 2, Thomas Sedgwick's favourite sister, Elizabeth, was only a year his senior. It is clear from her correspondence that Elizabeth was both well educated and enlightened and had excellent powers of observation and description.[1] Thomas Sedgwick doted on her only surviving daughter, Frances Elizabeth Sage, from a very early age.[2]

He adored Elizabeth and had more than one painting of her, one of which he kept with him all his life and from which the engraving below was made. The affection seems to have been mutual. A few years after her marriage, in a letter dated August 1773, she wrote,

> But in what instance through life has the fondest
> and best of brothers, omitted to show a sister,
> unworthy of so much attention, every proof of
> affection which was in his power. All the return I
> can offer him is the sincere and warm regard, and

---

[1] Her description of her sea passage to India and her first impressions of life there, contained in her letters to Thomas, deserve special mention - JCTSW I pp.282-311

[2] ibid I p.294

such a one as can only cease with my existence.

Since ever I was capable of making distinctions, you, my brother, were the dear loadstone of my affections; and, except the claims as a wife and mother, my heart can never admit to a rival to the love it bears you. Your absence from Wells [he was at the time a curate in Wales] was such a vacancy as nothing could supply; I myself did not imagine I could have missed you so much.[3]

4.1 Elizabeth Whalley

How Elizabeth met her husband, Isaac Sage (1741-1818), is

[3] JCTSW I p.272

unknown, but it is likely to have been in Bath, probably at the Assembly Rooms. He was the third youngest of nine children of John Sage and Elizabeth Sage (née Beresford) of Stanmore in Middlesex.[4] In 1762 Isaac or, more likely, his father had petitioned the East India Company in London for admission into its service as a writer.[5] This was the usual route of entry to the Company but was no simple matter. Although it recruited a dozen men to enter its service each year, this was undertaken by competition, for which there was an entry fee equivalent to £50,000 today.[6] Such applications were normally made at age 16 years, so Isaac was slightly older than average, but this was by no means unusual. Robert, later Lord, Clive was nineteen years old when his father acquired for him a similar position as writer, in 1744.

According to Hill Wickham, Isaac eventually became paymaster to Robert Clive's Indian army before his return to England in 1768/9, but this seems doubtful.[7,8] Such a post would normally have gone to a more senior individual. In 1765 Isaac was in the Company's employ in East Bengal, working as a junior to William Bolts, the factor at Patna. Bolts was a clever, devious and corrupt adventurer whose full story in all its complexity has been recorded in great detail by Hallward.[9] It seems most likely

---

[4] Lysons, D., *The Environs of London*: Vol. 3 - County of Middlesex, 1795, pp.391-403

[5] National Archives. *Records of the East India College*. 1762 IRO /J/1/4/380-383

[6] Williams, C., *The Nabobs of Berkshire*, Goosecroft Publications, Purley on Thames, Berkshire, 2010, p.112

[7] JCTSW I p.6

[8] At this time, because Britain was at war with the French, there was a very flexible relationship in India between the Company and the British Army. For his famous escape from Fort St David in 1746, Clive was given an ensign's commission by Major Stringer.

[9] Hallward N L., *William Bolts, a Dutch Adventurer under John Company*, University Press, Cambridge, 1920

that Hill Wickham's understanding of Isaac's role as 'paymaster to the army' applied to the brief period which followed Bolts's downfall and Isaac's promotion over him.

It is not clear quite when Isaac Sage arrived back in England from his first period in India. This was probably in 1767, when many senior servants of the Company in Bengal were either dismissed or resigned.[10] The last date on which we have proof that Isaac was in India was 12th December 1766, when he wrote to the Council in Calcutta and presented them with:

> a bill upon Mr. William Bolts for Rs. 8167/4/9 for
> grain sold by him out of the garrison of Chunar,
> and requests them to demand payment.[11]

Isaac seems to have returned from India a rich man – not unusual in those days – with the intention of finding a wife and settling down. Quite what size fortune he had amassed during his 5 years in India can only be guessed at. General Smith, who was of a similar age and with whom Isaac and his wife spent two weeks in July 1773,[12] had returned in 1770 with a fortune believed to be equivalent to £20-£30m today.[13] However, Smith had spent three times as long in the Company's service.

As Isaac's father and mother were still very much alive, Isaac would probably have lodged with them on his return, before renting a house in Bath ready for the 1768 season, which started

[10] Williams, C., *The Nabobs of Berkshire,* Goosecroft Publications, Purley on Thames, Berkshire, 2010, p.339

[11] The Council at Calcutta agreed this should be paid by Bolts, but Isaac had not been paid 2 years later. Bolt's prevarication and mischief continued for another two years, but there was no reason for Isaac to be involved.

[12] JCTSW I p.269

[13] Williams, C., *The Nabobs of Berkshire*, Goosecroft Publications, Purley on Thames, Berkshire, 2010, p.152

in October and was where many in his position went to find a wife. At that time Elizabeth Whalley was still living in Wells and Thomas Sedgwick was on his Grand Tour. As Elizabeth was now aged 23, her widowed mother would probably have been actively seeking a husband for her, and it would have been likely that she too had arranged for her daughter to spend time in Bath to that end.

Elizabeth Whalley married Isaac Sage in Wells at St Cuthbert's Church in July 1769. Elizabeth was then 24 years old, and he was a year older. Her first daughter, Frances Elizabeth, was born later the same year. Hill Wickham, in his synopsis of Thomas Sedgwick's life in the first volume of his book published in 1863, gives the year of their marriage as 1768, but church records clearly state otherwise. This was perhaps the intervention of Victorian morals. The book, after all, was published more than 90 years later, and it is well documented that more than half of 18th-century brides were pregnant at the time of their marriage, since a key requirement of marriage was to be able to produce an heir.

After their marriage Isaac and Elizabeth lived in London. Their first address was Queen Anne Street, and it is clear that they were in close contact with the Sages at their family home at Stanmore and also with Isaac's younger brother Joseph and his wife who lived at Reading. Joseph was to be Isaac's executor and for 40 years was Assayer to the Royal Mint.[14]

There is no correspondence recorded by Hill Wickham between Elizabeth Sage and her brother during the early years of her marriage. It is unlikely that any correspondence from this time would have survived, since Thomas was still undertaking his Grand Tour and Elizabeth would have been busy with her

[14] There is more than one account of Joseph appearing in court as an expert witness for the Crown when silver coinage had been tampered with by "clipping".

first pregnancy. As Thomas was ordained Deacon in 1770, he probably arrived back in England soon after his niece Frances was born. His absence at her birth may explain why he was not her godfather but was to the Sages' second daughter, Emily.

During the early years of their marriage, Isaac and Elizabeth moved in the very best of social circles. Elizabeth's first recorded letter to Thomas dates from July 1773 and is written from the Sage's London house at Queen Anne Street. In it she relates the very full social life of Nabob Society, recording balls and weeks spent at Epsom Races. The couple were clearly on nodding terms with the nobility and the very rich. In the same letter there is also the following news:

> Did you know that the society of which you are a member have elected Mr Sage? Your friend Count Hippisley [Sir John Cox Hippisley] put him up. Mr. Sage has never been among them. [15]

Quite what this society was remains unknown, but membership clearly was advantageous to both men. Sir John was ambitious and politically active. Born in Bristol, he had been called to the bar in 1771 and was engaged in confidential communication with the English Government during a residency in Italy from 1779 and 1780. Returning home in 1781, he was recommended by Lord North, First Lord of the Treasury, to the directors of the East India Company, from whom he received an appointment in India as paymaster at Tanjore in 1786. Thus one might suppose that, a few years earlier, he and Isaac would have had much in common. Other members of the East India Company they met or visited during this time include General Richard Smith of

---

[15] JCTSW I p.268

Chilton Lodge, Mr Stanlake Batson of Winkfield Place, Sir Thomas Rumbold, a Director of the Company, Mr Stables (a Director of the Company), Mr Wheeler (another Director of the Company).

In August 1773 Isaac bought Thornhill in Dorset, a large country estate, the house having been built in 1730 by Sir James Thornhill the artist. As Elizabeth said to her brother:

> ... the place is but five and twenty miles from Wells, so that if we live there, I may hope to see you often. We have been to see the estate which is a sweet one, [earning] between 300l and 400l a year [equivalent to about £30,000 today] and a good house on it.[16]

4.2 Thornhill, Dorset: 'the estate….. is a sweet one… and a good house on it'

Four months later, Elizabeth describes Christmas at Lovell Hill,

16 JCTSW I p.272

the home of another wealthy East Indiaman Hugh Watts, who had been born and married in India but whose family came from Berkshire. He had bought the house Lovell Hill in Berkshire in 1767 on his return from India and may well have travelled back on the same boat as Isaac Sage, which is perhaps how the two families came to know each other.

> Lovell Hill
> Christmas 1773
>
> Wish my dear you were of our party here, which is a very agreeable one. We sat down a large company to dinner yesterday and spent a most joyous evening. In the morning we went to church and in the afternoon engaged at the card table; and after supper music took place, and we sung songs and catches till twelve o'clock. Two-and-fifty dined at the house yesterday; and the servants were as merry as their masters.[17]

This letter, which was written before Thomas was married, shows that Frances and her sister and nurse were staying with their mother in Wells, where Thomas had recently returned from Wales. She hopes that Thomas is recovering from the fall from his horse. The fall, and Mrs Sherwood nursing him, would lead to their marriage (see Chapter 3). Elizabeth also asks Thomas to give her love 'to my dear Fanny and Emily with a kiss and remember me to nurse'. The Sage's daughter Frances was destined to spend several years of her early life with Thomas Sedgwick Whalley and his wife (see Chapter 5).

---

17   William C., *The Nabobs of Wiltshire*, Goosecroft Publications, Purley on Thames, Berkshire, 2010, pp.338-341

Hill Wickham records that Elizabeth Sage always had a delicate constitution.[18] It is clear even by this time that Elizabeth's health was not robust. In an earlier letter to Thomas, dated August 1773, written from the Hotwells in Bristol, Elizabeth says:

> You will see by the date of this letter that we are at the Hot Well, where I am very sanguine in my hopes of receiving benefit. The waters have greatly relieved my complaints already. I have brought my dear Fanny with me, and left Emily with my mother [Mrs Whalley senior at Wells] who was to carry her over to Winscombe to be there while I am here, which will be 6 weeks if the waters continue to agree with me.[19]

Her address, which she gives as 'Mrs. Brotherton's on the Parade, Bristol Wells' is likely to mean Dowry Parade, which was convenient for visiting the original Hot Well beside the River Avon. In the same letter she says

> My Fanny is so good a girl, and so very sensible, (I think I may say so impartially) that she is a very agreeable companion to me. Your god-daughter [Emily] is a sweet cherub and now runs quite alone and begins to chatter.

She adds a footnote which indicates the keen interest Thomas had in her life, as well as the frankness which existed between them: 'You ask me whether I am in the way of bringing another

18 JCTSW I p.6
19 ibid I p.273

81

brat, or whether you dreamt it? Certainly the latter.'[20]

Return to India

Quite who persuaded Isaac to return to India or when he agreed to do so is not known. There had been a severe famine in Bengal between 1769 and 1773, when the population of Bengal declined by a third. It was argued that the activities and aggrandizement of company officials – particularly using the monopoly rights on trade and land tax for the personal benefit of company officials – was partly to blame for this. Perhaps the Company sought a proven steady servant to take matters in hand.

Isaac was clearly not intending to return to India in the summer of 1773 as his wife speaks of his impatience to complete the purchase of the Thornhill Estate, whose farm they proposed keeping in hand 'for profit and amusement'.[21] Perhaps the possibility of his returning to India was raised with Isaac during the 1773 Christmas he and his wife spent at the home of Hugh Watts (see above). On the other hand, in a letter only a few weeks earlier from London, Elizabeth had said that Isaac had a great deal of business to attend to there, so perhaps it was raised before then.[22]

Isaac left for India some time in 1774, and in a letter to Thomas Sedgwick from Clifton, dated October 1st 1775, Elizabeth reported that she had received news from her husband in an earlier letter dated 5th February which he had written 'on the boat going up to Patna'. Since it usually took six months to get to India, and it had taken four months for his letter to return,

---

20 JCTSW I p.274

21 ibid I p.270

22 ibid I p.278

82

this would confirm his departure as early in 1774.

So, by March 1775 Isaac was ensconced as Governor and Chief factor in Patna, dealing with the complexities of managing the opium trade, which at that time contributed twenty five percent of the East India Company profits and which would lead to the Opium Wars. Various letters to and from him are known.[23],[24] Back in England in the same month, Thomas Sedgwick's goddaughter, the 3 year old Emily Sage, died; yet there is no mention of this event in any of the correspondence which his great nephew Hill Wickham published. Given the grief which Elizabeth and Thomas would have shared, this is so out of character as to be impossible. It is most likely that Hill Wickham, with his Victorian sensibilities, omitted such letters as being too personal for his Victorian readership. In the next recorded letter which Hill Wickham includes, dated October 1st 1775, Elizabeth has already decided to join her husband in India. Although she writes from Thornhill, she reports that she has already been on board the boat which will take her to India.

> Mr. Wheeler who is one of the Directors (of the
> East India Company) and was Chairman when Mr.
> Sage was appointed and was most helpful in mak-
> ing arrangements...[25]

The helpful director was Edward Wheeler, a director of the East India Company from 1765-1776 and its Chairman from 1773-4.

It is hardly surprising that Elizabeth should then want to join

---

[23] Dutt, G.N., *History of the Hutwa Raj*, 1904 p.209

[24] Letter from Gregorious Herklots to Isaac Sage 30th August 1775 and Sage's reply 31st August 1775. *Enclosures to memoir of outgoing Dutch Director Bacheracht to his successor*, HRB 253 (unfoliated) Archives and Records Association.

[25] JCTSW I p.283

her husband. As a letter took 6 months to get out to India, perhaps she wished to break the news of their daughter's death to him personally. Certainly, it is clear that Isaac had no idea of her intention of joining him until she arrived in Patna. Hill Wickham states that it was ~~an~~ unwise for someone who had always had a delicate constitution to attempt to travel to India.[26] However unwise, this she was determined to do, and their newly purchased house in Dorset was let. This advertisement appeared in the Salisbury & Winchester Journal in October 1775.[27]

STALBRIDGE, DORSET.

To be LETT, and entered upon immediately, ready furnished, THORNHILL HOUSE, belonging to Isaac Sage, Esq.; consisting of a hall, breakfast parlour, dining parlour, house-keeper's room, servant's hall, butler's pantry, kitchen, and other convenient offices on the first floor; a gallery (ninety-three feet by twenty-one),[28] drawing room, dressing room, and six handsome bed chambers adjoining, on the second floor; stabling for 14 horses, double coach house, kitchen garden, with walls planted with young fruit trees.

The house has been lately elegantly fitted up, and furnished, is pleasantly situated, and commands rich extensive views, and is within the parish of Stalbridge in the county of Dorset, distant from Sherborne 6 miles, Blandford 12, and Shaftesbury

---

[26] JCTSW I p.6

[27] See
http://freepages.genealogy.rootsweb.ancestry.com/~dutillieul/ZOtherPapers/NewS&WJ2Oct1775.html

[28] This would later be converted into living rooms by the Revd W Boucher.

14.

The land belonging to, and lying round the house, consisting of about 500 acres of arable, meadow and pasture, to be also let, and entered upon immediately, or at Lady-day next, or the whole or any part of it may be taken with the house, and the Stock thereon bought at a fair appraisement.

Further particulars may be had of Francis Edwards Whalley, Esq.; of Winscombe, near Axbridge, or of Mr. Wickham, of Frome, Somerset. - Mr. Clift, at the house.

One curiosity is that the letter in which she tells her brother-in-law James Wickham, a lawyer, that she now wishes to let Thornhill is dated December 1775.[29] However, it is clear from entries elsewhere in the two volumes that the dates of some letters have been estimated by the editor Hill Wickham. In the same letter Elizabeth gives very clear details of payments to be made to her brother Thomas Sedgwick, for her daughter's upkeep, out of the anticipated rent from the let of Thornhill. These are to be of £100 per annum plus £10 for the cost of six-year-old Fanny's nurse and £25 for Mrs Mazell, who one assumes was her governess. In addition, James Wickham is to reimburse 'Tom' for 'any little bills' which he might send him.

The letter to Thomas Sedgwick from Pall Mall, dated December 6th 1775, in which she apologises for having no time to visit him, was to prove prophetic:

My spirits keep up; nor should I cast one look behind but for the friends I leave, they ever must

[29] JCTSW I p.285

be dear! No time or distance can remove their idea, or the remembrance of the tenderness I have received, particularly from my dear Sedgwick and my sister (i.e. his wife). All the love you would continue to show me, bestow on my poor Fanny, your Fanny now; I give her up to you with this confidence, that she will never feel the loss of father or mother while under your care. Protect her innocence and foster her virtues.[30]

Elizabeth sailed from Gravesend at the end of December 1775 and left Portsmouth on January 6th 1776, arriving in India sometime before November of that year. Her vivid descriptions of her 11 month voyage via Madeira and Cape Town deserve special mention. They demonstrate her intelligence, education and vivacity, as well as the closeness of her family. It is interesting to note that all these letters are addressed to her sister Mary Wickham, the editor's great grandmother. She must have written similar letters to Thomas Sedgwick, but these are not included. In the one letter written by her to Thomas at this time, from London one month before she sailed and dated November 2nd 1775, she asks him to send her twelve dozen bottles of Bristol (Hotwells) water in two chests. She points out that while she could purchase these in London, she 'could not depend in its being fresh; and it would answer little purpose to carry it stale'.[31] Such concerns were well known, and in 1789 the Merchant Venturers had received a letter of complaint about Bristol water bought in London, asking that in future the retailer be denied further supplies.

30 JCTSW I p.288
31 ibid I p.284

To her surprise, Elizabeth Sage found the sea passage suited her very well. She reported that she did not suffer from seasickness, was putting on weight and was feeling better than she had been since the birth of her 'dear Fanny'.[32] This seems to imply that she had been unwell for the six years since Frances birth.

She arrived in India some time in 1776, and in letters to her sister Susan, from Bankipore on November 1st, paints another picture. In it Elizabeth, after describing their life in India, says:

> You may imagine us fixed here for some years but
> that is far from our intention. Had I not taken this
> resolution of coming out, Mr. Sage would have set
> sail for Europe probably in the very ship which
> conveys this (letter) to you, unable as he told me to
> support a longer separation. He was settling his
> affairs to return when the account of my intention
> arrived and he left it entirely to me to resolve
> whether I would go this season or the next; the
> latter I preferred both from a pecuniary motive,
> and as my mind rejected, however pleasant the
> voyage had been, a repetition of it so on. One year
> my dear sister will soon elapse... [33]

However, this would prove to be an unwise choice. Williams reports that there was a low life expectancy among East India Company employees, and during the period 1707-1775 when it appointed 640 writers, 58% died.[34] Hill Wickham states that because of Elizabeth's ill heath Isaac was forced to relinquish his

[32] JCTSW I pp.292-3

[33] ibid I p.308

[34] William C. *The Nabobs of Wiltshire*, Goosecroft Publications, Purley on Thmas, Berkshire, 2010, p.113

lucrative post and return home to England.[35] Other accounts say she returned to England in 1777, followed shortly by her husband. The latter seems more probable, since Hill Wickham states she died in Bath on December 17th 1778.[13] This was possibly in the house of her brother Thomas Sedgwick. Bath was the logical place to come; not only was her daughter living there with the Whalleys, but during the season there would have been the best doctors of the time serving the needs of the elderly rich. Sadly, Hill Wickham includes no correspondence of any kind for the period from November 1776, when his sister arrived in Bankipore, until August 1779, nine months after her death. She was buried in the Lady Chapel of Wells Cathedral on 24th December 1778. One suspects the hand of Thomas Sedgwick as a prebend of Wells Cathedral in seeing that his sister was buried there, rather than at St Cuthbert's church, Wells, where she had been married 9 years earlier and which was presumably the family church. It is also very likely that Thomas arranged for the placing of the memorial tablet, which his great nephew Hill Wickham would later restore in 1867.[36]

Hill Wickham states that on the death of his sister, Thomas transferred his affections to her daughter, his niece, Frances Sage, who thereafter spent a great deal of her time with him and his wife in Bath. This is certainly borne out by comments in his later correspondence with his niece.

---

[35] JCSTW I p.6

[36] See Jewers, A.J., *Wells Cathedral: its monumental inscriptions and heraldry*, Mitchell and Hughes, London, 1892, pp.171-3

Tablet in East Cloister

Burial register of Cathedral states Dec 24 1778 buried in Lady Chapel

Near this place lies the body of
Elizabeth Sage
who departed this life the 17th December 1778
aged 33 years.
In testimony of most sincere affection
for an amiable, tender, virtuous wife
her disconsolate husband Isaac Sage Esqre
of Thornhill in the county of Dorset
caused this memorial to be erected.
With her mother lies also the Body of
Emily Sage
daughter of Isaac and Elizabeth Sage
who departed this life the 27th March 1775
in the 3rd year of her nge.
Restored by the Revd Hill D. Wickham.
Rector of Horsington
Great nephew of the above Elizabeth Sage 1867.

4.3 The memorial to Elizabeth in the East Cloister of Wells Cathedral

CHAPTER 5
Travel in Europe and Frances's Early Life

William Lowndes, in his book on the profiles of important people who came to Bath, states that when Whalley heard of the death of his sister, he 'immediately offered her daughter the hospitality of his comfortable home'.[1] As we have seen from the previous chapter, this is far from the truth, for by this time, having spent three years with the Whalleys while her parents were in India, Frances had become almost a daughter to her uncle and aunt. It is also clear that even before this time Frances was frequently left with one or other of her grandmothers while Elizabeth and Isaac were pursuing a very active social life. When his sister died in December 1778, Hill Wickham says that Thomas Sedgwick's fondness for his sister was transferred to her only surviving child,[2] and as will be seen, he continued to dote on her in her adult life despite her misdemeanours.

Sometime in 1779, a portrait of 9 year old Frances was painted by George W. Romney for £50. It would be charming to think of this being commissioned by Isaac Sage as a momento for the Whalleys of the time Frances had spent with them, but the portrait, although painted in London where Romney was working, was paid for by Thomas Sedgwick. Such a portrait does still exist and was sold by Sotheby's to a buyer in South America in July 1987. Sadly, a letter forwarded by them to the new owner

---

[1] Lowndes, W., *They came to Bath,* Redcliffe Press Ltd., Bristol, 1982, p.89
[2] JCTSW I p.6

failed to elicit any response.

Quite how much of the time Frances spent with the Whalleys in Bath and Langford after the death of her mother is not clear. Certainly, she spent some time with her father in London and also at the family estate at Thornhill, where her father would become High Sheriff of Dorset in 1784.[3]

Frances's introduction to social life at Bath had been by the early age of 11 years, when the following account was recorded by Fanny Burney in her diary entry of May 27th 1780:

> In the midst of this Rattle, Mrs. Whalley proposed that Miss Thrale should go down stairs to hear a Miss Sage play upon the Harpsichord. Miss Sage is a Niece of Mrs. Whalley, & about 9 years old. I offered to be of the Party, – Miss Weston joined us, as did the Miss Ansteys, & down we went. And terribly wearied was I! – She played a Lesson of Giordani's, that seemed to have no end, & repeated all the Parts into the Bargain! – And this, with various little English songs, detained us till we were summoned to the Carriage. I had an opportunity, however, of seeing something of (the) Miss Ansteys, – & I found them such precise, formal, composed & dull young Women, that the same opportunity also served to acquaint me that I never need desire to see any thing more of them. [4]

Nothing is known directly about Frances's education after her mother's death. Maybe initially Mrs Mazell, mentioned in

3 Boswell, E., *The civil division of the county of Dorset*, Crutwell, Sherborne, 1795
4 Rizzo, B., *Early Journals and Letters of Fanny Burney Volume IV The Streatham Years*, Part II, 1780-1781, Oxford University Press, 2003, pp.126-9

Chapter 4, was retained. Had Thomas Sedgwick any influence during this period? He certainly was a highly educated man whose views on women's education are likely to have been those of the bluestocking circle with which he was now associated. It is also clear that Frances's mother had been well educated, and it clearly would have been her wish that Frances was no less enlightened. Whatever influences were brought to bear, there is no evidence that Frances maintained a circle of intellectual friends in later life. In 1784 she spent the winter 'under the protection of Mrs Blair', something of which Mrs Whalley thoroughly approved.[5] This was possibly Mrs Patricia Blair, the widow of the Rev Dr John Blair Prebend of Westminster but whose family seat was Balthayock in Scotland. This tutelage clearly came to pass, as in February 1784 Mrs Whalley's letter to Frances asks for the Whalleys regards to be passed to Mrs Blair.[6]

By 1785 Frances was placed with the Honorable Mrs Gordon, who we are told received a few young ladies 'who wished to profit by London masters' into her house.[7,8] Whether this was in music or painting, one can only guess at, but in a later letter Thomas Sedgwick includes many references to the paintings he and his wife were seeing and adds that he is glad that Fanny's drawing and instrumental music are not being neglected. In May 1785 Mrs Whalley is expressing satisfaction that Frances is so happily placed with Mrs Gordon, to whom she claims to be distantly related. The Honorable Mrs Gordon was the granddaughter of Lord Portsmouth and the daughter of Lord Lymington, and we are told that Mrs Whalley's late father had been on intimate terms with the latter and his brother

5 JCTSW I p.404
6 ibid I p.422
7 ibid I p.431
8 ibid I p.483

Colonel Wallop.[9] Thomas Sedgwick would later write that in his wife's eyes this tutelage produced a great benefit in Frances's correspondence:

> It is impossible to tell you how much delighted your excellent aunt was with your letter. Not only the tender regard glowing so artlessly throughout its pages, but the style also in which it was expressed, charmed her. Indeed my dear it was convincing proof to us that Mrs. Gordon's letters are full of graces, and that you have profited by them. It is truly kind in [sic] her to have corresponded with you, and shows not only her attention to your improvement, but that she knows also how to appreciate your understanding, and draw out those emulations which are the spur to excellence and which excite us and enable us to go on from strength to strength. While you are emulating the charms of Mrs. Gordon's style, think also my sweet girl that you are imitating that of you dear and incomparable mother, who eminently excelled in letter writing, and whose example in every respect it should be your pride, as it will be your advantage to follow.[10]

By the age of 16 years, Frances had acquired all the other attributes considered desirable in an eligible lady of breeding; she was beautiful, played the harpsichord and guitar, she sang, drew, spoke Italian and French and was much admired as a witty

---

[9] JCTSW I p.431
[10] ibid I p.440

conversationalist.

5.1 Frances Sage, by Cosway, aged perhaps 18 years

Early in 1783 the Whalleys were already considering moving to the continent for an extended period.[11] The war with France had ended, but peace with America was not finally ratified until 3rd September that year. By this time Thomas Sedgwick's lifestyle was beginning to eat into his wife's fortune. In that year the Whalleys had mortgaged Langford Court, 2 houses and approximately 270 acres of land for £3000.[12] Langford Court was now let to General Gunning,[13] and their house in Royal Crescent was also let at this time.[14] Hill Wickham states that their

[11] JCTSW I p.384

[12] Fryer J., 'Langford Court', in *Every House Tells a Story*, Langford History Group, Langford, 2006, p.28

[13] The Gunnings would continue to live there until 1788.

tour of Europe was undertaken 'at no mean expense' but was nonetheless intended to permit financial recovery from what had been a period of lavish entertainment at their house in Bath,[15] but there could have been other reasons. Not only had Mrs Siddons departed the scene, but Mrs Miller was proposing a similar European tour, and the loss of this literary figurehead in Bath and the death of his sister must have also influenced Thomas Sedgwick.

Travels on the Continent

It is possible to follow the Whalleys' movements from the accounts given in the three diaries Thomas Sedgwick wrote of the tours he undertook, and from the letters which he and his wife sent home to friends and relatives. The first tour made by Thomas began at Chambetry, which was then the capital of Savoy. There is no record of how the Whalleys had made their way to Savoy, but it seems from Hill Wickham's introduction that they had done so via Paris and Versailles, where Marie Antoinette had afterwards alluded to Thomas Sedgwick as '*le bel Anglais*'.[16,17]

In Savoy Baron Joseph de Châtillon Rambert was President of the Savoy Senate, and it seems from the familiarity between the two that he and Thomas Sedgwick must have met before, and this can only have been during Thomas's supposed Grand Tour in 1769-1771. Thomas introduces his journal of the 1783

---

[14] Lowndes W., *The Royal Crescent in Bath*, Redcliffe Press, Bristol, 1981, p.50

[15] JCTSW I pp.15-6

[16] ibid I p.16

[17] This seems to have been something of a habit of the French Court. Some years earlier, Louis XV had referred to the young Sir William Draper as '*le beau garcon anglias*'. See Dreaper J, *Bristol's Forgotten Victor*. Bristol Branch of the Historical Association, Bristol, 1998, p7

first tour by saying that it was written at his wife's insistence as she was left behind at the Castle of Châtillon.[18] The castle where she remained had been built in 1768 as a hunting lodge by Baron Châtillon and must have been only recently completed when Thomas first visited it on his Grand Tour. It was later decorated by the Baron's son, who *'Ce dernier créa aussi, à la même date, un jardin anglais en prolongement du jardin potager existant déjà'* [at the same time created an English garden as an extension to the pre-existing kitchen garden]. This might have been Thomas Sedgwick's influence or more likely that of his wife drawing on her experience at Langford Court. Thomas was much taken by the local scenery, and his later tree planting on the northern slope of the Mendips around Mendip Lodge did much to change the local scenery to something similar to that of Savoy.

In late November 1783 Thomas and the Baron set out for Aix-Les Baines on the shore of Lac de Bouget, then went on to Bellay and the Chateau of Lunes, visiting several monasteries on the way, before returning to Chambery. The second tour, described as 'an excursion into the Province of Tarantese', appears to have started in June 1784. The party this time consisted of Count Vivaldi and the young Chevalier Count Galateri, later to become the distinguished politician and soldier General Galateri, another lifelong friend.[19] The group reached St Pierre on the first night and soon after made their way to Miolin, the capital of the Tarantese, which Thomas Sedgwick describes as very old and ill-built![20] Then on to Conflan, where it seems they met the Marquise de la Pierre, an English woman who was to become another lifelong friend and correspondent. After a lunch at her chateau, they went on their way to Moutiers to lodge with

18 JCTSW I p.79

19 ibid I p.17

20 ibid I p.101

its commandant; then to Bell Autre and Tamier, calling in at three convents in the Alps, before returning to Chambery. It is not clear how long all this took. Despite the fifty pages of description it cannot have represented more than a few nights away from his wife (who for some reason he refers to in this account as Amelia), since the third tour also took place in the same month of June 1784. Whalley again travelled without his wife and again was accompanied by the Baron, who provided numerous entrees to the local nobility but who sadly seems to have died towards the end of this tour.

Mrs Thrale's first recorded letter to the Whalleys is dated March 6th 1784, when she replies from Bath to Thomas Sedgwick's earlier letter.[21] In this she congratulates him on his vivid description of Savoy and says that she has passed his letter on to Dr Johnson, who is ill in London. The tone of the letter, though, does not suggest that they are particularly close friends. She was living in Bath as early as the Spring of 1776, when her husband and Dr Johnson joined her,[22] but there is no evidence that she had met Thomas Sedgwick by this time. Mrs Whalley's first recorded letter to her niece Frances Sage is from Chamberty and dated July 27th 1784.[23] Frances was then aged just 15 years, but it is clear that there had been earlier correspondence. It would seem from the references in the letter that at the time Frances was living with her father but also leading an active social life in Bath. It is unclear whether her father had a permanent house in Bath at this time. Lowndes states that although the Whalleys let their house in Royal Crescent, Frances 'continued to live in the house'.[24] This seems unlikely unless she was still accompanied by

21 JCTSW I pp.402-4

22 Lowndes W., *They came to Bath*, Redcliffe Press, Bristol, 1982, p.53

23 JCTSW I pp.404-8

24 Lowndes W., *The Royal Crescent in Bath*, Redcliffe Press, Bristol, 1981, p. 50

her governess or perhaps the house was let to her father. In the same letter she hopes that Frances will be able to come to the continent 'next summer'.

In February 1785 we detect the first and only rebuke from Mrs Whalley to her niece, when she gently chides Frances from Avignon for not replying to earlier letters:

> I know the goodness of your heart too well my beloved Frances, to ever suspect that your silence proceeds from want of affection towards an uncle and aunt who love you with all the tenderness of parents and who are removed near a thousand miles distant from you. But I cannot say I so entirely acquit you of negligence… for depriving me for six long months…of the pleasure of hearing from you.[25]

However, by May 1785 all is restored, following receipt of Fanny's 'most affectionate letter'.[26] Mrs Whalley, now writing from near Lisle, says:

> I cannot quit the subject of your present establishment, without repeating my dearest girl, the joy it gives me that the Almighty has blessed you with a parent whose every wish seems to centre in your happiness nor does he think any expense too great that may contribute to your advantage.

She then goes on to tempt providence by adding:

> I am sure your heart must expand with filial love

---

[25] JCTSW I p.420
[26] ibid I pp.33-5

and gratitude towards him, and make no doubt but you will in return be everything, both in conduct and accomplishment, that he can wish- that you will gild his days with joy in the meridian of life and crown his latter years with peace

She concludes her letter with:

I will therefore bid you adieu my beloved child. Do not let the term give you umbrage, for I know we are very delicate on certain points at 15 (years of age); but I will always consider myself as your mother, if I live to see you thirty since I never can yield myself second in affection towards you to any human being but your father as believe me every maternal feeling every tender solicitude for your welfare expands the breast of your ever affectionate

Eliza Whalley

It has been said that no child is strong enough to bear the love of two parents alone. Frances had lost her younger sister and mother but acquired two indulgent would-be parents in addition to her own wealthy father. In these exchanges there are pointers to a degree of indulgence on the part of her father and Mr and Mrs Whalley which would not bode well for a later marriage to a husband who, although he had the promise of wealth through inheritance, had little of his own in the first years of their marriage. For example, in October 1784 Thomas Sedgwick writes to Frances from Avignon:

Though I consider you as your aunt's

correspondent, yet my dearest Fanny, I cannot deny myself the pleasure of now and then encroaching upon her rights, and assuring you, with my own pen, that absence only serves to increase my affection for you. It is impossible, my darling niece, to describe the satisfaction that the account of your merits gives my from all quarters. To see you grow up amiable and accomplished has always been my chief ambition, and I cannot hear that you are equal to my fondest hopes without the most sensible joy and pride. How delightful also must it be to you, my sweet girl, to see yourself as the blessing of your dear father's life; and that you find it in your power, by your talents and your tenderness, to recompense him for all his cares, and almost restore to him all the domestic delights and comforts that he lost in losing your charming and excellent mother. What happiness to myself, as well as him, to see her living again in you; to see all her graces and all her virtues blooming and ripening with your years![27]

Not perhaps the sort of thing one should be telling a 15 year old. Mrs Whalley also asks if Frances's father is 'in town', so one wonders who was providing day-to-day support for Fanny. Was there still a Governess as there had been 7 years before when her parents were in India? Little more is heard of Isaac Sage after the death of his wife, apart from his visit to join the Whalleys on the continent (see below). He became High Sheriff of Dorset in 1784 and still had his country house at Thornhill at this time. Later, he would move to Gatton in Surrey, a large estate belong-

27 JCTSW I p.408

ing to Mark Wood, before dying in Brighton in 1828. Hill Wickham states that Isaac never remarried and no evidence to dispute this has been found. Despite this two underage daughters, Marianne and Julia, are recorded in his Will of 1818, which was written at Gatton. There was also a son, Frederick, who died in either August 1811 or August 1812, and who was buried in Gatton Church.[28,29]

To return to the Whalleys' continental travels, one deduces from their subsequent letters that Thomas and his wife then visited Geneva and Lucerne, taking in Mont Blanc, before spending the winter of 1784/5 in Avignon, where they joined the English enclave led by the Duke of Cumberland. By February they had tired of the gaming tables and had retreated to L'Isle sur la Sorgue, where they seem to have stayed for three months.[30] While Mrs Whalley describes the town as they approached it as being a 'poor dirty hole', the house they rented from a previous English owner was much to their liking, being by the river and surrounded by olive groves in which nightingales sang.

Some years earlier, in 1766, William Patoun observed that Grand Tourists often met up with friends abroad, and wrote,

> The Consequence in general of the English herding together are these, a great increase of expences [sic]: vying with each other in Equipage, dress &c, Loss of time, temptation of gambling for want of other amusement, with many other pursuits, which are needless to mention.[31]

---

[28] *Church of England Parish Registers 1538-1812*, London Metropolitan Archives, London

[29] Bannerman, W.B., *The Parish Registers of Gatton and of Sanderstead in Surrey*, The Surrey Parish Register Society, 1908.

[30] JCTSW I p.432

Given that the main reason of his tour was the need to economise, the Whalley's might well have had this as the underlying reason for their departure. During the summer of 1785 Thomas made an excursion to the convent of La Grande Chartreuse, near Grenoble again, accompanied by the young Count Galateri.

5.2 The Whalleys' travels in Europe 1784 -1787

In the autumn of the same year, the Whalleys made the sea crossing to Italy, arriving in Leghorn in November. This voyage was not without incident, and Thomas recounts, in a letter to his mother, that during the first two days of the attempted voyage they were compelled to put back first to Nice and then Marseilles because of bad weather.[32] Soon after they arrived in Leghorn, their travelling companion Theodore von Luders died. He was born in 1753, and his family had come to Bath in 1766. Theodore was a consumptive who had been ill for some time

31 Patoun, W., 'Advice on travel in Italy', in *A Dictionary of British and Irish travellers in Italy 1701-1800*, (Ingamells, J Ed.),Yale University Press, Newhaven, 1997
32 JCTSW I p.455

when they set out, and he died aged only 32 years.[33] He had been a Captain in the Dragoons but had to resign his commission when he became ill. He is buried in the English cemetery at Leghorn.[34] The Whalleys' man-servant Vincent and Mrs Whalley's maid had also been ill, though what with is not stated, but were now recovered.

The Whalleys spent the winter of 1785/6 in nearby Pisa, where there were many English families, and during this time visited Bologna, Padua, Venice and Verona. In Venice in May they met up with Mr and Mrs Piozzi[35] and other English friends including Leonard Chappelow, another cleric and amateur poet, who had been Thomas Sedgwick's contemporary at Cambridge. Then, early in the summer of 1786, they set out on their return journey, which would eventually take them back to England. From Italy they travelled through the Tyrol to Switzerland, arriving in Zurich in June, and then progressed down the Rhine via Basle, arriving in Strasbourg a month later.[36] From here the Whalleys wrote to Frances Sage at Thornhill in June 1786, and in July to her uncle Joseph's house in London. By this time it had been agreed that Frances and her father would join the Whalleys in Brussels on 13th or 14th August, and Thomas adds a footnote to Mrs Whalley's letter of July 23rd, telling Frances not to forget her Italian songs and her 'drawing apparatus'.[37] By early August the Whalleys are in Malines (now known as Mechelen), between Brussels and Antwerp. It would seem that it had been the Whalley's original intention to include Holland in their final

[33] JCTSW I p.435, 459

[34] *Miscellanea Genealogica et Heraldica*, (Howard, J.J., ed.), 3rd Series, Vol IV, Mitchell and Hughes, London, 1902, p.66

[35] TPL I p.195

[36] JCTSW I p.472

[37] ibid I p.477

travels, but this idea was abandoned, probably because of their niece's arrival. Hill Wickham says that Frances spent 1787-8 with the Whalleys in Brussels. While there, they made the acquaintance of the Duke d'Arenberg, and his daughter, who invited the Whalleys and their niece to visit his country seat. This would mark the beginning of Frances's life long friendship with Princess D'Arenberg, who was of the same age.[38]

Louis Engelbert of Arenberg (1750-1820), nicknamed the blind duke, was the 6th Duke of Arenberg. Between 1803 and 1810 he ruled a Duchy in North-western Germany. His was one of the most prominent noble families in the Austrian Netherlands, but he had been blinded during a hunting party at the age of 24. Hill Wickham states that this was 'by the gun of the English Minister'. Unable to follow a military career, the Duke had turned to science, art and music. It was under his patronage that the first manned gas-filled balloon flight in history took off, from the front lawn of Arenberg Castle on November 21, 1783. His daughter Pauline (1774-1810) married Count Joseph Johann von Schwarzenberg (1769-1833) but was later to die tragically, trying to rescue her child from a fire. According to Hill Wickham:

> In the summer [of 1787] they visited the Duke at his country residence. He was totally blind... but was able to enjoy riding often accompanied by Miss Sage in a gallop across his park, a servant directing the horse with a loose bridle. Several letters are extant, written by the young Pauline Princess D'Arenberg, to Miss Sage, after her return to England [sadly only two are published in Hill Wickham

---

38 JCTSW II pp.78-9 (Footnote)

Vol 2]. This amiable Princess married one of the Schwartzenberg family and met her death at a ball given by her brother-in-law, July 16th 1810, then Ambassador at Paris from the Court of Vienna. The Emperor and Empress and all the Court, were assembled in a temporary saloon erected for the purpose, when one of the gauze curtains took fire and, immediately communicating to all the other hangings, the whole apartment was speedily in flames. The Emperor with great coolness sought the Empress and led her out. Princes Pauline Schwartzenberg escaped likewise with her child; but being separated from her in the confusion and fearing she might be still behind, the Princess rushed back into the saloon and was burnt to death.[39]

(See also Alison A., *History of Europe during the French Revolution*, Volume 7, 1843, Chapter LIX)

Hill Wickham says that while at Brussels the Whalleys 'met up again' with Mrs Piozzi. This was the former Mrs Thrale, who had recently remarried following the death of her first husband and was now on an extended European tour. Mrs Piozzi's letter to Mr Lysons, dated 11th May 1786, reveals that their first meeting with the Whalleys had been in Venice.[40] When they met up in Brussels at the beginning of 1787, Mrs Piozzi records:

Mr Merry lodges in our Hotel here and we talk of you [Mr William Parson, to whom the letter of

[39] JCTSW I p.20
[40] TPL I p.195

February 5th is addressed] and Mr. and Mrs.
Greathead by the hour. The Whalleys too help to
make our Time pass very agreeably; I always loved
'em , and they are grown more amiable now than
ever.[41]

In their footnote Bloom and Bloom refer to a letter from
her daughter Queeny (Hester Maria Thrale), who three days later
wrote: 'Here are crowds of English here [sic] - we wait for a fine
assembly at Mrs. Whalley's'.[42]

From this it would seem that such assemblies were the way
in which the Whalleys made connections with the many influential people they met on their travels. Indeed, given the timing of
this particular assembly, it may be that this was the one where
they met the D'Arenbergs.

The continental tour ended in early summer 1787. Perhaps the
group returned to England together. Thomas Sedgwick's first
letter to Frances, dated June 15th 1787, is addressed to her father's
house now in St. James Street, London. In it Thomas Sedgwick
alludes to her possible marriage. She would then have been 18
years old:

Young Horner is now at Wells, and who knows
but that Frank may bring him to you in his hand.
I say this to prepare you in case of accidents, and
that you may have time to consult your heart at
leisure. God direct you for your happiness, my
dear girl. If that is secured I care not how, or by
whom whom.[43]

[41] JCTSW I p.227
[42] ibid I p.228

This was likely to have been Francis Horner, who was related to the ancient Somerset family of Mells Park, of whom Sir John Cox Hippisley was also a member. This marriage clearly did not happen. The portrait by Cosway, reproduced as a miniature by Joseph Brown (Fig 5.1), which appears in Hill Wickham's book, has no date but may well have come from this time. In May the following year (1788), Whalley was again writing to Fanny. This time her address, presumably that of her father, is George Street, Hanover Square, where she had acquired a new pianoforte. In his letter of the 19th of that month, Thomas, having bemoaned the dirt, rubbish and confusion produced by work on his Langford Cottage, (see Chapter 6) says:

> When all these hurries and flurries are over...you shall come and be as much the shepherdess as you please; and feed the lambs and sing with the birds and lead about a lap dog in a rose-coloured ribbon and be all over sentiment and romance .

More significant to her future, bearing in mind she would be married almost exactly two years later, he goes on

> But a shepherd you must bring with you, if any such can be found in your sphere, for here we have none that will answer your ideas. Country shepherds, alas are in these our iron days mere clowns, with clod pates and filthy faces unknowing of garlands and crooks and pretty fancies. I am glad you and Mr. -------- are so rational in your tête a têtes. Reason is so often banished on such occasions.

It is difficult to judge Frances's character nearing adult life. There are no letters from her included in Hill Wickam's biography of her uncle, and one has to gain an insight from the eight letters to her written by Thomas Sedgwick and his wife. Thomas claims in his letter to his niece of October 6th that she is growing up amiable and accomplished and acquiring all the graces and virtues of her mother.[45] Clearly she was accomplished, but one gets the impression that she was a spirited and independent and worldly young lady, having something of the character of Mary Crawford in Jane Austen's *Mansfield Park*.

---

[45] ibid I p.408

CHAPTER 6
The Building of Mendip Lodge 1787-1790

The Estate of Langford

Langford Court and its estates were originally part of the Manor of Wrington, which at the time of Domesday was held by Glastonbury Abbey.[1] Upon the Dissolution the Manor of Wrington became part of the hunting seat of the Capel family, Earls of Essex,[2] and in 1636 the estate was bought by Francis Creswick, a Bristol merchant, for his younger son, John. In 1654 John Creswick's daughter married Cadwalladar Jones, and the estate then remained in the Jones family until Thomas Sedgwick Whalley married Cadwallader Jones's granddaughter, the widowed Elizabeth Sherwood in 1774.

When, in the early summer of 1787, Thomas and Elizabeth returned to England, they had no house in Langford, though they still owned their house in Bath.[3] Langford Court was still let to Colonel Gunning, who would leave in June the following year.[4] However, by this time it seems the Whalleys had no intention of returning to live there, and Langford Court was

---

[1] *The Domesday Book, Somerset* (Thorn, F. & C., Eds), Phillimore, Chichester, 1980, 8: 90,d

[2] Rutter, J., *Delineations of the north western division of the County of Somerset*, Longman Rees and Co, London, 1829, p.126

[3] JCTSW II p.14

[4] ibid II pp.23-4

immediately re-let to Mr Henry Bosanquet (1760-1816).[5] Henry's widowed mother, Elizabeth, had lived in Bath in Berkeley Square, which is perhaps how this rental came to be arranged.[6]

The Building of the Cottage (Later Renamed Mendip Lodge)

According to Hill Wickham, the first thing the Whalleys did on their return in May 1787 was visit his mother at Winscombe Court,[7] but this is not strictly true, since they came via Bath. Mrs Whalley senior was by now living there with Thomas' elder brother, Francis, who had bought the lease of Winscombe Court from the church.[8] Three months later, Anna Seward was still writing to Thomas there,[9] but a letter in October from Mrs Siddons is addressed to him at Bath. A further letter the following month is addressed to him at Frome, which indicates he either visited or stayed there with his sister Mary and brother-in-law James Wickham.

Thomas now set about building his 'Cottage' on the north slope of the Mendips above Langford. Hill Wickham says that this was on land that belonged to the Langford estate,[10] but it may in fact have been leased from the church.[11] Work on the

---

[5] He would be married to Caroline Anstey in 1790, Thomas Sedgwick Whalley performing the ceremony.

[6] *Bath Chronicle*, 17th January 1799

[7] JCTSW I p.21

[8] This is not the present building of that name but an earlier one. The present Court was built in 1880 by Mrs Lethbridge, who purchased the former Parsonage House rather than lease it. She was the Vicar's sister and had married Sir Thomas Buckler Lethbridge's younger son and became a major landowner in Winscombe.

[9] JCTSW II p.17

[10] ibid I p.21

[11] As part of the 'Exchanges' which were included in the 1797 Enclosure Act for Banwell and the Churchill Wastelands, the site was given by the Bishop of

house started in late 1787 or early 1788 and seems to have been added to intermittently until at least 1791. It is clear that Thomas took a great personal interest in its initial construction, and by May 1788 he was writing to his niece from 'The Cottage' for the first time, apologising for the delay in doing so. He explains that 'Hammer and saw have been my music; my occupation a deal of dirty work among masons and mortar makers' but says that when all the work was finished she should come and visit him there.[12]

A great deal of stone would have been required both for the house and in due course for the walls around the estate. For the latter this seems to have come from small, shallow scrape quarries, which can be found at several places to the west of the Stoney Lane. For the house itself a rather better quality material would have been required. This probably came from the quarry further west, at the level of the 500 foot contour in the 1881 Ordinance Survey map. This is marked as the 'Old Quarry' in the OS map of 1900.

It was not until the Cottage was habitable that Thomas and his wife could resume their former custom of spending the winter season in Bath and the summer at Langford, which he later regarded as his home ('Bath is but my visit , the dear Lodge is my home'[13]), and by May 1788 he was telling his niece to write to him at 'The Cottage, Langford'. Even so, in September the following year, when the Whalleys visited Anna Seward at Lichfield, it would seem the work on the house or surrounding garden was not quite complete, since she says: 'The former [i.e. Thomas Sedgwick] engaged in building, and opening, a little

Bath and Wells in exchange for other land which TSW had bought from the Enclosure Commissioners. One of these was his elder brother Francis (see Somerset Heritage Centre, ref Q/RDE/42)

12 JCTSW II p.23

13 ibid II p.287

Edenic habitation in a bloomy wilderness could only stay a week.'[14]

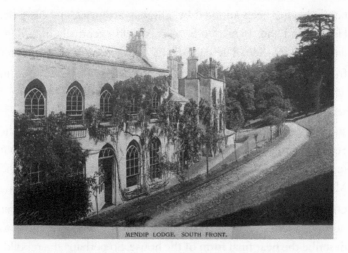

MENDIP LODGE. SOUTH FRONT.

6.1 The rear view of the completed Mendip Lodge. 'The Cottage' is likely to have been the building on the left with Gothic Windows

It is clear from the rear view of the house that several additions were made to the original Cottage. Although none of these can be accurately dated, it would seem that most had been built by 1791 and none were added after 1804.

Benjamin Edward Somers reports that his grandfather Benjamin (1782-1848) was present as a young boy playing on the Bowling Green (which starts just out of sight in the picture above) when the Cottage, thought at that time to have a thatched roof, burnt down.[15] Sarah, the widow of Edward Somers, had

[14] *Letters of Anna Seward, Written Between the Years 1784 and 1807*, (Constable, A., Ed), Vol 2, George Ramsay and Co Edinburgh, 1811, p.169
[15] Somers, B.E., *Pedigree of the family of Somers of Mendip Lodge – Somerset,* 1916, p.6

moved to Springhead Farm just below the house with her three children sometime after the death of her husband in 1790,[16] the family having been adopted by Thomas Sedgwick and his wife. Her second son, Benjamin Somers, would eventually buy Mendip Lodge in 1846. The date of the fire is confirmed in a letter from Mrs Pennington to Mrs Piozzi, dated 7th June 1793, in which she reports that it was caused by the carelessness of a servant but fortunately occurred during the day so assistance was soon obtained. One assumes this would have come from the Somers family and staff at Springhead Farm. No lives were put in danger by the fire, but there was £200 worth of damage, and Mrs Whalley returned to Bath while the repairs were being undertaken.[17] While this might suggest that a major rebuild was needed, a letter of 1791 to Lady Gresley (see below) appears to describe the near final form of the house. So perhaps the rebuilding after the fire was confined to repairing the original structure and replacing the roof with slate.

Descriptions of the Completed Mendip Lodge

As no plans exist for Mendip Lodge at any stage in its evolution, one has to be content with photographs and contemporary descriptions, the earliest of which occurs in a letter which Anna Seward wrote to Lady Gresley from Mendip Lodge, then Langford Cottage, dated July 30th 1791. In this she includes a report of her journey from Tewkesbury via Gloucester and Bristol to Langford, but the exact date of this visit is not given. Perhaps she came as far as Churchill Cross on the Bristol coach.

---

[16] By this time her eldest son Edward had been lost at sea.

[17] TPL II p.124 (Note 9)

At ten o'clock Mr. Whalley arrived in his chaise, to conduct me to his Eden, among the Mendip mountains, Singularly, and beyond my high-raised expectations, beautiful I did indeed find it; situated, built, furnished, and adorned in the very spirit of poetic enthusiasm, and polished simplicity. is about twelve years since Mr. Whalley began to cover with a profusion of trees and shrubs, one of these vast hills, then barren like its brethren. The plantations seem already to have attained their full size, strength, and exuberance of foliage.

By the addition of another horse, to help the chaise-horses, we ascended the sylvan steep. At about two-thirds of its height on a narrow terrace, stands the dear white cottage, whose polished graces seem smilingly to deride its name, though breathing nothing heterogeneous to cottage simplicity. The first floor consists of a small hall, with a butler's pantry to the right, and good kitchen to the left; housekeeper's room beyond that; scullery behind the kitchen; the offices at a little distance detached from the house, many steps below this bank. and screened from sight by trees. The second floor contains, in front, to the north west, three lightsome, lovely, though not large, apartments, whose spacious sashes are of the Gothic form. These are the dining-room, the drawing-room and elegant boudoir beyond, all opening through each other. My apartment from which I write, is behind the boudoir; its window, at the end of the house, looking to the east and upon a steep lawn, sprinkled over with larches, poplars, and woodbines, excluded by a circular plantation from all prospect of the magnificent vale upon which the front rooms look down, in instant and almost perpendicular descent. A gravel walk winds up this secluded lawn to the mountain top. Mr. and Mrs. Whalley, and their other guests sleep in the attics. The wide-extended vale beneath us has every possible scenic beauty, excepting only the meanders of a river. Scarce two hundred yards from the villa, on the left hand, a bare brown mountain intersects this its woody neighbour, and towers equal heights. The protection it extends from the north-west wind has been everything to Mr. Whalley, as to the growth and health of his plantations. Sloping its giant's foot to the valley, it finely contrasts, with barren sterility, the rich cultivation of the valley below, and the lavish umbrage which curtains these slopes.

With the sort of sensation that a beauteous country girl, in the first glow of youth and health, surveys an antiquated dowager of rank and riches, seems this little villa to look down on the large stone mansion of Langford Court, the property of Mr. and Mrs. Whalley, and their former residence. It stands in the valley, about half a mile from us encircled by its fine lawn of two hundred acres [sic], planted and adorned with great taste. Yet more immediately below us, nestles in a wood, the village of Langford. The smoke of its farms and cottages curling amongst the trees at early morn, imparts the glow of vitality and cheerfulness to our romantic retirement. I climb, by seven o'clock in a morning, the highest terrace, and 'drink the spirit of the mountain gale' which seems to invigorate my whole frame, and give my lungs the freest respiration. Never before did I breathe, for any continuance, an atmosphere so sublimated. The extensive vale finely breaks into inequalities by knolls and dingles. The beautiful fields, wearing from the late rains, the brightest verdure, have wave outlines of plenteous hedge-moss and appear, by their depth from the eye, shining and smooth as the lawns of our nobility. They are interspersed with thick and dark, though not large, woods. The whole wide expanse is dotted over by white rough-cast cottages, and here and there a village-spire and squiral chateau.

Fifteen miles in width and about seven distant from this elevation, the Bristol channel lies, a sheet of silver stretched longitudinally over the vale. Beyond, we plainly discern the Welsh coast, whose mountains bound the horizon.

Mr. Whalley's walks and bowers are finely diversified

"Shade above shade, a woody theatre"

The several terraces ascending over each other are connected by steep winding paths for the active, and by grassy steps for the feeble. These terraces are so variously planted and disposed, as to avoid all that sameness to which, from their situation, they were liable; now secluded and gloomy, now admitting the rich world below to burst upon the eye. Hermitages and caves cut in the rocky steeps contain rustic seats dedicated to favourite friends , by poetic inscriptions; one to Mrs. Siddons; another to Miss Hannah More; another to the accomplished Mrs. Jackson of Bath; one to Mr. Whalley's venerable mother; another to Mr. Inman, the excellent clergyman of this parish; one to Sophia Weston; and one to myself. These grottos relieve us perpetually by their seats amidst ascents so nearly perpendicular... I had the pleasure to find dear Mrs. Whalley tolerably well, though feeling at frequent intervals, severe memorials of her dreadful accident. Mr. W and myself talk of your Ladyship and Miss. Gresley frequently, and always with a most lively interest.

Mr. Whalley's mother is here, a miracle at eighty five, of clear intellects, upright activity, and graceful manners; also Miss Davey, a fine young woman, related to Mrs. Whalley; but charming Sophia is not here; the scanty number of these pretty bed-chambers forbids the accommodation of more than two or three friends at the utmost. [18]

[18] *Letters of Anna Seward, Written Between the Years 1784 and 1807*, (Constable, A., Ed), Vol III, George Ramsay and Co., Edinburgh, 1811, pp.96-101

6.2 Mendip Lodge from the Northwest, as it was in about 1923

6.3 Mendip Lodge as it was in about 1923, viewed from just inside the park. The new drive, which was added in 1826 and lead through the park from the Lodges from the turnpike road, is just visible on the extreme right.

In 1801 Hannah More, one of Thomas's closest friends and neighbours, suggested that he should adopt the name of 'Mendip Lodge', it being more appropriate for what was now an impressive country house.[19] The house was also later known by her as 'Mont Blanc', as its frontage was rendered and painted white, presumably with lime wash, and could be seen by her across the valley.

6.4 'Mont Blanc' – Mendip Lodge seen from the West

A later letter from Anna Seward to Mrs Powys, dated October 1804, reflects on the improvements made to the house since her earlier 1791 visit. This would have been at the happiest of times for Thomas Sedgwick, just before the tragedy of the death of his second wife.

---

[19] JCTSW II p.197 (Footnote)

I went thither on 29th September [1804]. Thirteen years ago [i.e. in 1791 soon after its completion] I passed six weeks in that Alpine habitation. Increasing wealth [i.e. following his second marriage to Augusta Heathcote in 1803] and fine taste have since transformed and enlarged an elegant cottage on the brow of the Mendips to an Italian Villa, superbly furnished; extended in everyway his steep and lawny walks; and placed before his house a Tuscan Veranda. It is the loveliest architectural luxury I ever traversed, peculiarly calculated for the almost dizzy elevation on which the mansion stands and for the extremes of light which it chastises, and which was given by large sashes, the whole height of the apartments, from every one of which on the second floor, we step out into the gay veranda. Those consist of two drawing rooms and a boudoir. The arches of the veranda are light ironwork, painted green. Its breadth allows three to walk abreast. The shelving roof is also painted green, the floor a mosaic sale-cloth [sic]; the circular seats at the end have each a large pier-glass reflecting a part of the beautiful vale below; the coved sides are fine painted glass. Twenty-four large china jars were filled with autumnal flowers and one of them placed under every arch. All the sitting rooms are on the second floor; servants apartments on the ground floor; but no culinary operations are carried out there. To this villa urbana there is a villa rustica which is the cooks region. It is placed sixty steps lower, and hid amongst trees, a covered way leading from it to the Arcadian palace above That is seen from the vale below for two miles on the great western road from Bristol, and it looks as if it had been dropt from the clouds; and indeed when we stand in the veranda or look from the bedroom windows on the third floor we seem suspended between earth and heaven and inhale an atmosphere peculiarly sublimated.

The vale below is of twelve miles extent, ere the amber waves of the Bristol Channel divide England from the Cambrian shores. Lesser hills, rich woods, lawns and fields, a profusion of gentlemen's seats, with villages, 'half hid in tufted trees' with their steeples or towers vouch for the enjoyment of social pleasures, and for the national advantage of great population.

There is a noble dining-room backwards [i.e. at the back of the house] on the second story adorned by fine pictures, the glory of which is a full-length portrait of Mrs. Siddons by Hamilton.[20] It is a speaking, a beautiful, an exquisite likeness, by which her charming face and figure, drawn in the prime of her life and beauty, should go down to posterity. She is in the character of Hills Zara at the moment in which she exclaims, with extended hands:

[20] This may be the 1789 original from which the engraving by James Caudwell, now held by the National Portrait Gallery, was taken. She had taken the role of Zara in twice during the winter in 1781/2 and was in correspondence with Thomas Sedgwick at this time about a possible performance of Edwy and Edilda, which he had completed in 1779.

121

"Can it be Osmyn speaks— and speaks to Zara?"

but I have not time to proceed in my description of
this grand saloon, nor of the result of that poetic
imagination which formed the wood-wild walks,
ascending and descending the sylvan steeps; or of
the green terrace which zones the whole mountain
to an extent of three quarters of a mile, command-
ing a perpetual change of the scenery beneath.

I staid at Mendip Lodge ten days. Its new mistress
[the second Mrs. Whalley nee Heathcote] is gentle
kind and good and sensible though reserved; three
other ladies were of our party.[21]

Anna Seward also sent Thomas Sedgwick a poem describing her
feelings on leaving Mendip Lodge after her visit.[22]

While Thomas Sedgwick and his wife usually spent the
winter in Bath, there is one description of Mendip Lodge in
winter, which he sent to Ann Seward, who in turn forwarded it
to her friend Miss Stokes in December 1791.

Our beloved cottage still has charms for us. Use
cannot pall nor custom stale its infinite variety.
Elevated as we are, the south-west hurricanes pass
innoxious over our heads, because we have
plantations of evergreens, as you know, and terraces
that rise above us to nearly the mountain's summit;

21 *Letters of Anna Seward, Written Between the Years 1784 and 1807* (Constable, A.,
Ed), Vol VI, George Ramsay and Co Edinburgh, 1811, pp.202-5
22 Seward, A., *The poetical works of Anna Seward*, (Walter Scott Ed), Vol. III,
Ballantyne and Co., Edinburgh, 1810, pp.362-4

and because the more lofty mountain which intersects ours on the left [i.e. to the west of Stoney Lane], forms our sheltering screen. But those hurricanes rush with tenfold violence through the vale beneath us, while our comforts within are undamped by the rain, and unchilled by the frost. A thousand cottages, undescried in leafy summer, now shew their white cheerful faces. The brook, which you called a nothing, and which, during the softer season, is, in truth, most shallow and simple, runs now expanded, and foams with turbulent pride at our feet; while the more distance moors, covered with water, perfectly resemble a majestic river, rolling between us and the sea.[23]

Quite why the Whalleys should have been there at this time and not at their house in Bath is not clear, but William Mullins and his wife, Thomas's favourite niece née Fanny Sage, had visited Mendip Lodge in October and maybe extended their time there, as William hated parties and balls and would not have wanted to go with the Whalleys to Bath.

Anna Seward's fuller account of the house at its zenith can be supplemented by a number of other descriptions. Sarah Siddons described the house as her 'Castle in the Air', and the Bishop of London, Dr Porteous, said he had never witnessed an entertainment so perfect in its appointment. Thomas De Quincey gives a less complimentary account of the house. This seems to have been written from memory, since it was published almost 10 years after Thomas Sedgwick's death:

---

[23] *Letters of Anna Seward, Written Between the Years 1784 and 1807* (Constable,A., Ed), *Vol. III,* George Ramsay and Co Edinburgh, 1811, p.107

From the Hotwells, Mrs Siddons had been persuaded to honour with her company a certain Dr. Wh--- whose splendid villa of Mendip Lodge stood about two miles from Barley Wood. [This is completely untrue. Sarah Siddons had been a lifelong friend of Thomas Sedgwick Whalley, who was godfather to one of her daughters and had who had long wanted to have a house in the same locality] This villa by the way was a show place in which a vast deal of money had been sunk, upon two follies of equally unproductive of pleasure to the beholder and of anything approaching a pecuniary compensation to the owner. The villa, with its embellishments, was supposed to have cost at least sixty thousand pounds, of which one half had been absorbed, partly by a contest with the natural obstacles of the situation, and partly by the frailest of all ornaments—vast china jars, vases and other 'knicknackery' baubles which held their very existence by so frail a tenure as the carefulness of a housemaid; and which at all events, if they should survive the accidents of life, never are known to reproduce to the possessor one-tenth part of what they have cost. Out of doors there are terraces of a mile long, one rising above another, and carried, by mere artifice of mechanic skill, along the perpendicular face of a lofty rock. Had they, when finished any particular beauty? Not at all. Considered as a pleasure ground, they formed a far less delightful landscape, and a far less alluring haunt to rambling steps, than most of the uncostly shrubberies which were seen below, in unpretending situations and upon the ordinary level of the vale. What a record of human imbecility! For all his pains and expense in forming this costly 'folly', his reward was daily anxiety, and one solitary bon mot which he used to record of some man, who on being asked what he thought of the house, replied, that 'He thought the Devil had tempted him up to an exceedingly high place'. No part of the grounds, nor the house itself, was at all the better because, originally, it has been beyond measure difficult to form it: so difficult that, according to Dr Johnson's witty remark, on another occasion, there was good reason for wishing that it had been impossible. The owner, whom I knew, most certainly never enjoyed a happy day in the costly creation; [This again is completely untrue] which, after all, displayed but little taste, though a gorgeous array of finery. The show part of the house was itself a monument to the barrenness of invention in him who planned it ; consisting, as it did of one long suite of rooms in a straight line, without variety without obvious parts, and therefore without symmetry or proportions. [Again this is nonsense. Given the steepness of the site the house had to be long and narrow] This long vista was so managed that, by means of folding doors, the whole could be seen at a glance, whilst its extent was magnified by a vast mirror at the further end.[24]

[24] De Quincey, T., *The Works of Thomas De Quincey*, (North, J., Ed.), Vol. 11, Articles from Taits Magazine and Blackwoods Magazine 1838-41, Pickering and Chatto London, 2003, pp.239-240

The Lodge's Water Supply

The sale details of Mendip Lodge from 1923 state that it had an 'Unfailing supply of pure water from a spring on the hills to a large reservoir 50 ft x 22ft x 6ft deep having a capacity of 40,000 gallons.' Quite where this spring was sited is impossible to say, but it must have been above the reservoir. The sale map of the same year shows a 'pool' which corresponds to this, lying about 100 feet directly above the house. The Langford Brook, formerly known variously as Hylisbrook, Hylsbrook and Hunters Brook, appears well below the house, starting at the level of the present Springhead Farm. It would seem that it always has done so. According to Knight:

> Much smaller...are the streams on the hill above, all three of which sink into the ground, and which, although experiments have failed to prove the truth of the theory, may unite by subterranean channels to form the Hunters Brook. One of the three, a stream which has which has been partly drawn off to supply Mendip Lodge and other houses, and which now runs only in wet weather, but whose source forms part of the parish boundary, arises on the northwest slope of Blackdown and disappears down Fox Hole Swallet just outside the upper edge of Mendip Lodge Woods.[25]

The fact that these only ran in wet weather would make the reservoir essential. Such a supply no longer exists at the Lodge but clearly was used from the earliest time. The springs on

---

[25] Knight, F.A., *Heart of Mendip,* reprinted by Chatford House Press, 1971, p .37

Mendip quite often vary, and in 1806 it would seem that a major revision of the water supply was necessary. Thomas complains in a letter to Anna Seward that he has been driven away from Mendip Lodge 'by the imperious necessity of rebuilding the great reservoir in the home plantation which supplies the house and gardens'.[26] It is not clear whether this is due to a failure or an enlargement of the original reservoir, but the work would seem to have taken three months.[27]

The West Harptree Turnpike 1793

At this time travel between Bath and Langford was not easy. One route was to take the turnpike from Bath to Bristol and then take the Bridgewater turnpike to Churchill Cross. These were good roads, the latter having been built by Macadam himself, but the total distance was 27 miles and travel would have taken perhaps 7 hours by coach. There were two alternatives which avoided going through Bristol. One was to take the Bath Turnpike Trust road (now the A39) as far as Hallatrow, where it met the Bristol Trust Road (A37), which soon became the Wells Trust Turnpike. Then you had to cut across country for 12½ miles, along the north side of the Mendips, through West Harptree, Blagdon and Ubley, on an unmade-up road, now the A368 but then no more than a track. Alternatively, you could take the old Fosse Way, now the A367 but then still part of the Bath Turnpike Trust, as far as Stratton on the Fosse, but once again, here you would then have to take the same unmade up road but this time further to the east, giving 17 painful miles. Such a route would have been very hazardous, if not impassable, in the winter.

Thomas Sedgwick needed to make regular visits to Wells as

26 JCTSW II p.288
27 ibid II p.304

a prebend of that Cathedral. For this there was no alternative but to take one or other of the unmade roads, either to the north of the Mendips, as already described, or to the south via Shipham, Cheddar and Westbury-sub-Mendip. He would also wish to visit his mother and elder brother Francis, who were living at Winscombe, and also his younger brother the Reverend Richard Chaple, initially Rector of Horsington, south of Wells, and later Rector of Chelwood. There was also Thomas's sister Mary Wickham and her family, living beyond Wells at Frome, and finally his favourite sister and her daughter Frances, who spent some time at Isaac Sage's house Thornhill in Dorset.

In the light of this it is not surprising that the Whalley brothers, together with local landed friends and relatives such as Wickham, Hippisley Coxe, Tooker, and Popham, set out to sponsor an Act to build the West Harptree turnpike. This would run from the Bristol to Bridgwater turnpike at Churchill, along the foot of the Mendips, to West Harptree, then turning north-east to connect with the Bristol to Wells turnpike at Chelwood Bridge. The Act received its second reading in June 1793.

6.5 The state of the roads in 1792

Notable also amongst the trustees of the new Turnpike was Thomas Sedgwick's friend Henry Bosanquet, who was renting Langford Court at the time, and John Hiley Addington, brother of the Prime Minister Lord Sidmouth, who by 1797 had taken over the lease at Langford Court and would eventually buy the Langford estate in 1804.

Although this late Turnpike Trust did not make a huge profit, it certainly facilitated the lives of the Whalley family and their friends. So while Atthill finds the layout of the new turnpike rather a puzzle,[28] it makes complete sense when one understands the distribution of the Whalley family and their powerful friends. As no public coach service ever ran along the West Harptree turnpike, letters for Mendip Lodge came via the Bristol mail coach to the turnpike gate on the Bridgewater road at Churchill Cross. The turnpike keeper's boy then took the letter the mile to Mendip Lodge and was paid on receipt, the normal practice in the days before the penny post.

The Final Form of the House

Thomas Somers (1812-1862), who acquired Mendip Lodge from his father in 1848, did much to restore the gardens. The only change he made to the buildings was to add the new stables and coachman's house adjacent to what had been the kitchen.[29] Somers also installed water closets. Before this Miss Seward described 'Offices at a little distance detached from the house, many steps below this bank'. One assumes this means an earth closet well away from the house. There was originally a kitchen

---

[28] Atthill, R., *Old Mendip*, David and Charles, Newton Abbot, 1971, p.116

[29] Somers B.E., *Pedigree of the family of Somers of Mendip Lodge,* 1916, p.16

block to the west of the main house and a covered walkway between this and the Lodge, but by Somers's time cooking was undertaken in the main building. Quite what the kitchen block was then used for is unknown.

6.6 The stables and coachman's house (left) built by Thomas Somers, circa 1850

The plan of the house, however, and most of the rooms remained as Whalley had built them, though Somers added to the furniture which was already there. It is sad that the dimensions of each room cannot now be measured, since the foundations are buried under the remains of the demolished house. However, from the sale map of 1903, it would seem that the overall length of the house was about 90 feet, with a front to back depth of about 30 feet, excluding the veranda which might have added another 6 feet. If the original Cottage was confined to the section of the building seen at the rear with the distinct gothic windows, then this original building would have been about 35 feet in length.

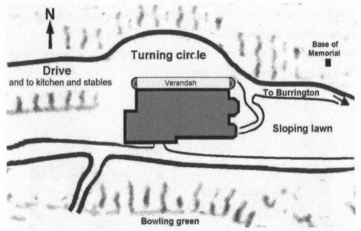

6.7 The site plan of Mendip Lodge, compiled from contemporary descriptions and maps

6.8 The rear of Mendip Lodge in 1906, viewed in from the SE

6.9 Bowling Green

Because of the sloping site, rooms viewed at the front and back are on different floors. The entrance was on the SE corner of the first floor

Ground Floor

Large entrance hall (23ft x 15ft) with cloak recess
Kitchen with range (though an earlier account also says no culinary activities took place in the Lodge and presumably did so in the kitchen block during the Whalleys' occupation of the house)
Scullery with close range and circulating boiler
Two larders
Butlers Pantry
Servants' sitting Room
Lamp room
Coal House
Boot and Knife Room

Two beer and two enclosed wine cellars

An earlier account says there was also a housekeeper's room. While the 1903 description has this on the ground floor, because of the sloping site, it is in fact at ground level at the rear but connects with all other first floor rooms.

First Floor

Dining-room 30ft x 18ft with arched sideboard recess facing south (i.e. at rear)
Morning room (Bow Room) 26ft x 15ft with large bay window facing east
First Drawing-room 18ft x 15ft with two china cupboards
Second drawing room 23ftx 15ft
Two painted rooms 28ft in length (Described as all opening through each other, which would fit with De Quincey's description) and each opening on to the veranda 84 feet in length
Oak panelled library 17ft x 12ft
Smoking Room/WC

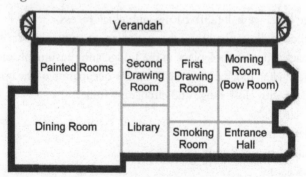

6.10 Possible 1st floor layout, deduced from available descriptions and measurements

133

6.11 One of the two painted rooms

Coyshe also says the Painted Rooms were painted by a French Prisoner of War drafted in from Bristol. This, however, seems unlikely in view of the terms of parole at that time.[30] Certainly, at least one painted room existed in Mendip Lodge, and this decoration was retained during the time of the Somers family's occupation, though by the time Coyshe visited the house in the early 1950s, these hangings had been stripped.

6.12 The Dining Room

---

[30] Vintner, D., *Prisoners of War in Stapleton Jail near Bristol,* Bristol and Gloucestershire Archaeological Society Transactions, 1956, pp.134-169

6.13 The Drawing Room

This image and figures 6.14 and 6.15 below are reproduced
with the kind permission of the Somerset Heritage Centre,
who have made unsuccessful attempts to contact the original
depositor of documents DD/X/MT/5 held at the Centre.

6.14 The Morning Room (The Bow Room)

6.15 The Balcony from the east

The upper floor and attic rooms were grouped together in the 1903 sale catalogue. The upper floor, at least, was reached by both a principal and secondary staircase

The Upper floors

A Suite of Sitting Room, Bedroom and Dressing Room. One assumes this was usually the Whalley's bedroom
Five family bedrooms and dressing room. It is not clear where the dressing room was

Bathroom
A pretty boudoir facing south
Lavatory, etc.

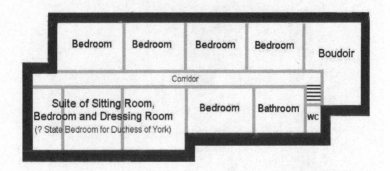

6.16 Suggested 1st floor layout from available data.

Miss Seward's earlier account says, 'Attic rooms for Mr. and Mrs. Whalley and their other guests but not more than three at a time could be accommodated'. There was a guest room which looked out to the east and was at the end of the building.

Attic Floor
Four servants' bedrooms
A large boxroom

CHAPTER 7
The Estate and Gardens

Hill Wickham gives his great uncle the credit for the innovative experiment of planting trees on the north slope of the Mendips.[1] There seems good reason for believing this, as the claim is repeated by his son J.D.C. Wickham, who calls Thomas Sedgwick 'this first reviver of local afforestation'.[2] Lady Miller of Bath Easton referred to this activity in November 1780 as probably the reason for his late appearance in Bath.[3] But 'planting clumps', at which he was supposed to be engaged at Langford Court, was the outdated practice of those such as Capability Brown, who felt that nature should be managed. By 1787, perhaps because of his travels in Savoy, Whalley's views were now the same as those of Sir Uvedale Price,[4] namely that the natural 'picturesque' landscape was more desirable, and there is no evidence of trees ever having been planted in clumps on the Mendip Lodge Estate.

So was the idea of planting trees on the north slope of the Mendip really Whalley's own? It seems more likely it had become a local trend in the pursuit of profit. The only secure reference

---

[1] JCTSW I p.31

[2] Wickham, J.D.C., *Records by spade and terrier,* Harrison and Sons, London, 1912, p.422

[3] JCTSW I p.315

[4] Price U. *Essay on the picturesque, as compared with the sublime and the beautiful,* J Mawman, London, 1794

to tree planting in the area occurs in a letter of 1788 from a Somerset contributor to the 'Society for the Encouragement of Agriculture, the Arts, Manufactures and Commerce at Bath', the precursor of the Bath and West Society.[5] In this the correspondent, identified only as R.E. of Somerset, commends the planting of trees on thin soils and remarks:

> On the north slope of the Mendip Hills in particular, (a situation as unfavourable as most, on account of it being a bed of rocks exposed to the bleak north and east winds), we see beautiful woods of large extent hanging over the parishes of Compton Martin, Ubley, Blagdon, Hutton and Churchill. In these woods although the timber is not large, the growth of the pollarded trees and copse wood must every twelve years bring considerable sums to the owners, although the land for any other purpose would not be worth one shilling per acre.

This would imply that if trees did exist on the slopes above Upper Langford at this time, they would have been planted some years earlier in order to have reached a size where coppicing or pollarding could be contemplated. This all fits with the idea that Whalley was engaged generally in planting trees on the Langford estate shortly after he married Elizabeth Sherwood in 1774, but is somewhat at variance with the account of Anna Seward dated to 1791, which would put the date of the first planting as 1779.[6]

---

[5] *Letters and papers selected from the correspondence book of the Society, Instituted at Bath for the Encouragement of Agriculture, the Arts, Manufactures and Commerce,* Vol. II, Bath, 1788, p.352

[6] *Letters of Anna Seward, Written Between the Years 1784 and 1807,* (Constable, A.,

The earliest painting of Mendip Lodge which is known to exist is reproduced as a print in Rutter's book of 1829.[7] It shows that the tree planting extended no further than Stoney Lane. This is not entirely surprising as it was only after the Enclosure Act of 1795 that Whalley was able to gradually acquire the land further to the west.

7.1 Mendip Lodge as it appears in Rutter's drawing of 1829[8]

The Landscaping of the Grounds

The author maintains that the development of the site around Mendip Lodge reflected Whalley's enthusiasm for the picturesque, which had become popular in England at the

Ed), Vol III, George Ramsay and Co., Edinburgh, 1811, pp.96-101

[7] Rutter, J., *Delineations of the North Western Division* of the *County of Somerset, and of Its Antediluvian Bone Caverns, with a Geological Sketch of the District.* Printed and published by the author, 1829

[8] Whalley had only died the year before the book appeared, and yet the engraving in Rutter (Plate 8) is entitled 'The property of Anthony Wickham of North Hill'. Maybe his subscribing to two copies of the book made this insertion possible in the hope of producing a sale.

end of the 18th century.[9] Whether Thomas Sedgwick employed any professional advice on the layout of his estate is uncertain. Two exponents of the picturesque, Humphrey Repton and William Mason, were part of the Whalley circle. The latter was described by Anna Seward in 1788 as being 'intimate' with Thomas Sedgwick at the time when the house was being built.[10] Also, in a letter of October of that year, she had told Repton, whom she held in high regard, that she had interested Thomas Sedgwick in his work. Repton, who saw himself as Capability Brown's heir, had published the first edition of his book in 1791, using his *Red Book* of Wellbeck Abbey as a basis. Thomas Sedgwick would have had great interest in such a book, as he had always regarded Wellbeck Abbey as his 'old family seat'[11] (see Chapter 2).

It is not known if the grounds around the house were laid out while the house was being built, or carried out later, but it would seem that the work was largely complete by 1791. According to De Quincey, the landscaping around Mendip Lodge cost the Whalleys around £30,000 (£3M today). This sum presumably included the planting of trees around the house and may have included buying the land around the house. Apart from the trees, very little of this now remains. The avenues of yews which used to line the various walks around the house can still be recognised in places, but nothing remains of the 50 hermitages and grottos which Anna Seward mentions. Somers gives details of two further grottos: one, containing the statue of the King of Mendip, was at the east

9 See Hunt JD., *The picturesque garden in Europe*. Thames and Hudson Ltd, London, 2003

10 *Letters of Anna Seward, Written Between the Years 1784 and 1807,* (Constable, A., Ed), Vol. II, George Ramsay and Co., Edinburgh, 1811, p. 172

11 JCTSW II p.288

end of the wood, and the other, for the Queen of Mendip, was at the 'top'. These were already in ruins at the time when Thomas Somers set out to restore the house and gardens, some time after he bought the estate in 1846.[12] Nor is there anything to indicate the site of the 'rustic seats' dedicated to Whalley's friends Hannah More, Mrs Siddons, Mrs Jackson, Miss Weston, Reverend Inman (the local clergyman) and Thomas Sedgwick's venerable mother, described by Seward.[13] However, Thompson, in his book the *Life of Hannah More*, provides a drawing of three of these, made by him in 1838 with the permission of the then occupant of Mendip Lodge Colonel Fawcett, who had married Thomas Sedgwick's niece and was living there.[14]

7.2 One of the yew tree lined walks

[12] Somers BE., *Pedigree of the Somers family of Mendip Lodge* 1916, p.16

[13] *Letters of Anna Seward, Written Between the Years 1784 and 1807*, (Constable, A., Ed), Vol. III, George Ramsay and Co., Edinburgh, 1811, p.100

[14] Thompson, H., *Life of Hannah More with notices of her sisters*, W Blackwood and Sons, Edinburgh, 1838, p.62

7.3 The dedicated seats in the grounds of Mendip Lodge.
(See above text)

Enclosure of West Mendip

Up until 1795 Stoney Lane had provided the only access road to
'The Cottage'. This was little more than a steep sheep track.

7.4 Stoney Lane today – restored to be much as it would have
been in 1790

By this time the enclosure of common land by Act of Parliament was taking place all over Somerset.[15] Sometimes, it involved open arable fields but more often was of moorland or *'upland waste'*.[16] Thomas's elder brother, Colonel Francis Whalley J.P., who had already been involved in the enclosure of Cheddar, played a significant part in the Act of 1795 to enclose Banwell and the wastelands of Churchill. Such an enterprise was not cheap. Billingsley gives the costs of upland enclosure at this time as £1951,[17] equivalent to perhaps £200,000 today.

As with all other Acts, the enclosure of Banwell and Churchill was ostensibly aimed at increasing agricultural production. The wars with France and America had a disastrous effect on the import of food, and the price of wheat had nearly doubled from £2-14s a quarter in 1794 to £4 1s 6d in 1795,[18] leading to civil unrest in some parts of the country. Despite this such Acts were often used by wealthy landowners as a means of increasing their estates. This was achieved by buying up the land allocated to commoners as compensation for loss of grazing rights. These independent cultivators were frequently in debt to tithes and rents and were persuaded to sell their rights, but in so doing, they became the landless labourers who would power the industrial revolution.[19] As Thomas's brother Francis Whalley was one of three commissioners appointed to implement the Act, this was

15 Tate, W.E., *Somerset Enclosure Acts and Awards*, Somerset Archaeological and Natural History Society, Frome, 1948

16 Williams, M., *The enclosure and reclamation of the Mendip Hills*. The Agricultural History Review, 1971; 19: 65-81

17 Billingsley, J., *A general view of the agriculture of Somerset*, 2nd Ed., London, 1798, p.57

18 Wright, Sir J., *Observations on the important subject of preserving wheat from vermin*, London, 1796, p.34

19 Trevelyan, G.M., *English Social History*, 2nd Ed., Longmans Green and Co, London, 1946, pp. 379-F

easily achieved, and Francis was also able to ensure that the paragraph in the Act which required that the water supply of 'The Cottage' remained undisturbed was upheld.[20]

The enclosure of Churchill also provided Thomas Sedgwick with the opportunity to improve access to Mendip Lodge. Three new roads were proposed in the Act: The Cottage Road, Lower Cottage Way and Upper Cottage Way. Ostensibly, these were to improve public access to the new enclosures, but in reality they were to improve access to his Cottage, which could now be approached from Burrington Combe on the more gradual incline of the new Cottage Road.

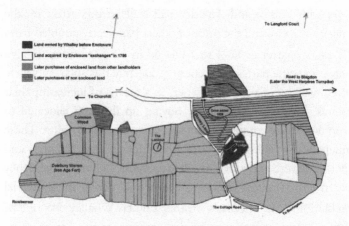

7.5 The final extent of the Mendip Lodge Estate

Over the following years Thomas Sedgwick gradually acquired more of the enclosed land, until he eventually owned 1200 acres. The enlarged estate now included Dolebury Warren, where Thomas and his friends were able to hunt. Thomas's dogs were always a very important part of his life. By this time he

---

[20] *Banwell and Churchill Enclosure Act 1797*. Somerset Heritage Centre, Q/RDE/42

owned Duke and Duchess, two large Danish dogs described as being of spotted white and liver colour and 'of great sagacity'. They were known to absent themselves from Bath and make their way back to Mendip Lodge to engage in their favourite pastime of hunting rabbits on Dolebury Warren.[21]

The Drive and the Lodges

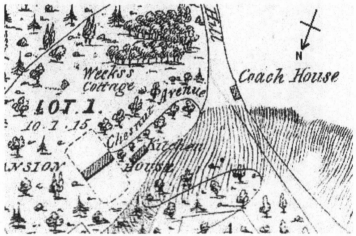

7.6 Mendip Lodge, taken from the sale map of 1844, showing the old coach house and the new drive. This image and figures 7.7, 7.9 and 7.11 are reproduced with the kind permission of the Somerset Heritage Centre, who have made unsuccessful attempts to contact the original depositor of documents DD/X/MT/5 held at the Centre.

From 1814 onward Thomas was trying to sell Mendip Lodge and its estate,[22] but the asking price of £30,000 was generally considered to be unreasonable. When after ten years it had still not sold,

---

[21] JCTSW II p.22
[22] ibid II p.385

Thomas, who now owned the land below the mansion, added a drive with two lodges in the hope that it would improve the chances of a sale. This work was undertaken during 1826/7. The drive still runs across what is known as The Park and zig-zags up the slope above. At the time of writing it is still used by a local shooting syndicate to reach the site of the Lodge and stables.

7.7 The new drive through the Park, constructed in 1826/7

7.8 The Lodges and drive, added in 1826

Writing to his great nephew in March 1828, having just driven from his newly acquired house in Clifton to view the work, Thomas is exultant:

> I have crept out of my winter nest twice, swaddled like a mummy and furred like a Russian, tempted abroad before even the butterfly by bright sunshine. The first time was to handsel [sic] the new road up to Mendip Lodge which is completely formed and only wants stoning. Though the earth was not yet settled, yet two rips of post-horses draw my carriage with ease up the now winding gentle ascent. Huzza!
>
> Thus what was a great objection is now converted into a great recommendation and what was a striking blemish into a striking beauty.[23]

As with the house, no builder or architect of the two Lodges is known, but they bear a striking resemblance to the Toll House at Stanton Drew, which was built for the West Harptree Turnpike. According to local accounts, the west lodge contained the kitchen and living quarters for the lodge keeper and his wife, and the east their bedroom. Sadly, the lodges were damaged by fire and demolished in the late 1950s (see Chapter 14).

---

[23] JCTSW II p.505

7.9 The view of the house, park and gardens from the north
as it appear in a the sale documents of 1844

The sale painting of 1844 shows two further garden
features: an obelisk to the east of the house and a small temple
in the park below. The obelisk can also be seen in a 1923
photograph, and there is still the base for what might have
been this feature situated in its intended location, but it seems
to be too small and lightweight to have supported such a
structure. Maybe it was used to carry the epitaph for Thomas
Sedgwick's dog Sappho, which certainly had a tomb on the
estate;[24] moreover, the map which was included in the 1903
sale catalogue for the estate identifies this as a 'monument'.
There is no trace today of the temple or its foundations.

[24] JCTSW I p.258

7.10 This base to the east of the house might have been for the obelisk or, more likely, carried an epitaph

The Kitchen Garden

At Langford Court, as at any large country house of the time, the Whalleys had an extensive walled garden adjacent to the house. However, this would have been unavailable to them once Langford Court had been let in the summer of 1783. The land around 'The Cottage' was quite unsuitable for growing anything but grass or trees. Not only was the site very steep, but it had almost no topsoil and, being north facing, was in shade for almost all the year. It must have been for these reasons that the garden for the Cottage was sited on the flat land at the foot of the estate, on the north side of the road which would become the West Harptree turnpike (now the A386). This land must originally have been part of the Langford estate. It was in such a position that it would receive some sun even in winter. At the time of the sale in 1844, this was the only land belonging to the Mendip Lodge Estate that lay north of the turnpike road, and so one must assume it had been reserved by Whalley for himself when he finally sold the Langford Court estate to Hiley Addington in 1804.

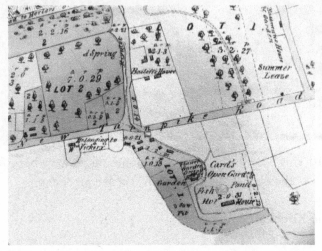

7.11 The garden as it appears in the map accompanying the 1844 sale details. Note the Flower garden and the Green and Hot Houses.

The soil here was very fertile, having been washed down from the Mendips by Langford Brook over many centuries. Around 1900 the area would be taken over by the successful Mendip Nurseries.

There are several buildings between the garden and the road shown in the 1844 plan, which by this time belonged to the Mendip Lodge Estate. Dove Cottage, formerly known as the Pigeon House, would certainly have provided Mendip Lodge with pigeons and their eggs.

7.12 Dove Cottage (Pigeon House)

The adjacent Brook Cottage may have housed the gardener and other staff.[25] There is a gardener's house mentioned in the advertisement of 1904,[26] and the siting of the door still present in the wall surrounding the Flower Garden would have provided direct access to these cottages.

25 Dornton, U., 'Dove Cottage', in *More Stories from Langford*, (Friar, J. et al., Eds.), Langford History Group, Langford, 2009, pp.75-88
26 *Residential Property Sales*, The Times, May 24th 1904

7.13 The gate probably leading to the gardener's cottage

When the Mendip Lodge estate was finally sold in 1846, the garden was included with the house and park as Lot 1. It is only described as having 'walled gardens of considerable extent, large hot and green houses', but as can be seen, there are several subdivisions. The area marked 'Garden' was presumably for vegetables. The separate 'Flower Garden' contained both a green house and a hot house. There was an open area containing the saw-pit. Mr Card owned the adjacent garden, which contained a fish pond fed by the brook. All this area has now been built over to accommodate buildings for the Blagdon Water Garden. Who Card was, and the nature of his relationship was to the Whalleys or the Langford Estate, is unknown, but there were families of that name living in nearby Cheddar and Chew Magna at the time. Beyond Card's

Garden, Pear Tree Farm was never part of the Mendip Lodge estate. There is an excellent published account of this farm's origins and life there in the 1950s by Pat Wilson, who was brought up there.[27] The Pear tree Industrial Estate now occupies the site.

What now remains of Thomas Sedgwick's garden is Grade II listed. Its garden walls to the east and north are in good condition, and the area within them is laid down to grass under restrictions imposed by English Heritage. The Grade II listed heated wall also remains in good condition, apart from the attached furnace house. The heated wall was once thought to be a simple wall containing 32 bee boles, but this is clearly not the case as it contains soot lined heating ducts running below the two rows of 16 arched recesses which provide access for flue cleaning. The concrete area to the north, in front of the heated wall, formed the floor of the hot house, and the whole would have been enclosed by an iron or wooden framed glasshouse.

The identity of the heated wall has now been corrected; however, the author would dispute English Heritage's suggested date of construction as 1816.[28] By this time Thomas Sedgwick would not have been prepared to put money into his garden as he was no longer resident and was attempting to sell the estate. In May 1814 he had separated from this third wife and was living on the continent and would never return to live at the Lodge. It must be that the heated wall was constructed earlier, perhaps even at the same time as the house.

---

27 Wilson, P., *Pear Tree Farm*, in 'More Stories from Langford', (Friar, J. et al., Eds.), Langford History Group, Langford, 2009, pp.57-74
28 English Heritage 1816- /9/10018

Original 18th century chimneys

Later Victorian addition

Non-original brickwork

Later doorway

Recess to probably to receive iron corner post

7.14 The Heated wall

Its design fits well with contemporary descriptions of heated walls as to the size and the location of the flues, fireplaces and chimneys.[29] Thomas Sedgwick could have had an excellent source of advice on its construction through his friend Erasmus Darwin, who died in 1803.[30] Whalley's heated wall hothouse might have served several purposes, but it is almost certain that one of its uses was growing grapes, as it had at Langford Court. Mrs Siddons, writing from Bristol on 16th July 1782, where she had come to undertake a benefit performance,[31] thanked Thomas Sedgwick for the grapes she has sent her. A month later, she passes on her husband's

[29] Loudon, J.C., *The Encyclopaedia of Gardening.* Longman,Rees, Orme,Brown,Green. Longman, London, 1835

[30] Stephens, C.D., 'Mendip Lodge Garden', in *More Stories from Langford*, (Friar, J. et al., Eds), Langford History Group, Langford, 2009, pp.97-106

[31] *The Theatre Royal Bath.* Hare A. (Ed). Kingsmead Press, Bath, 1977, p.84

thanks for the fruit which Thomas had sent him, which he had enjoyed.[32] Very much later, in March 1810, twenty years after Mendip Lodge had been completed, the Whalley's neighbour Hannah More wrote to Thomas Sedgwick to say his gardener had given her a few hours of his time to direct the construction of a 'grape house' at her new house at Barley Wood.[33] This would strongly support the idea that the heated wall for Mendip Lodge had been built much earlier than 1814. Heated walls could also be used to cultivate exotic fruit such as nectarines, peaches and pineapples; however, to do so would have required additional heat provided by a fermenting pit at the base of the wall, but there is no sign that this ever existed. Certainly, though, the wall or the adjacent greenhouse would have been used for the forcing of flowers and the protection of tender plants throughout the winter, prior to planting out in the flower garden. Thomas Sedgwick was known to be very keen on flowers: 'twenty-four large china jars were filled with autumnal flowers' on his veranda when Annas Seward visited the Lodge in September 1793.[34] Heated walls were also built to impress, and any visitor would be able to view the heated wall with its attached glass house as they looked down on it from the veranda of Mendip Lodge, 400 feet above.

Quite what material was used to heat the wall is unknown. It is unlikely to have been wood, since until Whalley started planting trees on it the north side of the Mendips, these slopes were treeless; on the other hand, the nearby saw-pit is interesting. Generally, these were only used for making planks, but there

---

[32] JCTSW I p.375

[33] ibid II p.338

[34] *Letters of Anna Seward, Written Between the Years 1784 and 1807*, (Constable, A., Ed), Vol VI, George Ramsay and Co Edinburgh, 1811, pp. 203

would perhaps have been sense in siting the pit near the hot wall, where brashings and other off cuts could be used for kindling. Coal was certainly available in Langford. There were local pockets mined at Longbottom Valley near Shipham, only 2 miles from Mendip Lodge,[35] and also at Blagdon, a few miles away along the West Harptree Turnpike.[36] There is a contemporary account of coal being provided for the poor in the nearby parish of Winscombe at '13s.0d per load'.[37] Other Trustees of the West Harptree turnpike included Whalley's friends Hippisley and Tooker, who were both involved in coal mining.[38] As there was a turnpike gate near the Bromley Colliery at Stanton Drew, on the West Harptree turnpike, which must have been used for collecting tolls for the transportation of coal,[39] it most likely came from here. This is supported by the fact that the tolls on the West Harptree turnpike were adjusted to be particularly favourable for moving coal; 'every horse, mare, gelding, mule or ass not drawing or loaded with coal' was charged one penny while one of these animals carrying coal was only charged a halfpenny![40] It is also true that Thomas's elder brother, Francis, had interests in coal and was a member of the committee which proposed and built the Somerset Coal Canal, although there is no evidence that coal ever came by road from the canal at Bath to Langford.

---

[35] Gough, J.W., *The Mines of Mendip*, Clarendon Press, Oxford, 1930 p.253

[36] Bulley, J.A., *To Mendip for coal - a study of the Somerset coalfield before 1830*, Somerset Archaeological and Natural History Society Proceedings, 1952, 47: 46-78

[37] Forbes, M., *The Church in Winscombe*, Winscombe and Sandford Millennium Series, Locking, 2000, p.17

[38] Wickham, J.D.C., *Records by spade and terrier*, Harrison and Sons, London, 1912, pp.244-249

[39] Atthill, R., *Old Mendip*, 2nd Ed., David and Charles, Newton Abbot, 1971, pp.116-7

[40] *West Harptree Turnpike Act*, 3rd June 1793, 1048-9

The Lookout

This is the only other surviving garden feature. Its name seems to have been added later. The account given by Anna Seward of her visit in 1791, part of which is included in Chapter 6, also describes this structure and its use:

> On the summit of this pendant garden we find a concave lawn, with a large root-house (a house made of tree roots) in the centre of that semicircular bank, whose thick curtains of firs, larches, poplars &c. form a darkly verdant fringe that, rising above the root-house, crowns the mountain-top (now known as The Lookout). This rustic pavilion supported by pillars made of the boles of old trees, and twined round by woodbine and sweetpeas, is open in front, and commands the whole splendour of the vale below. It contains a large table on which we lay our work, our writing or our books, which we carry thither in a morning, whenever the weather will permit. Hitherto the skies have not shone upon us with much summer warmth and brightness.[41]

While this was certainly built by Whalley, some believe that it used an earlier structure connected with the Dolebury Iron Age Camp above it. It has been pointed out that any force attacking the fort would likely have approached along the foot of the Mendips, either to the north or the south. But while the fort would have a good view of any southern approach, the rising land of Blackdown to the east would obscure an attack coming

---

[41] *Letters of Anna Seward, Written Between the Years 1784 and 1807*, (Constable, A., Ed), Vol III, George Ramsay and Co., Edinburgh, 1811, pp.96-101

from the north. A lightly defended outpost in the location of The Lookout could have provided warning of this. It also gave a line of sight for any signals from the Iron Age Camp at Little Down north of Bath.

Path Profile from Lookout (ST458591) to Lansdown (ST717689)

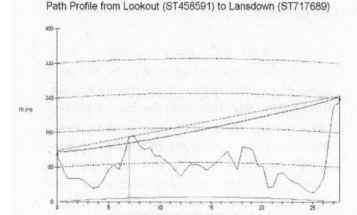

Path Profile (km), Path Length = 27.6, Min clearance = -13.9m at 7.0 km from t

7.15 The line of sight from the Lookout to Lansdown above Bath

Whatever its origins, the Lookout consists of a flattened horseshoe area thirty metres in diameter, open towards the northwest and retained on all other sides by a raised earth bank of about eight feet in height. There is an outer ditch, and it appears that stone quarried from this ditch was used to build a mortared outer retaining wall for the bank. There is a small shelter built of brick, which is thought to have been clad in stone, built to the thickness of the encircling bank on its south east aspect. It appears to have had a floor and may well have been where Thomas Sedgwick kept writing and drawing material for himself and his guests.

7.16 The inner flattened area of the lookout

7.17 Looking northwest from the Lookout across the
Severn to the Welsh hills

7.18 The shelter built into the retaining wall on the south east corner. Its function remains unknown

7.19 Restoring the above retaining wall

CHAPTER 8
Frances's First Marriage and Divorce

Shortly after the Whalleys had returned from the continent in 1787, their 18-year-old niece Fanny Sage joined them in Bath and was busy enjoying life there at her uncle's expense but also to his delight. Her relationship with her uncle and aunt was described in a later letter from Anna Seward to a friend, dated April 1795:

> Miss Sage was in her infancy recommended to his care by the maternal tenderness of a beloved sister, expiring in the bloom of life. This sacred and precious trust Mr. and Mrs. Whalley executed with the most sedulous attention and fondest indulgence. She grew, she bloomed;- the pride and delight of their hearts. Genius and wit aided, by rapidly acquired endowments, the fascinations of beauty.- The creations of the pencil glow beneath her fingers. Her skill, taste and invention on the harpsichord is scarce inferior to that of the first masters*; and to a voice of exquisite tone, power, compass and inflexion, she adds the touching graces of harmonic expression, in a degree of excellence that approaches to enchantment. She was abroad with the aunt and uncle Whalley in the year 1786 and, mistress of French and Italian, she con-

versed, sung- she played, she danced, the day-star
of our island; so that nothing was more talked of in
the then happy French cities than the charming
English woman.[1]

*There were other similar reports of her playing. In
one she is compared to Mrs Miles. [2,3,4]

She was by now known as the "Queen of Bath", for her good
looks, wit and conversation, her singing and her playing of the
harpsichord and guitar. Lowndes records that in 1939 there
remained a notice in one of the rooms of 20 Royal Crescent, then
occupied by the British Boxboard Agency, bearing the inscription
'Fanny Sage, known for her beauty as the Queen of Bath, lived
here in 1787'.[5] She was not the first to hold this unofficial title; a
Miss Wroughton (1754-1825) of Wilcot House Wilton was also
so known.[6] She was the patroness of Rauzzini (the composer and
friend of Joseph Haydn), and Thomas Sedgwick had once
addressed verses to her.[7] By May 1789 the 19 year old Frances

[1] *Letters of Anna Seward, Written Between the Years 1784 and 1807,* (Constable, A.,
Ed), Vol. IV, George Ramsay and Co, Edinburgh, 1811, p.43

[2] JCTSW II p.41

[3] Jane Mary Guest (Mrs Miles) was a leading keyboard player of the day who
was at the height of her powers at this time. She performed at Rauzinni's
concerts in Bath and at the Hannover Square Concerts in London. She was
teacher to the daughters of George III and was also a composer of concertos
and other works including "Six progressive lessons for the harpsichord or piano
forte" (See Salwey, N., 'Women pianists in the late 18th century',in (Wollenberg,
S., McVeigh, S., Eds) *Concert life in the 18th century.* Ashgate Ltd, Farnham, 2004.
pp.282-284

[4] *Letters of Anna Seward, Written Between the Years 1784 and 1807,* (Constable, A.,
Ed), Vol. III, George Ramsay and Co Edinburgh, 1811, p.379

[5] Lowndes, W., *The Royal Crescent in Bath.* The Redcliffe Press, Bristol,1981. p.50

[6] Tearle J., *Mrs. Piozzi's Tall Young Beau William Augustus Conway.* Associated
Universities Press, London, 1991, p.80

[7] JCTSW I p.255

was clearly still having a wonderful time in Bath but was causing Thomas's cousin Sophia Weston some anxiety:

> Has our lovely Fanny made any new conquests and may I dare to drop a hint that I wish you would not let her run so much about Bath in a morning? Walking is certainly good for her health, and necessary; but the misfortune of Bath is that young people cannot take the advantage of exercise without being too much exposed to observation. Fanny is too attractive not to be much sought after, but she should not be too easily or too frequently found. When you and Mrs. Whalley think she is walking in the Crescent, she is often flying all over the Parades. The dear thing is wonderfully prone to flirtation, and hunts after a new beau, who has happened to strike her fancy, with a degree of activity and interest more natural than fit. I am sorry to say that her cousin, Miss Wickham, seemed much more inclined to lead her into this sort of thing than, as she ought, to be a check upon her. Miss King is also intolerably giddy. Perhaps the indulgence of always having a young friend to run about with her, may be ultimately of the most serious disadvantage to Fanny. Be assured, though I heard many remarks upon this subject, I have not ventured to speak from the observation of others. Fanny loves me, and my time of life is not formidable to her. I had, therefore, ample means of making my own observations, such as even yourself or Mrs. Whalley could not have.

I know how delicate interference of this sort is amongst friends; but I also know that I am influenced only by motives of the purest attachment to Fanny's interest, and I know moreover the candour and liberality of my dear cousin Thomas. Therefore however ill judged these remarks may appear, I have no fear in submitting them to your indulgence.[8]

Miss Wickham 'who should have known better' was probably the 26 year old Elizabeth Mary Wickham (1763-1823), her cousin, who was to remain a spinster. Less likely, it could have been Ann Wickham, who was of the same age as Frances but died later that year. Miss King could perhaps have been a daughter of James King, Master of the Ceremonies (1744-1816), who is mentioned in Jane Austen's *Northanger Abbey*.

8.1 'A view of the Parades at Bath', attributed to Humphrey Repton. © Bath in Time

---

[8] JCTSW II p.33

The cartoon above, which is attributed to Humphrey Repton in 1787, if not of Frances herself, gives a clear illustration of what Miss Weston was concerned about! Repton was a member of the Anna Seward circle and at this time was attempting to establish himself as a garden designer.[9] He was also an excellent artist, and Anna Seward, in a letter to him the year before, says 'You tell me Mrs. Repton reads to you in an evening while you draw'.[10] She had a high regard for Repton and made a point of introducing him to Thomas Sedgwick in a letter of October 1788:

> I should suppose that nobody has ever been so well
> qualified as yourself for the profession you purpose
> [sic] to assume, that of landscape gardener;...Mr.
> Whalley will be in Bath this Winter, he is very warm
> hearted and oratorically persuasive and I have
> interested him in your fame and success.[11]

At that time Thomas Sedgwick was very much engaged in completing the house and laying out the gardens for his "Cottage" at Langford,[12] and if Repton took up the offer of this introduction, he may well have met Frances, as the Whalleys were in residence at Royal Crescent by the following January.

Perhaps as a result of Miss Weston's concern, Frances was married a year later to William Townsend Mullins, a widower and an heir to a large fortune. She was 20 years old; he was 29

---

[9] It has also been suggested that the tall gentleman with the white hair is Thomas Sedgwick himself

[10] *Letters of Anna Seward, Written Between the Years 1784 and 1807,* (Constable, A., Ed.), Vol. I, George Ramsay and Co., Edinburgh, 1811, p.128

[11] *Letters of Anna Seward, Written Between the Years 1784 and 1807,* (Constable, A., Ed), Vol. II, George Ramsay and Co Edinburgh, 1811, pp.172-3

[12] ibid p.204

and already had two young daughters. His first wife had died in 1788,[13] and his two daughters Anna (b.1785) and Elizabeth (b.1786) would spend all their lives in Ireland.

William had been educated in Limerick at the School of the Reverend Daniel Monsell and then had entered Trinity College Dublin in June 1779, where as *Socius Comitatus* (a Fellow Commoner) he paid double fees in order to graduate in three years rather than the usual four.[14] How he and Frances met or how the marriage was arranged is not known. The Mullin's family seat was Burnham House, County Kerry, Ireland, and his father, who was to become the first Lord Ventry, was immensely wealthy, and so his son must have seemed a good prospect for a husband. The marriage settlement of £17,000, equivalent to £1.7m today, was paid jointly by Isaac Sage, Thomas Sedgwick Whalley and his wife. Such a dowry was intended, through investment by her husband, to provide £1000 per annum for Frances in the event of his death.[15]

Yet the choice of husband was an odd one for the beautiful and talented Frances Sage. Certainly, William Mullins's father was extremely wealthy, but he did not yet have a title. As Thomas Sedgwick would not have had anything to do with imposing a choice of husband on Frances, and as he was happy to put up half the dowry, one must assume that he, Isaac Sage and Frances were content with the match. But where were all the young, dashing, rich and titled gentlemen who had come to Bath to find such a talented beauty as Frances? Could it be that she was already a woman with a reputation? Maybe the title "Queen of

---

[13] To Sarah Anne, the youngest daughter of Sir Riggs Falkiner first Baronet of Anne Mount, County Cork

[14] *Alumni Dublinenses,* (Burtchaell G, Sadleir T, Eds.), London, 1924.

[15] *An Act to dissolve the Marriage of William Mullins and Frances Elizabeth Sage.* 36 Geo III 1795/6

167

Bath" carried a warning. By this time sensuality had become the antonym of respectability,[16] and Miss Weston's remarks about Frances and her friends allude to a dangerous disregard for propriety.

The marriage took place on 12th May 1790 in Walcot Parish Church Bath.[17],[18] It is to be assumed that one or more of her three uncles were in attendance at the wedding and perhaps their mother too, who although in her 84th year was due to live for another 10 years. The marriage was not conducted by either of her ordained uncles but by the Rector of St Swithin's Walcot, John Sibley.

Romney painted a full-length portrait of Frances at about this time; sadly, the whereabouts of this remains unknown. There exists another portrait by him, 'Lady in a White Dress', which might well be that of Frances; her facial appearance, the position of the head and the sheet of music in her hand bear a striking similarity to the earlier painting by Cosway.

16 Porter, R., *English Society in the 18th century*, Penguin Books, London,1982, p.307

17 White, G.H,. Lea, R.S., *The Complete Peerage, or a history of the House of Lords and all its members from the earliest times*, St. Catherine Press, London, 1959; XII, pp.238-241

18 Greenwoolers, C., Witness statement. Divorce papers, 1795

8.2a Frances Sage aged 18 years

8.2b "Lady in a White Dress" by Romney

Why the Marriage Failed

According to Porter, once married, a lady in polite 18th-century society had four functions:[19] to obey her husband, produce heirs, run the household and be ladylike. While in the early months of their marriage there seems little doubt that Frances was obedient, after a few years she had not produced an heir nor had she a house to manage. In due course, perhaps after reading Mary Wolstonecraft's book *A Vindication of the Rights of Women*, published in 1792, she seems to have ceased to be either obedient or ladylike.

Six months after the marriage, though, Thomas Sedgwick thought that all was well and had communicated this to Anna Seward, who replied in December 1790: 'I am glad…that the temper and disposition of him to whom your darling niece has

[19] Porter, R., *English Society in the 18th century.* Penguin Books, London, 1982, pp.27-8

given her herself, is so amiable'.[20]

William was due to inherit his father's title and estate. According to Thomas Sedgwick, he would then have acquired an income of £32,000 a year (i.e. £3.2m at today's value).[21] However, as matters turned out, his father was exceptionally long lived, and William would not inherit until he was 63 years old and just two years from his own death.

After their marriage the couple and Frances's father, Isaac Sage, went to Ireland and, according to Isaac Sage's valet James Daxon, stayed at William Mullin's house at 'Tarbutt in the County of Kerry'. This could not have been Tarbot House, near Killarney, as this was then in the ownership of the Leslie family, but it may have been Piermount House, Tarbert, on the shores of the River Shannon, William's family home, which was still being lived in by a members of Mullins family in 1944. If so, one can only imagine the shock which the prospect of a future lived on the West Coast of Ireland made on Frances, and she never again visited Ireland, though William clearly did.

---

20 *Letters of Anna Seward, Written Between the Years 1784 and 1807,* (Constable, A., Ed.), Vol.III,. George Ramsay and Co Edinburgh, 1811, p.47
21 JCTSW II p.414

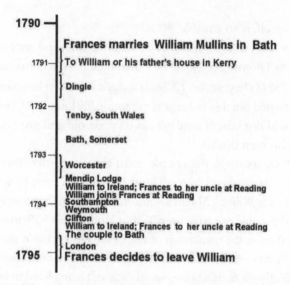

1790 —

Frances marries William Mullins in Bath

1791— } To William or his father's house in Kerry

} Dingle

1792 —

Tenby, South Wales

Bath, Somerset

1793 —

} Worcester

Mendip Lodge
William to Ireland; Frances to her uncle at Reading
William joins Frances at Reading
1794— Southampton
Weymouth
Clifton
William to Ireland; Frances to her uncle at Reading
The couple to Bath

London
1795 — } **Frances decides to leave William**

8.3 The movement of William and Frances Mullins after their
marriage as far as they can be deduced

Frances may well have expected that William would now buy a
house in England, but he did not; perhaps he was unable to do
so. According to Thomas Sedgwick, William Mullins's father was
avaricious and a mean skinflint, so one can suppose that Mr and
Mrs Mullins were now rather less well off than Frances, her father
and Thomas Sedgwick might have imagined when the marriage
was arranged.[22] All this may explain why the couple seem
henceforth to have to lead a peripatetic life around England,
relying on the hospitality of their many wealthy friends and
relatives to accommodate them.

When a woman married in the 18th century, she became
'mistress of the family', and her domain was the family home. Her

---

[22] At the end of his life, Thomas Sedgwick was still trying to recover a loan
which he had made to William of £500, on which even the interest had not been
paid (see Chapter 13, Letter to William Bromley 27th April 1827).

role as a dignified, efficient housekeeper and mother was a source of satisfaction and public esteem, and her husband was expected to honour his wife's authority on all domestic matters.[23] If there was no prospect of her owning a house in England, Frances could not entertain. Furthermore, William hated 'balls, assemblies, suppers and late hours', all of which were a major feature of Frances's life before she married.

By 1793 it is clear that things were not well. In October 1793 Mrs Siddons had written to Thomas Sedgwick, saying how sad she was to learn of Frances's 'unhappy situation' and hoping her beautiful hands will soon be fully restored.[24] Quite whether the unhappy situation referred to her hands or the unhappy marriage is not clear from the context. Was this perhaps a psychosomatic skin disorder, or had Frances self-harmed? Two months later, in December 1793, Frances received a letter from Princess D'Arenberg, who was of a similar age and with whom she had formed a close friendship when they met in 1786 (see Chapter 5). In this the Princess mentions that William might be going to the continent to join the war with France and suggests:

> If Mr. Mullins crosses the sea for the sake of military
> glory you should for his sake come nearer the centre
> of military operation; and why would you not stay
> in Brussels where you have left many friends and
> certainly you would hear more frequently news of
> your husband... [25,26]

---

[23] Vickery, A., *The gentleman's daughter – womens' lives in Georgian England*, Yale University Press, London, 2003. p.160.

[24] JCTSW II p.90

[25] ibid II p.85

[26] There is no evidence that he did so but in October 1803 a William Mullins (Gent) enrolled as an Ensign in the first East Somerset Regiment.

By April 1795 there was knowledge of the breakdown of the Mullins marriage, but this was confined to Thomas's close friends. Later, we learn from Ann Seward that the breakdown was longstanding.

> After a twelve month's ardent attention to him, repaid on his part by the most devoted indulgence, she grew cold, apparently oppressed by every instance of his regard, and charmed by the admiration of other men. She racked his heart with jealousy, and received his expostulations with scorn; grieved and alarmed from time to time by her levities, those tender friends who had been the guardians of her youth [The Whalleys]; and at last, a few month since, eloped with Captain Tothe [sic: clearly a missprint] of the Guards, with whom she now lives in total disgrace, reckless of having blasted her constellation of talents- reckless of this dire apostacy from gratitude, from love, from honour, and from duty [27]

Whatever the cause, it is very clear that after only a few months of marriage both partners were deeply unhappy. At that time there were only three options in such a situation: mutual acceptance, legal separation or divorce. As a male heir must have been the main reason for William's second marriage (as it was for his later third marriage), he must have realised that the only way out for him was divorce, since legal separation did not permit remarriage.

---

[27] *Letters of Anna Seward, Written Between the Years 1784 and 1807,* (Constable, A., Ed.), Vol. IV, George Ramsay and Co., Edinburgh, 1811, p.44

Separation and Divorce in the Eighteenth Century

Before the Matrimonial Causes Act of 1857, which set up special courts to deal with divorce, the only way to obtain a divorce (as opposed to a legal separation) was by a private Act of Parliament. Before 1700 even this was not possible, but between 1700 and 1857 there were about 350 Divorce Acts passed in the House of Lords. Divorce was granted only for adultery, and women could not obtain a divorce from their husbands unless the adultery was compounded with other offences, such as bigamy or incest. In reality, divorce was invariably given to men, there being only 4 Divorce Acts granted to women before 1857.[28]

Before the House of Lords would consider an Act for divorce, it required a divorce '*a mensa et thoro*' (not allowing remarriage) from an ecclesiastical court, together with a verdict of 'criminal conversation' (adultery). The procedure of the church courts was very different from the civil court system of today. The parties to a case provided witnesses to attempt to persuade the court of their case (or defence). These witnesses were known as deponents, as their evidence was given not orally but by deposition: a written statement of the facts. Depositions were taken in response to written lists of questions (called interrogatories) drawn up in advance. These appear in the statements as 'articles of the aforesaid libel'. The court required there to be statements from seven independent witnesses. Once this had been achieved, the House of Lords re-heard the cases tried by the ecclesiastical court to ensure that adultery was proven and that there had been no connivance, collusion or condonation by the husband.[29] Such trials were held in public.

---

[28] Woolfram, S., *Divorce in England 1700 – 1857*. Oxford Journal of Legal Studies 1985; 5: 162

[29] ibid 5: 155-185

While divorce was not legally confined to the nobility and landed gentry, most cases involved these classes, as it concerned the matter of inheritance, and it was also not a cheap undertaking. The estimates are that the overall cost of a divorce might have been £70,000 at today's prices, excluding damages which might be sought. Legal costs were not borne by the plaintiff but by the adulterer, and damages awarded to men who brought successful cases against their wives were high. The Mullin's divorce is the only one recorded between an heir to a title and his wife before 1800 and probably had a large element of mutual consent.[30]

One can imagine that from William's standpoint there was nothing he could do to bring about a divorce, and if there was anything to suggest he had been involved in planning the infidelity of his wife, then the case would be rejected by the Ecclesiastical Court. However, it would appear that Frances had already provided clear evidence of infidelity.

The Divorce

What happened in January 1795 is recounted through the various depositions presented to the Ecclesiastical Court, taken during May and early June 1795, and also in the press.[31] It seems that on January 26th Frances and her husband were planning to leave Osborns Hotel, London to visit the Whalleys at Langford. Under the pretence that she would go via her uncle Joseph, who lived at Reading, Frances left accompanied only by her maid. Having set out, Frances told the maid that she and her husband were about to part and she would not be going to Langford. Instead, having failed to find suitable lodgings in Piccadilly, she directed the coach

---

[30] Woolfram, S., *Divorce in England 1700 – 1857*. Oxford Journal of Legal Studies 1985; 5: 165

[31] *The Times*, 28th July 1795.

to Kensington Gravel Pits (about where Notting Hill Gate is now) and stopped at what the maid thought was a friend's house for the night. Soon after she arrived, Frances wrote a letter, which she sent out, and later that evening Captain Abel Rous Dottin of the Life Guards arrived and stayed talking to Frances until 10 or 11 o'clock.

8.4 Isaac Sage's House in Albemarle Street, St James as it is today

The following morning, her husband and father arrived and talked with Frances for some while but then departed. Two hours later, her father returned in his carriage and took Frances and the maid back to his house in Albemarle Street. She stayed there until the 30th, whereupon she ordered a sedan chair which took her to the coach stand in Oxford Street, from where she took a Hackney Coach to the Castle Inn at Richmond, where she met and stayed with Captain Dottin, acting as man and wife. When on the following evening Mr Sage and Mr Mullins arrived, the innkeeper at first denied that the couple had shared a room but was later told by Captain Dottin to tell the truth. Mr Sage and Mr Mullins then departed, but the couple stayed for a further three days before leaving to stay at the Grassiers Hotel in Jermyn Street, where they registered as Mr and Mrs Dottin. This location was clearly more convenient, since it was exactly midway between her father's house in Albemarle Street and Dottin's barracks! The maid was summoned from Albemarle Street to attend her mistress for several days thereafter, which must have been with the agreement of Isaac Sage. They then moved to lodgings in Grosvenor Square and finally lodgings at 6 Brook Street, these various locations together ensuring that there would be at least seven reliable witnesses who could provide independent statements of 'criminal conversation' between the couple, as required by the ecclesiastical court .

The divorce became public knowledge at the end of July 1795, when the Bath Gazette and Weekly Advertiser, the Ipswich Journal and The Times all contained reports of the hearing on Tuesday 21st July, when Consistory Court of the Bishop of London found the adultery of Frances with Captain Dottin of the Guards proved.[32,33,34]

Captain Abel Rous Dottin

Abel Rouse Dottin was the same age as Frances and the eldest son of very wealthy parents. Though Abel and his brother were born in London, both sides of his family were plantation owners in Barbados,[35] and had been for several generations, but their

[32] *The Bath Gazette and Weekly Advertiser,* July 23rd 1795, p.2

[33] *The Ipswich Journal,* July 25th 1795, p.2

[34] . *The Times* July 28th 1795, p.1

[35] See Smith, S.D., *Slavery family and gentry in the British Atlantic,* Cambridge University Press, Cambridge, 2006

parents married and lived in England. Abel Dottin senior went on to become High Sheriff of Oxford. The Dottin family had a London House as well as a substantial house in Princes Buildings, Bath, which was described as having a double staircase, a large garden, a coach house containing a post coach and 2 phaetons, and stabling for 4 horses.[36] Princes Street and Royal Crescent were only a few hundred yards apart, and the Dottins must have attended the same church in Walcot as the Whalleys and Frances Sage when she was in Bath. The Dottin boys attended a boarding school in Bristol. Abel, his father and grandfather were Oxford graduates, and Abel attended Queen's College.

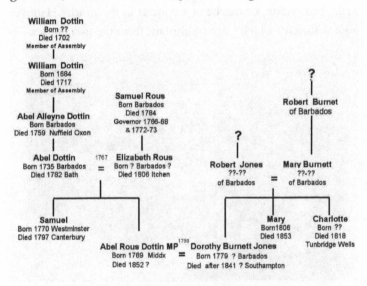

8.5 The Dottin family tree

As Frances and he were of the same age, and because his father had a house in Bath, they must have known each other in their

---

36 Bath Chronicle, February 26th 1784

teens, especially as Abel was known for his 'good minuet'. By the time of the divorce, Able Dottin was aged 26 years and had risen to the rank of Captain in the 2nd Life Guards, so it is likely that he entered the army directly after leaving University. This would have removed him from the Bath social scene before Frances reached an age to contemplate marriage, but they could still have met at social functions when he was on leave. By 1790 Abel was based at St James Palace barracks at the bottom of Albermarle Street. This was only a few hundred yards from the Sage's house and on the direct route between the Officers Mess and Dottin's house in Argyle Street. So this is perhaps how they met, or met again, in London, or maybe at a concert in the nearby Hanover Square Rooms, which were equidistant from the two houses.

8.6 'Loyal Souls' – the Mess Room at St. James. Capt Abel Rous Dottin proposes the loyal toast © National Portrait Gallery, London

While the witness statements and the picture of the Officers' Mess

179

at St James paint a picture of Captain A Dottin as a typical 18th-century rake, there is a much more flattering representation in an engraving by H.B. Hall of a painting by Sir Thomas Lawrence. (Lawrence was a lifelong friend, from the time when, in 1782 as a precocious 13 year old, he sketched Abel and his brother in Bath.37,38) Although entitled 'Abel Rous Dottin MP', the subject in Fig.8.7 looks to be no more than 25 years of age, not much before his entanglement with Frances Mullins. As Dottin didn't become MP until the age of 49, the portrait by his friend Lawrence must have been undertaken much earlier.

8.7 Abel Rous Dottin, the engraving by HB Hall of the painting by Sir Thomas Lawrence, published in 1830

37 http://www.holburne.org/muse/search/item.cfm?MuseumNumber=2008.1 [accessed 24/09/2013]

38 Holburne Museum of Art Annual Report, Bath, 2007, p.9

William Mullins obtained damages and costs against Dottin of £500 in the Court of the Kings bench.[39] He was then free to petition the King to bring about an Act of Divorce. The first reading of this was held on the 3rd of December 1795 and the second reading on the 4th of February 1796. The Bill was then considered by a Committee of the House of Lords on 18th of February, and the divorce was made effective from March 1796.

The divorce included a generous settlement to Frances of £1000 per year for life.[40] This sum was derived from the income arising from her dowry, which remained the property of William Mullins. This would have been enough to keep a single woman in considerable comfort. In *Sense and Sensibility*, written only a few years after Frances's marriage, Jane Austen includes a conversation between Marianne and Elinor in which Marianne considers a suitable income for setting up house.

> And yet two thousand a-year is a very moderate income," said Marianne. "A family cannot well be maintained on a smaller. I am sure I am not extravagant in my demands. A proper establishment of servants, a carriage, perhaps two, and hunters, cannot be supported on less.

All parties appear to have remained on the best of terms after the divorce. William Mullins still had no male heir and was now free to remarry. This he did 18 months later in September 1797. His son Thomas was born the same year, which suggests that William was not going to be caught out again by marrying a barren wife!

---

[39] A senior court of common law at that time.

[40] *An Act to dissolve the marriage of William Mullins and Esq. And Frances Elizabeth Mullins* 36 Geo III 1795/6

Thomas Sedgwick Whalley remained on the closest terms with William Mullins, to whom he seems to have lent a large sum of money against the day when William would inherit from his father.[41] Many years later, in November 1815, Thomas visited William and his family in Brussels and stayed there for several months. In his correspondence at that time to his friend Arthur Anstey, he speaks in the warmest terms of both William, whom he describes as 'my old and steady friend', and 'the lovely and amiable' third Mrs Mullins and their son.[42,43] Some four months after Frances left her husband, Maria Brazier, her maid, was in the service of the Reverend George Markham, who was soon to become Dean of York, and it was from here that she wrote her deposition in 2nd May 1795. One cannot believe this position had been obtained without help of the well-connected Whalley family. She was of course the only weak link in the carefully arranged scheme and must have overheard much of the planning, so it was better that she was out of the way as soon as possible.

What Happened to Captain Abel Rous Dottin?

The involvement in the divorce did not hold Captain Dottin back. Three years later, in March 1798, he married Dorothy Burnett Jones, who was from another extremely wealthy West Indies family. Her father had been Attorney General of Barbados, and her sister was to become Lady Arundel.[44]

Dottin's means of election to parliament also adds further

---

41 Letter from Thomas Sedgwick Whalley to Wm Bromley April 1827 (See Chapter 13)

42 JCTSW II p.413

43 ibid II p.412

44 Burke, Sir B., *A genealogical and heraldic history of the commoners of Great Britain and Ireland*, 1895

weight, if any were needed, to the idea that Frances' divorce was engineered with the agreement of all parties, for he achieved his seat with the help of Isaac Sage, via the Constituency of Gatton, near Reigate in Surrey. This was possibly the most rotten of all rotten boroughs at the time and, in spite of its tiny size, returned two members of parliament. Sir Mark Wood, Baronet, who owned Gatton, and his son (also later Sir Mark) held one of these from 1802 to 1818.[45]

The village of Gatton had 23 houses, of which perhaps as few as 6 were within the borough, so electors were never more than a handful, and the most important was the Lord of the Manor, living at Gatton Park. It was, of course, pointless for any candidate to stand in opposition to the Lord of the Manor of Gatton. A delightful account of the election of 1816, just two years before Dottin's election there, is recorded by Henry Stook Smith, who describes the circumstances which are likely to have pertained for Mr Dottin. It appears that in 1816 there were, uniquely, two candidates for the one vacant seat, and in the event Mr Wood the younger defeated a Mr Jennings by one vote. However,

> Mr. Jennings was Sir Mark Wood's butler and there were only three voters Sir Mark, his son and Jennings. The son was away and Jennings and his master quarrelled, upon which Jennings refused to second the son and proposed himself. To get a seconder for his son Sir Mark had to second Jennings, and it was ultimately arranged, and the vote of Sir Mark alone given. This was the only contest within memory. [46]

[45] Arundell, T.R., *Obituary Sir Mark Wood*, Gentleman's Magazine, Vol. XCIX, 1829, p.276

Isaac Sage, having sold Thornhill, had been living at Gatton Park, a fine Palladian Mansion, since sometime before 1811, when he rewrote his will as 'Isaac Sage of Gatton'. It would seem he was renting the estate from Sir Mark Wood, who had been created baronet in 1808. In 1802 Sir Mark's wife, Rachel, had died and was buried at Gatton, as was his son, Alexander, in 1808. Perhaps this led to Sir Mark vacating Gatton, which left the house empty for Isaac Sage to rent in that year. Both were members of the East India Company until its dissolution in 1818, and both men were keen race goers. Sir Mark had been a colonel in the Company and had become its Chief Engineer in Bengal when Isaac had been Governor of Patna.

Sir Mark eventually died on 6th February 1829 in his London House in Pall Mall, only half a mile from Isaac's house in Albemarle Street. Thus, even if Isaac had not himself been acting as the Lord of the Manor of Gatton in 1818, he clearly had it in his power to either promote or bar Abel Rous Dottin's election to Parliament via that route and must have chosen to do the former.

So by 1826 Dottin was MP for Southampton and a pillar of Southampton society. He became a JP and later High Sheriff of the County but does not seem to have been a particularly active MP, though he notably chaired the committee which proposed the establishment of the Southampton Docks Railway.[46]

What Happened to Frances Mullins (née Sage)

In July 1795, only a few days after the hearing at the Court of the Kings bench became public, Mrs Piozzi's daughter Cecilia was referring to Frances as *'that dreadful Mrs Mullins'*. She even suggests,

46 Smith, H.S., *The Parliaments of England 1715-1847*, 2nd Ed., (Craig, F., Ed.), Parliamentary Reference Publications, Chichester, 1973

in her letter dated 2nd July, that the death of Thomas Sedgwick's first wife had been brought about by the distress which Frances had caused her aunt.[47] (This was wholly incorrect, since the first Mrs Whalley did not die until 8th December 1801!) Anna Seward also reported that the Whalleys were 'both ill, distracted and depressed this time',[48] although six months later she reported finding them 'well and cheerful'! [49]

Some weeks earlier, Mrs Piozzi had pressed her close friend Penelope Pennington for details of Mrs Mullins's disgrace. It is clear that she never had a high opinion of her.[50] Penelope, who, as Sophie Weston had in earlier days, regarded herself as a friend and confident of Frances (Sage), replied in unusually severe terms:

> After alarming and teizing [sic] her Friends with great Impropriety of conduct for above these two years past; [her] Husband was about two Months since too well convinced, that he had still more to complain of. Think however of her Depravity, when in the same Week that she confessed to a Criminal Connexion with One Man, and was pardoned [sic] on fair promises of better things, She commenced an intrigue with another! no less a Person than the Dancing Mr. Dottin, who you must recollect at Bath – famous for his Debaucheries and Good Minuet – On the discovery of which poor Mullins immediately carried her to her father in London, – from which she eloped twice in one week, – Once

---

47 TIL p.129

48 *Letters of Anna Seward, Written Between the Years 1784 and 1807*, (Constable, A., Ed.), *Vol IV*, George Ramsay and Co., Edinburgh, 1811, p.44

49 ibid p.127

50 TPL II p.239

they traced her to a House of no good Fame in Kensington and the second time to the Castle at Richmond, where she had been two days and two night with Dottin – passing for his wife – and when her Father in tears and agony requested, that she would not let him leave her in a Brothel; she treated him with the utmost Contempt, – did every thing but laugh in his Face, and refusing to return with him, remained there with her Paramour, with whom she continues in London where her Husband is preparing, with Mr. Erskine's assistance, to obtain such redress as the Law will afford him [51]

One interpretation of such a description was that Frances had become a high class prostitute, another that she was bored with her husband and was seeking the only way out available to her. What does not fit in this is that Frances remarried only three weeks after the Divorce Act had its third reading. Was this a marriage of love or one of convenience, enabling her to continue to live the life of a courtesan? If the former, she could not let her second husband be the co-respondent, as technically divorce was granted to the plaintiff, allowing him or her to remarry, a permission not given to the guilty party. In reality there was no way in which the law could prevent this from happening. However, at the time of her divorce, efforts were being made in the House of Lords to change the law so that the guilty woman could not marry her paramour. While this failed to become law, at the time it was a real threat. If a love match, then what Frances and her husband-to-be needed was someone they could trust to act the part of adulterer without putting Frances's honour at risk.

[51] *Letter from Penelope Pennington to Mrs. Piozzi 27th March 1795,* The John Rylands Library, University of Manchester, 567.57

So on the 26th of March 1796 Frances married the Rev Robert
Boyle Sullivan in Westminster.[52]

No. 1328.} The Reverend Boyle Sullivan of this Parish
Bachelor and Frances Eliza Sage of the
same Parish spinster were
Married in this Church by Licence
this Twenty sixth Day of March in the Year One Thousand seven Hundred
and Ninety six By me Benjn Lawrence Curate
This Marriage was solemnized between Us { Boyle Sullivan
{ Frances Eliza Sage
In the Presence of { Sophia Louisa Egerton
{ Fra^s Rowe

8.8 The marriage of the divorced Frances Mullins to Robert
Boyle Sullivan, Marylebone, Westminster, March 1796

This was by special licence, rather than the cheaper option of
having the banns read. Perhaps this was to avoid the possibility
of an objection being voiced! The officiating clergyman, the
Reverend Benjamin Lawrence (BA Oxon, 1782), is described in
the Oxford University Alumni (1500-1886) as a gentleman of
Builth Wells who was ordained in Lincoln in 1795 and became
Curate of St Mary's Marylebone; although he was later (a largely
absentee) Rector of Carsington, in 1798 he remained a Curate of
St Mary's (as he did all of his life).[53] It is quite possible, though
unlikely, that he also was unaware that Frances had been married,
since she is recorded in the licence as being a spinster. It is
perhaps also a deliberate obfuscation that the Reverend Robert
Boyle O'Sullivan, for that is who he was, signed himself in the

52 London England Banns, 1754-1921

53 Bigwood, R., *Lawrence families of the Builth Wells and Llanelwedd area in the 18th
and 19th centuries*, Radnorshire Society Transactions, 1989, 59: 96-99

marriage register as 'Boyle Sullivan' not Robert Boyle O'Sullivan. It is of course true that many Irishmen dropped the "O" on coming to England, but why exclude his Christian name in a Christian marriage register?

The witnesses at the marriage, Sophia Louisa Egerton and Francis Rowe, appear to have had no family connection with either the Sages or Whalleys, and this too points to the importance of not giving any suggestion that the divorce, only a few weeks before, had been mutually arranged by the two families. Sophia Louisa Egerton, on the other hand, appears to be related to Francis Sutherland Egerton, 1st Earl of Ellesmere. She was born about 1775 and would go on to marry Thomas Havelock in 1796. Francis Egerton had links with the Boyles, and a poem ascribed to him is about Boyle Farm, a mansion in Thames Ditton and home of Charlotte Boyle Walsingham.[54] The Sullivan Baronets also lived at Thames Ditton, notably Sir Richard Joseph Sullivan, 1st Baronet, who had been born in Dublin in 1752. This all suggests family links between the Boyles, Egertons and Sullivan.

Who Was the Reverend Robert Boyle Sullivan?

The closeness of the date of the second marriage to the divorce supports the idea that Frances must have fallen for this man sometime earlier, since with a divorce settlement of £1000 per year from William Mullins there was no real reason for her to remarry. So who was he and how did they meet?

Frances Sullivan's Will of November 1850 identifies the late Major General John Stafford, who was to marry her close friend and cousin Frances Maria Whalley, as 'the nephew of my late husband Robert Boyle Sullivan'. Hill Wickham also refers to

---

54 *Boyle Farm* 4th Ed., S and R Bentley, London 1828

Robert Boyle Sullivan as a relative of General Stafford.[55] Further investigations have shown that Robert's sister Thomasine Sullivan married Hugh Stafford in Cork in 1780. Her father was Rev H. Sullivan of Clonakilty, Co. Cork, from which it might be assumed that their mother was a Boyle. The Staffords must have soon moved to Somerset, as their son John Stafford was born in Winscombe in 1785, and thus the family became neighbours of Francis Edwards Whalley and his family at Winscombe Court.

Most unusually, the Database of the Clergy of the Church of England gives nothing of Robert Sullivans's early life. His BA degree is not recorded at an English University nor does his name appear in the Alumni Dublinienses.[56] However, a Boyle O'Sullivan appears in the *Catalogue of Graduates of Dublin University* as obtaining a BA in 1782.[57] This would make him the same age as Frances Sage. The Boyles and O'Sullivans were prominent families in the Cork and Youghal, County Cork, at the time, and there is a Reverend Boyle O 'Sullivan listed by the Cork Historical and Archaeological Society as being in Cork in 1788. has already been pointed out that many Irish living in England would drop the 'O' from their surnames, which may explain why the Clerical and Parochial Records of Cloyne, Cork and Ross have a Boyle Sullivan listed as being appointed a Deacon of Cork in September 1783, which would have been the year after Boyle O'Sullivan's graduation.[58] The Boyles are likely to have had a more relaxed attitude to infidelity and divorce, since Edmund Boyle, the 7th Earl of Cork, having tried unsuccessfully to divorce his wife, went

55 JCTSW I p.38

56 *Alumni Dublinenses ,* (Burtchaell, G., Sadleir, T., Eds.), London, 1924

57 Todd, J,H., *Catalogue of Graduates of Dublin University who have proceeded to Degrees in the University of Dublin*, Hodges Smith and Foster, Dublin, 1868

58 Brady, W.M., *The Clerical and Parochial Records of Cloyne, Cork and Ross,* Alexander Thom, Dublin, 1863, Vol. 3, p.254

around openly with his mistress Miss Greenhill.[59]

The Effect of the Divorce on the Whalleys

While it seems almost certain that the divorce was carefully stage managed by Frances, her father and William Mullins, it does not appear from later correspondence that Thomas Sedgwick and his wife were part of the plot, though they clearly had been aware of the couple's estrangement. Correspondence shows that they were devastated by the divorce. Anna Seward, writing to her friend Mrs Powys one month after Frances had left Mr Mullins, states:

> The 13th of March brought Mr. and Mrs. Whalley
> to me, whose dear society I have also very recently
> lost. One of the heaviest afflictions that can wring
> the feeling bosom, after having tormented them
> near two years with terror of this descent, because,
> some four months since, complete: and affliction:
> the corrosive bitterness of which must inevitably
> mingle with all of comfort which they may hereafter
> taste till human evil, neither by immediate pressure,
> nor cruel recollection , may annoy them more. [60]

Their friends were horrified at Frances's defection, some of the more straight laced thereafter avoiding any further contact with the Whalleys,[61] and by their own choice the Whalleys cut themselves off from their close friends for many weeks.[62] It would

[59] See *Town and Country Magazine*, 3rd April 1783.

[60] *Letters of Anna Seward, Written Between the Years 1784 and 1807,* (Constable, A., Ed.), *Vol. IV,* George Ramsay and Co. Edinburgh, 1811, p.50

[61] ibid V pp.111-2

[62] ibid III pp.42-5

seem that Frances did make contact with the Whalleys, as one year later, in October 1797, Anna Seward, writing to Thomas Sedgwick, expresses her sympathy at some new indiscretion, hoping that 'her [Frances's] new dereliction will for the present prevent the repetition of those letters of hers which must torture you to no purpose'.[63] Quite what the new dereliction was or what the earlier letters from Frances were asking is not clear; perhaps it was money (see below).

Life after the Second marriage

A letter from Mrs Piozzi (Mrs Thrale/née Hester Lynch), who was one of Thomas Sedgwick's lifelong correspondents to Sophia Pennington (née Weston), dated April 4th 1799, suggests that despite Frances's £1000 p.a. divorce settlement, the couple were soon short of money.

> His unfortunate niece, cydevant+ Fanny Sage sent
> to me yesterday for £20; and said she was detained
> (for debt I trow) at our poor petty town of St Asaph
> two miles off. A tall ill looking man on horseback
> brought the letter but will not, I hope revenge my
> refusal of his lady's request, when Dumouriez shall
> have set all the wild Irish at full liberty*. I was half
> afraid, sure enough, yet little disposed to give what
> would make 40 honest cottagers happy for a gay
> lass (she was just 30 years old) who I never liked in
> her best days, and who never had any claims on my
> friendship which she now talks so loudly of.[64]

[63] *Letters of Anna Seward, Written Between the Years 1784 and 1807*, (Constable, A., Ed.), Vol. VI, George Ramsay and Co. Edinburgh, 1811, p.395
[64] TIL p.171

+A misspelling "of ci-devant", a derogatory comment from the French meaning "from before" and technically applied to members of the French nobility.

* A reference to the French General Charles-François Dumouriez, who was thought to be about to bring Ireland into the War on the side of Napoleon, providing confirmation that the messenger was Irish – clearly Frances's husband Robert Boyle Sullivan!

Mrs Piozzi seems to have shared her daughter's low opinion of Frances. It is also clear that she had never met the Reverend Boyle Sullivan. Perhaps her dislike for Frances stemmed from the early days of her marriage to William Mullins, when Frances had ignored her in London. Clearly, this affront upset her enough to relate the matter to her friend Anna Seward, who in turn relayed it to Thomas Sedgwick.[65] Since Mrs Piozzi was hugely rich, by her first husband's fortune, she would normally have regarded £20 as of little consequence when dealing with a friend, which is perhaps why Frances sought her out. By July she was aware of the couple's relationship, for she wrote to Sophia Pennington:

> Mr. and Mrs. Sullivan certainly were in this Neighbourhood together, whether they have parted since or not; and they had a niece of his with them, and they were much liked at St. Asaph till People found out who and what they were. He was said to

65 JCTSW II p.48

be a Clergyman – Is he in orders or no? Sure Fanny
Sage's Life must be beyond all Novels ever written.
When will she finish her mad career? People
hereabouts admired her accomplishments, but said
there was very little Beauty to boast.[66]

At the time that the Boyles were in St Asaph, Thomas Sedgwick
was in London on tenterhooks, waiting on the production of his
play the *Castle of Montval*. In January 1799 Anna Seward had
written to him at Sir Walter James's house in Greenwich,
expressing her concern at the rise of Bonaparte's power, saying
how she longed to read his play and hoping that it would have a
successful reception.[67] From March to June 1799 Thomas seems
to have lived at Hampton Court. These apartments were made
available, by the grace and favour of the monarch, to royalty,
aristocrats, military heroes, and after 1730, clergymen. They
became common after George III determined not to live at
Hampton Court. There is no record of Thomas Sedgwick having
such an apartment, but his friend of 30 years Mrs Horneck, whom
he was later to marry, did (Apartment 12a; Suite XXIV on the
ground floor). One must assume that this was through her
husband, by this time a General.[68,69] The play finally appeared on
April 23rd at Drury Lane, having been delayed by the indisposition
of Mrs Siddons, who played the leading role of Countess Montval.
The play had eight performances between then and May 22nd
1799 and was never put on again. Hill Wickham says that its

66 TPL III p.115

67 JCTSW II p.111-2

68 See Parker, S.E., *Grace and favour*, Hampton Court Palaces, Surrey, 2005, p.44

69 However, according to Parker, there were strict rules attached to the warrants:
apartments were not to be sub-let, and boarders were forbidden, so perhaps
there was another explanation.

chances had been damaged by an earlier version of the play by Matthew Gregory Lewis, which had appeared at Drury Lane in December 1797 under the title *Castle Spectre*.[70] While we are told that Thomas Sedgwick left other plays in manuscript, none were ever put on (see Appendix 2).

The next mention of Frances occurs in a letter that Hill Wickham quotes in connection with the "Blagdon Controversy", which was raging at this time.[71] This is given the date of June 1802, and we are told that Mrs Sullivan was then living in 'Sydcot', not far from Winscombe. A further letter to Mrs Sullivan is quoted on the following page, in which her uncle, the unworldly Reverend Richard Chaple Whalley, berates his elder brother Colonel Francis Whalley as 'an enemy to serious religion'. But he clearly still holds Mrs Sullivan, who according to Hill Wickham he addresses as such, in high regard, despite her divorce and remarriage.

In October 1803 the London Gazette recorded that the Reverend Boyle Sullivan had been appointed Chaplain to the Western Regiment of the Mendip Legion, a volunteer regiment whose Commandant, appointed the same year, was Thomas's elder brother, Lieutenant Colonel Francis Edwards Whalley Esq.[72] Since Francis Edward's daughter Frances Maria and Frances Sullivan were close friends and living close by, this was perhaps inevitable. The Provisional Cavalry was supplemented by conscription in November 1796 into the Volunteer and Yeoman Cavalry, otherwise known as the 'Hunter Corps', but this was only paid for by the Government until February 24th 1800, after a debate in the House of Commons, when Lord

[70] JCTSW I p.23

[71] ibid I p.24

[72] *London Gazette*, 1803, Issue 15637 Oct. 26th, p.1498

Dundas, as Secretary of State for War, successfully argued that such expense was no longer warranted.

The Database of the Clergy of the Church of England first records Robert as being licensed by Bishop Beadon as the curate of the church of St James the Great, Winscombe, on 5th August 1806.[73] One wonders if his appointment is yet another example of Thomas Sedgwick's influence. Bishop Beadon and Thomas Sedgwick were related on their mother's side,[74] and it is clear from earlier correspondence that they were very good friends and also that the Bishop knew Frances.[75]

8.9 The church of St James the Great, Winscombe, where Rev Robert Boyle Sullivan was curate

---

[73] *St James Winscombe Banns 1754-1811,* Weston super Mare Family History Society, 2004

[74] Dr Beadon was in turn Archdeacon of London (1775); Master of Jesus College Cambridge (1781); Bishop of Gloucester (1798) and in 1802 was translated to the see of Bath and Wells over which he presided for 22 years.

[75] JCTSW II p.35 (Footnote)

Two years later, in June 1808, Frances Maria Whalley married Major John Stafford at the same church, and his uncle, the Reverend Robert Boyle Sullivan (now of course married to her cousin Frances) is recorded as being a witness. Curiously, there is no second witness named, though perhaps Robert was also signing on behalf of his wife.

Robert was only to remain as curate at Winscombe from 1806-1810 and was removed from office in 1811 for neglecting his duties.[76] Perhaps the couple were indeed enjoying life outside the church. Notwithstanding this, in 1814 Robert was appointed as Stipendiary Curate at Bradford-on-Avon at the Chapel of Stoke (Limpley Stoke). How this came about is not known, but one suspects again that Thomas Sedgwick was instrumental. Another possibility is that it was through Mary Randolph, a friend of Penelope Pennington, who was married to the Reverend Dr Francis Randolph, Prebendary of Bristol. Dr Randolph had previously been Vicar of Bradford on Avon from 1799-1804. The Randolphs and the Penningtons were on sufficiently good terms for the Penningtons to be offered the Randolphs' house and servants when the latter went with the Duke of York to Germany.[77] It is also clear that Penelope enjoyed the company of Frances, who she had known since she was a girl.

Even so, such an appointment was only possible because Bradford on Avon came within the diocese of Salisbury, and so Robert Sullivan's earlier dereliction of duties would have been unknown or could be glossed over! This new appointment carried a stipend of £60 plus 'surplice fees of Stoke'. Robert was 'directed to reside at Holt, 3 miles away, the Vicarage house being occupied

---

[76] *Diocese of Bath and Wells presentation papers*, Somerset Heritage Centre, D/D/Bp/148-154

[77] *Mary Randolph letters to Penelope Pennington 1818-1819*, Princetown University Library Manuscripts Division, C1180

by Mr. Knight, resident curate of Bradford, to whom Sullivan is assistant'. Sadly, no details exist in the Church of England Database about Knight, not even his Christian name. It would seem that during this period there was no Vicar in residence. The living of £600 p.a. from 1793 had belonged to William Blomberg, who perhaps was instrumental in Robert Boyle gaining the appointment. Blomberg was a graduate of Thomas Sedgwick's College, St. Johns Cambridge, and like him had also been chaplain to the King. He had become Vicar of Banwell (1799-1808), and as this was only a few miles from Mendip Lodge, he must have continued to know Thomas personally. Blomberg's life is at least as interesting as Thomas Sedgwick's. The following account is given by Hill Wickham:

> The name of Dr Blomberg has often turned up in the course of the preceding correspondence, and we find it mentioned here in connection with Carlton House. His intimacy with the Royal Family arose from a very remarkable circumstance. His father was a British Officer, and in the earlier part of the reign of George III he was quartered in the West Indies with Major Torriano but in different islands, the latter being in St Kitts [His son would later attend Thomas Sedgwick Whalley's funeral in France, see Chapter 13]. One night as Major Torrianno and another officer were lying in the same room, they suddenly saw Blomberg standing before them. On expressing their great surprise, he informed them that it was only his shade (ghost) which they saw as he had just fallen victim to rapid disease; and was permitted to appear, in order that he might request them on their return home to

make diligent search in a certain house in Scotland, where, in a chest, documents would be found which would put his only son, then young, in possession of a small property. The officers gave their promise and the ghost disappeared. In the course of a few days intelligence reaches St. Kitts of the death of Blomberg on the night in question; and in due time search was made for the papers, which were found and the boy obtained his property. The story being much talked of at the time came to the ears of the Royal Family and (young) Blomberg was sent for by George III to be brought up with the young princes. There was apparently nothing remarkable in his character to call forth a special providence in his behalf, as he was only distinguished by his taste and skill in music. He was brought up to the Church, and under Royal favour obtained various pieces of preferment. Latterly he was Canon of St Paul's, to which he was appointed in 1822; Chaplain to the Queen; and incumbent of the valuable vicarage of St Giles Cripplegate.[78]

How long Robert Sullivan held the Curacy in Bradford on Avon is unknown, but it would have been a convenient location from which Frances could hope to enjoy Bath Society again. Soon though, following the Battle of Waterloo in 1815, Britons flocked to France, as they had done after the Treaty of Amiens in 1802. Maybe it had always been the Sullivans' wish to live in France, where they could live more cheaply. On the other hand, Frances may have discovered in Bath the social estrangement which an

78 JCTSW II p.449

unfaithful divorcee attracted at this time. Removal to France was not possible until the signing of the second Peace of Paris in 1816, but by 1820, and perhaps a few years earlier, the Sullivans were living at La Flèche to be visited by their uncle in May of that year.[79] The fact that the Sullivans and the Staffords moved at about the time to live not far apart in France suggests that the two Whalley cousins planned their removal together. By this time Colonel Francis Whalley had died (1813), as had Frances Sullivan's father, Isaac Sage (1818). Unlike Frances, her close friend Frances Maria Stafford (née Whalley) raised a large family.[80] She had come to live nearby at Saumur, Sarthe. Their youngest son was born there in August 1828, shortly after Robert Boyle Sullivan's death only a few miles away at La Flèche. He was named Boyle Torriano Stafford.[81]

---

79 JCTSW II p.473

80 The first 5 children of John and Frances Stafford were born in Winscombe. The first daughter, born in 1812, was named Thomasina, after her grandmother. Four other children were born there between 1814 and 1820.

81 A Mr Torriano also attended Thomas Sedgwick Whalley's funeral in La Flèche. He is described by Hill Wickham as being 'the son of one of his oldest and most intimate friends' (JCTSW I p.38). In fact, this was probably a grandson of Charles Stafford who does not seem to be mentioned in any letter of the two volumes but was born in Wells in 1716 and died in Bath in 1791. A Major Torriano, perhaps his son, is described as having been killed at Toulon when it was taken by Napoleon in 1793 (JCTSW I p.247).

CHAPTER 9
The Blagdon Controversy

This is only a brief summary of the events to show how Thomas Sedgwick Whalley came to be embroiled in this issue. A comprehensive account is provided by Elizabeth Harvey in her two chapters included in *The History of Blagdon*.[1,2]

Hannah More (1745-1833)

Thomas Sedgwick Whalley's lifelong friend Hannah More was successful in many fields of endeavour, of which education was only one. She has variously been called a counter-revolutionary, a bluestocking, an evangelical reformer and 'the first Victorian'. Many accounts have been written of her life and achievement, and only a synopsis will be offered here to put this event in context and throw further light on the belief and attitudes of the time.

Hannah showed a precocious talent for learning, which was initially encouraged at the school her father had established in Fishponds Bristol when his expectations of an inheritance were dashed. By the age of four Hannah was reading voraciously and had composed a satirical poem on the subject of Bristol. By 12 years she was fluent in Latin and French and had the rudiments

[1] Harvey, E.M., 'Hannah More and her connection with Blagdon', in *A History of Blagdon*, Vol.2. Bentham E (Ed), Blagdon Local History Society, 2006, pp. 75-96
[2] ibid Vol. 3 pp.31-85

of Spanish and Italian. In 1758 her two older sisters, with the support of their father, opened a boarding school at Trinity Street, College Green, Bristol for 'young ladies'. They were only nineteen and seventeen years old. Initially, the 13 year old Hannah was a pupil but soon became a junior teacher. The school prospered and was soon regarded as the foremost boarding school for girls in the south west, with more than sixty pupils.

THE FREE-SCHOOL, FISHPONDS, GLOUCESTERSHIRE.

9.1 The Free School of Hannah More's father Jacob More in Fishponds Bristol

9.2 Hannah More

When the school moved to larger premises in Park Street, the guardian of two of their pupils was the wealthy landowner William Turner of Belmont. He later proposed to Hannah, but having postponed the marriage twice, he seems to have taken fright. He was then persuaded by his friends to settle an annuity of £200 on Hannah and later bequeathed her £1,000 in his Will. This allowed Hannah to make the decision to give up any idea of marriage and to devote herself to writing. In addition to her many books and essays, she wrote a number of highly successful plays, notably *Percy*, which sold four thousand copies in a fortnight after its successful production at Covent Garden, and *Fatal Falsehood*. She came to enjoy the approval and friendship of many influential contemporaries, notably Horace Walpole, David Garrick, Sir Joshua Reynolds, Dr Johnson and William Wilberforce.

After Garrick's death in 1779 Hannah gave up writing plays but still visited Eva Garrick and through her attended the conversation parties of the so called "blue stocking" circle, of which she became a prominent member. She also came under the influence of the Clapham Sect, of which William Wilberforce, the anti-slavery politician, was a member.[3] This was an informal group of wealthy evangelicals, who sought to reinvigorate the Church of England with what could be described as a modified form of Methodism.

How she and Thomas Sedgwick Whalley met is not known. Hannah More's first play was performed at Bath in April 1775, when Thomas and his wife were at Langford. His younger niece, Frances's younger sister, had died the month before, and their mother had decided to sail to India to join her husband and would leave Frances in her brother and sister-in-law's charge. So it is unlikely, though possible, that Thomas would have seen this play. It was followed by the very successful *Percy* in 1778, which he would have been likely to have seen, and *Fatal Falsehood* in 1779. The first mention of Hannah More's name in any correspondence is in a letter from Anna Seward to Thomas Sedgwick and his wife, who were still on the continent, dated August 1786. From this it is clear that 'Miss More' was known to them both, though one gains the impression that this was only as a public figure rather than as a close friend. However, the year before Hannah had bought a house at Cowslip Green, near Wrington in north Somerset, where she settled down with her sisters to country life and writing,[4] much of it focused on the education of women.[5] The sisters divided their time between here and Bath, where they

---

[3] So named because many of its members lived close to Clapham and worshipped in the parish church there.

[4] Mary (1738-1813); Elizabeth (1740-1816); Sarah (1743-1817); Martha known also as Patty (1747-1819)

[5] See also Harvey, E.M., Hannah More and her Connections with Blagdon, In *A History of Blagdon,* Vol. 2. Blagdon Local History Society, Blagdon, Somerset, 2006, pp.75-96

had bought a house in Great Pulteney Street. Three years later she became a neighbour of Thomas Segwick Whalley and his wife, when they returned from their European tour, their new house 'The Cottage' soon visible across the valley. In August 1789 William Wilberforce and his sister stayed at Cowslip Green and visited Cheddar in order to see the cliffs, which at that time were a popular curiosity. On their return William retired to his room, apparently ill but in reality deeply shocked by the poverty he had seen. When he emerged, he said to Mrs More 'Something must be done about Cheddar.'[6] Later, after several hours discussion as to how they might proceed, he exclaimed, 'If you will be at the trouble, I will be at the expense'.[7]

In some areas of the country, weekday parochial schools had already been set up, encouraged by the Society for Promoting Christian Knowledge, of which Hannah was a member. Usually, this was achieved by the local Rector with support from the parish. In Gloucester the first Sunday schools had been set up in 1780 by the layman Robert Raikes, a publisher and philanthropist, and it was probably this which gave Hannah More the idea of running an independent school in Somerset.

6 From about 1787 onward she addressed herself as 'Mrs More'. See Thompson, H., *The life of Hannah More with notices of her sisters,* W Blackwood and Sons, Edinburgh, 1838, p.79

7 Thompson H., *The life of Hannah More with notices of her sisters* .W. Blackwood and Sons Edinburgh, 1838, pp.380-2

9.3 Cheddar School

But such education was not always welcomed. In Cheddar she faced opposition from the local landowner, who shared the view of many Mendip farmers at the time that the labouring poor were created for their use in the same way as their cattle. Anything which they thought might diminish the toils of their workforce they resisted, as they did any expense for their workers' welfare unless it was seen as likely to return a profit to their employer. Hannah and her sister Martha were told by the wife of a local farmer, who rented land at £1000 per year, that 'the lower class was fated to be poor and ignorant and wicked; and as wise as these ladies were, they could not alter what was decreed.'[8] To make matters worse, in Cheddar, unlike Gloucester, there was neither a resident vicar nor a resident curate to call upon for support – nor had there been for 40 years! Undaunted, Hannah More took a 7 year lease on a cottage for a Cheddar school house and appointed a Sunday school teacher. Soon, by her powers of

[8] Thompson H., *The life of Hannah More with notices of her sisters* .W. Blackwood and Sons Edinburgh, 1838, p.97-99

persuasion and her own prodigious hard work, local opposition was overcome and the school at Cheddar opened. William Wilberforce became a regular visitor to Cowslip Green. The school prospered. A master and mistress were appointed to instruct the children during the week in sewing, knitting and spinning, the profits of which went to the children. Two years after their first visit to Cheddar, an energetic and able curate was appointed, who supported the work, and together they saw the congregation increase from 16 to over 200. It should not be thought that the school was totally without local support. One patron was Mrs Stagg, the lady of the manor, who left a handsome legacy to the school and another to the Poor Womens' Club in Cheddar, on her death in 1802.

The Blagdon Controversy

Following the success of her school in Cheddar, Mrs More, as she now liked to be known, assisted by her sister Martha, went on to set up further schools at Axbridge, Banwell, Winscombe, Yatton, Congresbury, Wedmore, Shipham and Nailsea. In 1795 she was asked by the Curate of Blagdon, the Reverend Bere,[9] who was also the local magistrate, to set up a school in his village. This she did, financed by Henry Thornton, a philanthropist and friend of Wilberforce, having first drawn up guidelines for the instruction, which were approved by the Reverend Bere, as had been her practise elsewhere. There were soon 170 children and adults enrolled there. Five years later she described her teaching philosophy and methods in a letter to Thomas Sedgwick's niece Elizabeth Wickham, when the latter was considering undertaking similar work, one presumes in Frome.

[9] It is curious that the Clergy of the Church of England Database records him only as Rector of Butcombe 1781-1814

Any poor lights I have on the subject in question would be so much better communicated in conversation than writing, that I feel at a loss how to make my letter at all useful to you. I wish we had discussed these points when you were at the Cottage [her uncle Thomas Sedgwick's "Cottage"]. Should I be alive next year, I shall invite you to take what we call the 'Cheddar Round' as I think you would be better able to see what was right or wrong in our plans by personal inspection than by any written documents. My grand principle is, to infuse the minds of the young people with as much Scriptural knowledge as possible. Setting them to get by heart such portions of the Bible as shall take in the general scheme of doctrine and practice, then bringing that knowledge out by easy, simple and intelligible conversation, and then grafting it into their minds as a principle of action, and making all they learn practical and of personal application, seems the best method. I am extremely limited in my ideas of instructing the poor. I would confine it entirely to the Bible, Liturgy, and Catechism, which, indeed, include the whole of my notion of instruction. To teach them to read without giving them principles, seems dangerous; and I do not teach them to write even in my weekly schools. Almost all I do is done by conversation, by a simple exposition of texts, which I endeavour to make as lively and interesting as I can; often illustrating what is difficult by instances drawn from common life.[10]

---

[10] JCTSW II p.141-2

There are several other accounts which restate these principles.[11]

Mr Young, a trusted teacher who had already given reliable service at her Nailsea School, was appointed at Blagdon. All went well with the new school until January 1799, when Mr Young, unbeknown to the Mores, introduced Monday evening meetings for adults. Mrs Bere, the Curate's wife, attended one of these believed that she had been 'insulted by the arrogant assumption' of the schoolmaster who told her 'she had not sought the Lord in the same way that the young people had done and defied all opposition'.

Mrs Bere wrote to Mrs More, who was ill at Bath at the time, to express her concern. Being unable to reply herself, Hannah instructed her sister Martha to issue a reprimand to Mr Young, which she did. He was forbidden to hold instruction for adults and permitted to run only the Sunday school and weekly school 'industry classes'. He immediately complied, and this seemed to resolve the situation to the satisfaction of all parties, and a letter from the Reverend Bere to Hannah More in March 1800 confirms this. Soon afterwards, it came to Hannah's ears that the Reverend Bere had preached against the school. She immediately wrote to him, offering to close the school as she had never run a school without the support of the local minister. He replied that he had never preached against the school, only 'enthusiasm' (i.e. Methodism), and implored her to continue the school. Then at the beginning of April she learned that the Reverend Bere had submitted a sworn affidavit saying that Young had caused a man to decline entering his service because he had told him that to do so would risk his right to a house and orchard. (There would later prove to have been several other sworn affidavits which Bere had extracted from villagers.) As Mrs More was in London, she wrote

---

[11] Thompson, H., *The life of Hannah More with notices of her sisters,* W. Blackwood and Sons Edinburgh, 1838, p.100 & 354 (Footnote)

to the Reverend Bere, suggesting that the matter should be put in the hands of Sir Abraham Elton (he was known to Bere but not Mrs More but was trusted by her as 'a respectable and judicious magistrate in the neighbourhood'). This mediation the Reverend Bere declined and instead referred the matter to his Rector Dr Crossman. It seems that his submission did not include the sworn affidavits, which Hannah More later claimed 'were flatly contradicted by counter evidence, and which having no dates to the facts which they attest, could never have been admitted in a court of justice'. It would later become clear that some of these were written by Bere himself and signed under duress by local parishioners!

9.4 The Blagdon school opened by Hannah More in 1795

Dr Crossman, having heard the case put by the Reverend Bere, declared that he was entirely friendly towards the school but that he objected to the Methodist leanings of the teacher Mr Young and that they should be referred to Mrs More, and if this did not proceed to a satisfactory outcome, the Reverend Bere could 'punish Young's irregularities in his magisterial capacity'. Mrs More declined to dismiss Mr Young without sufficient proof against him. As far as she was concerned, the one error he had made had been immediately corrected to the satisfaction of herself and the Reverend Bere. She was also concerned that if the new charges were seen to have been sufficient proof for his dismissal, his prospects for further employment would be greatly damaged. She therefore opened correspondence with Dr Crossman to persuade him that the charges should first be properly heard. He consulted Dr Moss, the Chancellor of the Diocese, and the Bishop, who decided that a Committee be set up comprising local clergy, which met at the George Inn Blagdon in early November 1780 under the chairmanship of Colonel Francis Whalley JP.

9.5 The George Inn, Blagdon c 1910. From the George Symes collection, Blagdon Local History Society Archives.

It is clear from the various letters that, while Thomas Sedgwick and his younger brother the Reverend Richard Chaple shared very similar views to those of Hannah More, their brother Colonel Francis was rather different. According to Richard in his letter to Frances Sage dated June 11 1800,

> In your Uncle Whalley (who as a natural man is the best-tempered creature that lives, and one whom I dearly love as a brother) you will meet with a decided enemy to all serious religion – so entirely ignorant of himself, and perfectly wrapped up in his own sufficiency for understanding, willing and doing, that he treats the Gospel as trash, when it crosses his own conceits and opinions. His character helps to confirm me, more that that of any other person I have met with, in my opinion of the deceitfulness of the human heart, and how easy it is for a man to think himself a Christian, without the least foundation of faith in the word of Christ.[12]

Having only seen the original complaint against Young, and being unaware that this matter had been settled to the Reverend Bere's satisfaction, the committee could only come to one conclusion: the school should be closed and Young dismissed. Mrs More immediately complied, and the school closed on 16th November 1800 to the dismay of local residents.

---

[12] JCTSW I p.25-6

In the following months a number of letters were sent, and lobbying clearly took place, by Thomas Sedgwick and others.[13] Mrs More, in a letter to Thomas Sedgwick, also asks:

> Perhaps it may be of use to you and Mr. R. Chaple [the Reverend Richard Chaple Whalley] to write and inform Dr. Moss of the inveterate prejudices which Mr. Francis Whalley, though so amiable and respectable a man, has to the cause he was called upon to oppose and the many letters which Bere (knowing this) wrote to obtain his presence.[14]

This he clearly did, as a later letter acknowledges.

Local villagers and farmers, too, were concerned, not only at the loss of the school but also at what they believed to have been a miscarriage of justice.[15] In early January 1801 Mrs More wrote to Dr Whalley with surprising news:

> I have had two visits of some hours each time from the Rector of West Monckton and Blagdon [Dr. Crossman]. He is a complete convert (as far as I can judge), to the atrocity of his curate's conduct and the innocence and hard usage of Young. Margaret Thorne* I think wrought this conversion in the first instance, and my papers letters and conversation completed it. He owned her character destroyed the credit of all the affidavits. Between ourselves he has been kept completely in the dark. The Chancellor (of Wells

13 JCTSW II p.167

14 ibid II p.164

15 ibid II p.150

Cathedral) had not yet sent him a line of your
letters or even of mine.[16]

*She was a witness called by Bere against Young
the schoolmaster

On 17th January 1801 the Bishop decided that the school should
be reopened and the Reverend Bere dismissed, and on 25th
January the school duly reopened. Immediately after this it was
realised that, as the Reverend Bere had committed no
ecclesiastical or moral offence, he could not be deprived of his
curacy and so he was reinstated! During the following year the
"Blagdon controversy" raged and became a cause celebre.

> Pamphlets of the most violent character appeared
> on both sides: the charities and courtesies of social
> life were suspended between families associated
> by the great bond of coincidence of sentiment on
> all important subjects; opponents of the Blagdon
> controversy could not safely be invited to meet at
> the same table; [17]

These pamphlets were variously published in Bath and London
by the parties involved and distributed through
booksellers.[18,19,20,21,22,23,24,25,26] The notable exception was Mrs

[16] JCTSW II p.170

[17] Thompson, H., *The life of Hannah More with notices of her sisters.* W Blackwood
and Sons Edinburgh, 1838, p.189

[18] Bere T., *The Controversy between Mrs. Hannah More and the Curate of Blagdon [T.
Bere] relative to the conduct of her teacher of the Sunday School in that parish. With the
original letters and explanatory notes,* J S Jordan , London, 1801

[19] Bere T. *An appeal to the public on the controversy between Hannah More, the Curate
of Blagdon, and the Reverend sir A. Elton.* Richard Cruttwell, Bath ; G.G. and J.

More, who offered no public defence and remained aloof to the furore, though deeply affected by it.

In August 1801, facing continuing opposition from the reinstated curate, Mrs More again resolved to close the school, as it had been her invariable practice to only operate with the full consent of the resident minister; this she did in September. The teacher Mr Young was found alternative employment by her in a similar charitable school in Dublin. On 25th August The Times had carried a false announcement of the marriage of Hannah More to Dr Crossman, who was now known to be supporting her cause. This was followed by a published retraction on the 10th September. While many took this as laughable nonsense, Mrs More herself did not.[27]

Robinson, London, 1801

[20] *Boak J. A Letter to the Reverend T. Bere.* [A reply to certain statements contained in a pamphlet by him.]. Biggs & Cottle, Bristol, 1801

[21] Drewitt T. *The force of contrast, or, Quotations, accompanied with remarks, submitted to the consideration of all who have interested themselves in what has been called The Blagdon Controversy,* .S Hazard, Bath,. 1801

[22] Layman,A., *The Blagdon Controversy: or short criticisms on the late dispute between the curate of Blagdon* [T. Bere] *and Mrs. H. More, relative to Sunday schools and Monday private schools,* Bath, 1801

[23] Elton, Sir A., *Expostulatory letter to the Reverend Sir A. E. in consequence of his late publication addressed to the Reverend T. Bere,* Bath, 1801

[24] Elton, Sir A., *A letter to the Reverend Thomas Bere, Rector of Butcombe, occasioned by his late unwarrantable attack on Mrs. Hannah More : with an appendix, containing letters and other documents relative to the extraordinary proceedings at Blagdon,* Cadell and Davies, Bath, 1801

[25] Moss, C., *An Address to Mrs. Hannah More on the conclusion of the Blagdon controversy. With observations on an anonymous tract entitled "A Statement of Facts",* Richard Crutwell, Bath, 1801

[26] A friend of the establishment (Crosse, E.),*The Force of Contrast continued; or extracts and animadversions with occasional strictures on the Contraster [T. Drewitt,] and others of Mr Bere's opponents, and observations on Mrs H. More's schools. To which is added, a postscript, on the editors of the British Critic. Respectfully submitted to the consideration of those who have interested themselves in the Blagdon controversy.* Bristol, 1802

[27] TPL III p.336

On September 7th a meeting took place at the Langford Inn, chaired by Matthew Brickdale, the former MP for Bristol. It was attended by a number of local worthies, Dr Crossman and Mr Bere. After a good dinner and generous endorsement of both parties by the chairman, a reconciliation between them took place 'to the satisfaction of the whole company'.[28] After the meeting Dr Crossman wrote to Mrs More to inform her of this.[29] It seems she did not take this well, as by October Mrs Piozzi, Thomas Sedgwick and Martha More were all seriously concerned for Hannah's health and state of mind.[30] This became sufficiently serious for her to have to employ a scribe to write letters for her; but things were about to improve. Late in 1801 Martha More was able to write to Thomas Sedgwick, enclosing a letter Hannah had received from the Bishop of Lincoln. She writes: 'It is curious as well as gratifying to see our cause supported by the very man on whom Bere had placed all his hopes.'[31] Later in the same letter she asks:

> What think you of the Bishop of Lincoln's plan?
> However as the eyes of our neighbouring clergy
> seem to be opened, we are willing to spare them
> such mortification; and how, my dear sir, could
> we expose your brother Col. W [sic] Whalley, for
> whom we have really a great respect though he has
> such a dislike to us.

It is not clear what that plan was, nor whether it was ever put into action, but clearly a watershed had been reached.

28 *Morning Chronicle* 15th September 1801

29 JCTSW II p.201

30 TPL III pp. 332-3

31 JCTSW II p.199

The storm of public debate was finally brought to a close by the pamphlet of Thomas Sedgwick *Animadversions on the Curate of Blagdon's* [T. Bere's] *three Publications*, published anonymously in June 1802 and widely acknowledged to have been a masterpiece of logic and diplomacy.[32] This is not to say that Thomas Sedgwick had been delayed until then in coming to Hannah More's aid. Many letters passed between them from November 1800 onwards.[33] These indicate that he was very active behind the scenes. It is also important to remember that these were tumultuous times. The war with France was raging. In February 1801 George III's madness returned, and in March 1801 William Pitt resigned as first Minister. With rocketing food prices, there had been riots in several cities, including Bristol in April 1801.[34]

But to return to Thomas Sedgwick's pamphlet, he had been ill with fever for the early part of the summer of 1801 but was recovering by July.[35] By this time, though, his wife was sinking and would die in December. The draft was still being worked on in January and February 1802,[36] and the completed work was printed in early summer of 1802. When it did finally appear, Mrs More, who was again quite ill at the time, was delighted and wrote to Thomas Sedgwick:

---

[32] Whalley, T.S., *Animadversions on the Curate of Blagdon's* [T. Bere's] *three Publications, entitled, The Controversy between Mrs. Hannah More and the Curate of Blagdon &c., An Appeal to the Public, and An Address to Mrs. Hannah More, etc.* J. Hatchard, London, 1802

[33] JCTSW II pp.144-214

[34] *The Bath Journal* reported on April 13th, 1801 that Mr Whalley, Sir Abraham Elton and Dr Randolph and a number of other good men went to ' harangue and reason' with the Bristol miners and colliers but it is not clear if this was TSW or his brother Colonel Francis Whalley.

[35] TPL III p.298

[36] JCTSW II p.212

I will sit up in my bed and write my own self a line, for who but myself ought to thank you, my most able, zealous, and successful advocate? I have now got quite through your book: indeed it is admirable! You have embraced such a vast variety of objects. Nothing has escaped you. And not only the facts are important, but the writing is admirable. Sir A.E suspects you. How should he help it? He paid you, however, a great compliment, for he said 'If there was not such an exact knowledge of local circumstances, he should almost suspect it was done by Dr.Rennell'.[37] But whoever be the author, he says it is extremely well done. It only wants to make its way and be known to produce effect.[38]

But this was not quite the end of the matter, for during the course of the controversy there had been a number of scurrilous accusations made against Mrs. More herself, which she took very personally. These included that she had been tried and found guilty of sedition and imprisoned; that she was a Methodist,; that she had hired two men to shoot the Reverend Bere; that she was a Jacobin and had been concerned with Charlotte Corday in the assassination of Marat![39] So when Bishop Richard Beadon was translated to the See of Bath and Wells in 1802, Mrs More felt it necessary to write to him at great length, explaining all the events which had taken place.[40] This was almost certainly unnecessary,

[37] Rev. Dr. Thomas Rennell FRS, Dean of Winchester, Master of the Temple
[38] JCTSW II p.223-4
[39] Jean Paul Marat, a radical journalist assassinated in France in 1743 by the royalist Corday, who was tried and hanged
[40] Thompson H., *The life of Hannah More with notices of her sisters.* W Blackwood

since Thomas Sedgwick was a close friend and relative as well as a prebend of Wells and so would have been fully aware of her unblemished record. Not surprisingly, the Bishop replied to her in the warmest terms and promised her every protection and encouragement for her schools.

According to Hannah More the Reverend Bere, whom she forgave, later went insane and died a 'dreadful death' in October 1814.[41]

Further Reading

Collingwood, J., & Collingwood, M., *Hannah More*, Lion, Oxford 1990

Harvey ,E.M., 'Hannah More and her connection with Blagdon' in *A History of Blagdon*, Vol.2 Bentham, E., (Ed), Blagdon Local History Society, 2006. pp. 75-96

ibid Vol.3 pp.31-85

Hopkins, M.A.. *Hannah More and her circle*, Longmans, London, 1947

Jones, M.G.. *Hannah More*, Greenwood Press, New York, 1952

More, H., *The work of Hannah More,* 2 Vols., S.G. Goodrich, Boston, 1827

Stott, A., *Hannah More. The First Victorian.*: Oxford University Press, Oxford 2003

Thompson, H., *The life of Hannah More with notices of her sisters.* W Blackwood and Sons, Edinburgh, 1838

---

and Sons Edinburgh, 1838, p.200-222

[41] JCTSW II p.392

CHAPTER 10
The Second Mrs Whalley

O n the face of it, the sudden death of his first wife on 8th
December 8th 1801 caused Thomas Sedgwick less suffering
than either that of his second wife or of his mother. There is no
mention of his feelings of remorse with regard to this event in any
of his correspondence at this time. This does seem entirely out of
character for someone who had written so affectionately of his
wife on the first anniversary of their wedding.[1] However, it seems
highly likely that his biographer Hill Wickham omitted many
letters from his two volumes on the grounds that they were too
personal to include.

His feelings following the death of his first wife are suggested
by Anna Seward in a letter she wrote to Thomas two years later,
after the death of her close friend John Saville, vicar choral of
Lichfield. She says,

> I had always understood, my kind friend, that,
> from the first of your loss in the close of the
> year 1801, you had resisted all temptations to
> seclusion; that early on the event you were with
> Sir Walter James in town, and passed the
> ensuing summer in travelling about with a
> friend.[2]

---

[1] JCTSW I pp.231-4
[2] JCTSW II p.242

This conflicts with the report in a December letter from Mrs Pennington, which states

> He [Thomas] is, as you may suppose, violently affected and strictly and earnestly prohibits all letters and visits of condolence which he says his mind cannot bear in its present and perturbed state so that I am unacquainted with any particulars'[3]

Elizabeth Whalley had been in poor health for some while. In early April of 1789 she had been thrown from her "whisky" (a light, covered, two-wheeled carriage for two persons, drawn by a single horse) into Langford Brook.[4] She recovered only slowly and partially. According to Hill Wickham, her spine was injured and 'her body became much bent'. She nonetheless maintained her usual cheerfulness after the accident.[5] When called 'Mother Bunch' by a visiting child, brought by her mother to Mendip Lodge, she replied very kindly that she could not be the Mother Bunch who lived under the hill as she lived at the top of a hill.[6] We know little of her character apart from the poem written by Thomas Sedgwick on the first anniversary of their wedding (see Appendix 2) and the passing comments recorded by Anna

---

3 TPL III p.341 Note 10. Sadly no source to the letter referred to is given.

4 Constable A (Ed), *Letters of Anna Seward, Written Between the Years 1784 and 1807,* Vol II, George Ramsay and Co., Edinburgh, 1811, p.317

5 JCTSW I p.31

6 Mother Bunch, initially an evil Elizabethan folk character, had by the early 18th century become sanitised as a wise old country woman who told fairy stories. *Mother Bunch's Fairy Tales* were published in 1777 as a collection of elegant moralistic fairytales based on the translation of Pasquil's *Jests Mixed with Mother Bunches Merriments.* These would have been read by many middle class children of that time.

Seward, with whom she stayed for three weeks in September 1788.

> She is a pleasing rational companion, infinitely
> estimable, though genius may not have infused
> her ideas as those of her husband, in it ethereal
> dyes [sic].[7]

and later, on her death: 'And Mrs Whalley too in a gentler, quieter way, was arch and amusing, and most genuinely good.'[8]

Perhaps, as this quoted reference implies, her death at Langford Cottage was a blessed release to her and perhaps a great relief to her husband. Mrs Whalley was buried in Burrington churchyard, and another memorial tablet appeared beside that of her first husband, above the door of the church.

---

[7] Constable A (Ed), *Letters of Anna Seward, Written Between the Years 1784 and 1807,* Vol. II, George Ramsay and Co., Edinburgh, 1811, p.169
[8] ibid V p.427

Sacred to her Memory
Tho' unworthy to record her Virtue
This Marble has been erected by
The Rev^d THO^s SEDGWICK WHALLEY
Over the Grave of ELIZABETH WHALLEY
His belov'd excellent & deeply lamented Wife
who was Sole Heiress to EDWARD JONES Esqr
Of Langford Court
And Relict of JOHN WITHERS SHERWOOD Esqr
Of Sydcot
She died on the 8th of Decr 1801
In the 61st Year of her Age

If Mortal Goodness favor may obtain
Before the Great Eternal's awful Throne,
Where Time and Chance and Pain and Sorrow cease,
At the last Trumpet she shall rise again
From underneath this perishable Stone,
To Life immortal, And eternal Peace.

10.1 Elizabeth's memorial tablet in Burrington Church

As was to be the case following the death of his second wife, Thomas Sedgwick withdrew from Bath to London. By January 1802 he was staying at the house of his oldest friend, Sir Walter James, 22 Devonshire Place (see Appendix 1). The Blagdon controversy was at it height, and Thomas was working to assist Hannah More by composing the draft of his *Animadversions*,[9] which

---

9 JCTSW I p.31

would soon be added to the flurry of pamphlets which followed the reopening of the Blagdon school (see Chapter 9).

This was to be an unhappy time for him. He was now again not well, and while in London, he learnt of the death of another good friend, the polymath Dr Erasmus Darwin.[10] A few months later, Mrs Siddon's father died, causing her much distress. This was followed quickly by the severe financial difficulties of his cousin Sophia Pennington née Weston (see Chapter 11). Then on 14th September his venerable mother died in her 97th year.

It is suggested that his wife's death meant that Thomas Sedgwick was now distracted by an urgent need for money, as explained in Anna Seward's letter of that month

> ... I grieve for Mr. Whalley's irreparable loss, not only in a wife, so justly dear to him , but the means of obtaining a continuance of those expensive elegancies in his style of living, which long habit has rendered necessary to his comforts. I fear his wane of life will severely feel the inconvenience and deprivation resulting from the Quixotic generosity of his youth, when, as I have been informed, lest the world should think and say, and lest his beloved Mrs Sherwood should suspect, that his attachment was mercenary, he would not marry her till she had settled upon her own relations, after her death, all her maiden fortune except an annuity of £200.
>
> Her considerable jointure must drop with her.[11]

---

10 JCTSW II p.220

[11] Constable A (Ed), *Letters of Anna Seward, Written Between the Years 1784 and 1807* Vol. V, George Ramsay and Co., Edinburgh, 1811, p.426

Yet by September 1803, while Anna Seward is offering her condolences at the death of his mother, she was able to add

> I am glad this second deprivation was withheld
> till you have found an object of affection equally
> dear with the two you have lost within the short
> space of a couple of years.[12]

This was Augusta Utica Heathcote, a wealthy spinster whom he had married on 19th May 1803. She, like his first wife, was slightly older than him.

10.2 The marriage entry in the Southbroom church register

The Heathcotes were an extensive, wealthy and influential 18th-and-early-19th-century family, with branches based in Derbyshire, Leicestershire and Wiltshire (see Heathcote E.D, an account of some of the Families bearing the name Heathcote which have descended out of the County of Derbyshire. Warren and Sons Ltd., Winchester, 1899). Augusta was the only surviving daughter of George Heathcote (1700-1768). Although born in Jamaica, he had come to London in early life. He became a prosperous merchant and Member of Parliament and was later

---

[12] Constable A (Ed), *Letters of Anna Seward, Written Between the Years 1784 and 1807* Vol. VI, George Ramsay and Co., Edinburgh, 1811, p.115

Sheriff of London but declined to become Lord Mayor and retired to South Broom, Wiltshire.

Quite how Thomas Sedgwick and Augusta met is not known, but it seems likely this was through her brother Josiah. Their father owned a house in Walcot, Bath, and Josiah was born there in 1748 and seems to have lived there until 1792. Josiah's memorial in St Johns Church, Devizes speaks of his courtesy, hospitality, polite manners and animated conversation, all of which are things which would have appealed to Thomas Sedgwick's circle of friends. According to Hill Wickham, after her marriage to Thomas in 1803, Augusta wrote to her friends of her great happiness and good fortune in being united to a gentleman 'whom she had always admired beyond any of her acquaintances and who brought her a fortune equal to her own'.[13] It would seem, then, that she had known Thomas for some time before they were married, rather confirming that after the death of her father she either lived at Walcot or was a frequent visitor there.

As Augusta's father was said to be on very intimate terms with his cousins in Hursley,[14] it is just as probable that Thomas Sedgwick knew of her through the Rev Gilbert Heathcote (MA Oxon 1765-1829). An Oxford graduate (no less than thirty two Heathcotes graduated from Oxford and sixteen held holy orders), he was later Archdeacon of Winchester and eventually became Treasurer of Wells in 1814, under the patronage of Bishop Richard Beadon, who was Thomas Sedgwick's relative. As a former Vicar of Colerne, the Reverend Heathcote would have been well aware of Augusta's eligibility and wealth, as

<hr>

13 JCTSW I pp.31-2

14 Heathcote, D.E., *An account of some of the families bearing the name Heathcote which have descended out of the County of Derbyshir,*. Warren and Sons Ltd., Winchester, 1899, p.69

Colerne was only 16 miles from her home at South Broom House Devizes. (South Broom House, now a school, has a Heathcote House.) More likely, though, in view of the timing of these events, Thomas Sedgwick may have used his influence on Bishop Beadon, his relative and friend after his marriage to Augusta, to assist his new wife's relative Gilbert Heathcote to become treasurer of Wells Cathedral in 1814. It seems likely that the Heathcote influence came to bear as a quid pro quo when in 1815 Robert Boyle Sullivan, who had been dismissed as curate of Winscombe in 1811 for dereliction of duties, found another curacy at Bradford on Avon, within the diocese of Salisbury, where he took over the stipendiary curacy from Thomas Heathcote! (See Chapter 8.)

On the death of Augusta's father in 1768, her brother Josiah succeeded to the property at Walcot and also South Broom House. In 1792 he also acquired estates in Devizes from his maternal side. He moved to South Broom House, where he died unmarried in 1811. His move may have been precipitated by the view that two unmarried siblings living together under the same roof was improper, but in any case, Josiah bought out his sister's share of the Eyles property, and it would seem that she continued to live at Walcot. Quite what other property Augusta owned to give her the title of "heiress" is unclear. It is known that, on her father's death in 1786, his estate passed to her brother, who outlived her (and left no Will), but maybe some of the estate had passed to her with a lifetime interest.

The first indication that Thomas Sedgwick's proposal of marriage had been accepted was the Will which Augusta drew up on 18th May 1803, just before her impending marriage, but curiously this final Will was not signed until April three years later and only 6 months before she died. Also at the time of drawing up the Will in 1803, she gives the Royal Crescent as her address, but it may be that she was living there in the days before her marriage, as it would seem that at this time Thomas Sedgwick was back at Mendip Lodge, perhaps supervising the rebuilding mentioned below.

Thomas Sedgwick Whalley and Augusta were duly married in St James church, South Broom. This was a Chapelry of the parish of Bishops Cannings, so it is quite possible that they were married in the same church as Augusta's parents. Both parties were given as being 'of Walcot'. The witnesses were Augusta's brother Josiah, Eleanor Jones and Anna Cath Richards

By the 23rd of the month, the couple were in Clifton, but the new Mrs Whalley had yet to take up residence at Mendip Lodge, which was undergoing some further building work.[15] This may be indicative of the changes which the new Mrs Whalley brought to Thomas's life. Perhaps as a result of this expenditure in 1804, Thomas sold Langford Court to the Rt Hon John Hiley Addington, the brother of the Prime Minister, to whom it had been let in 1797.

There can be no doubt that the couple were exceedingly happy. Indeed, the new marriage seems rather to have gone to Thomas Sedgwick's head, incurring the disapproval of some of his friends. The first intimations of this occur in a letter from Anna Seward, 31st December 1803:

> I have heard much of the splendour of Mrs. Whalley's jewels, of your plate, chandeliers and other magnificent ornaments for your board. However inconceivable to me that such exteriors can contribute to the happiness of a mind like yours, they must possess that power, or you

---

[15] JCTSW II p.231

would not have taken the trouble to purchase them and therefore I congratulate you on their possession.[16]

Six months later, her further comments are more in sorrow than in anger. Her letter of July 27th 1804 starts out expressing sympathy over Thomas' recent poor health but soon focuses witheringly on its possible causes:

> ...it increases my wonder that its frequent and heavy pressure (of his continuing bad health) did not long since compel you to feel the comforts of leisure, rest, and the society of a few select friends, instead of condemning yourself in the decline of life, and loaded with pains and oppression, to the slavery of immense connections, which I understand was as little the taste of the present as of the late Mrs. Whalley. Eternal crowds of company and superfluous magnificence, however they may excite exterior respect and selfish flattery, are sure to lessen instead of exalting him who invites the one and displays the other.
>
> That I have heard many ridiculous exaggerations of Mr. Whalley's imitation of the customs and manners of our dashing youthful nobility, I make no question; and when Admiral Brown's lady amused a circle of company at Buxton with accounts of the permitted public display of his bride's night clothes decorated with lace at the

---

[16] JCTSW II p.245

most profuse expense, I venture to say that she must have been misinformed for that Mr. Whalley was a man of talents and however he might like to live splendidly could not have allowed a circumstance to exist so flagrantly open to just ridicule.

I mention these things with some hope of convincing you how much the reverse of respectability is all needless "prominence" as you term it from the station of life we were born and educated to fill. Increase of wealth and connection with those who are one step above us, can never make it our duty to follow the example of the light and vain in the higher ranks of society. Flatterers will not speak this language; a sincere friend will not repress it when its disclosure may possibly guard those beloved from future evils. [17]

Curiously, the earliest mention of the name Heathcote in Thomas Sedgwick's own correspondence occurs much later, in an undated letter addressed to Mendip Lodge in about the year 1805. This was an invitation from Hannah More to Thomas and a Mr Heathcote to share a meal of 'plain fare' with her and William Wilberforce, who was staying with her at Barley Wood for a few days.[18] This seems very likely to have been Augusta's brother Josiah, who would by now have been living at South Broom House and doubtless had been invited to view the newly refurbished Mendip Lodge. There is, though, the possibility that this could have been Gilbert Heathcote, mentioned above, who

---

[17] JCTSW II pp.249-50.
[18] ibid II p.278.

was then Vicar of Hursley parish, south west of Winchester, but who in 1814 would become Treasurer of Wells Cathedral. Whoever it was was clearly staying with Thomas and his wife at Mendip Lodge.

The letter goes on to state that at this short notice 'I dare not venture to request the honour of seeing Mrs Whalley to dinner'. This may have been Mrs More's way of suggesting that her presence would dampen the animated conversation. This would fit, as Anna Seward had described Augusta, as 'gentle, kind and good, and sensible though reserved'.[19]

In April 1806 Thomas Sedgwick found that extensive repairs were needed to the reservoir which supplied water to Mendip Lodge and its gardens. This rendered the house uninhabitable for the early summer, when he would normally reside there. He therefore took the opportunity to take his wife on a tour of England as far north as York. Setting out from Cheltenham, they visited Malvern, arriving on 26th April, where he stayed at Malvern Well House.[20] This was built in 1748 as a coaching inn but later converted to a hotel benefiting from the supply of Malvern spring water in its grounds.[21] There was also a post office close by, which would have been convenient for Thomas. The hotel was just the sort of location which would appeal to him. The surrounding landscape was similar to Mendip Lodge, and there were even more impressive views. From there the Whalleys travelled to Lichfield to visit Anna Seward, then on to Derby, Matlock, Chatsworth, Chesterfield and York. Their intended return journey was via Nottingham to Welbeck Abbey, Thomas Sedgwick's old family seat.[22] Then on to Leicester, Daventry,

19 Lucas, E.V., *A Swan and her friends,* Methuen and Co, London, 1900, p.201
20 JCTSW II p.288
21 Chambers J. *Malvern Guide.* Longman, Hurst, Rees Orme and Brown London. 1817 p184-186, 276-7

Banbury, Oxford, Newbury and finally to Devizes, his new wife's family home. Whether this intended itinerary was carried out as described is unknown, as there is a gap in the correspondence. The next letter is dated June 21st but whether 1806 or the following year is not clear. In this Hannah More writes to say that she had heard that Thomas would soon be returning home and asks if he and his wife would be able to attend her Shipham Anniversary on June 26th.[23] This was presumably the anniversary of the opening of her Shipham School.

Sadly, the second Mrs Whalley did not live long. According to Hill Wickham, Augusta caught a cold 'on leaving a crowded assembly in Bath' in the autumn of 1807 and died a few weeks later on October 10th. (The date of 1805 given by Hill Wickham seems to have been an error.[24]) Her death does seem to have been a real blow to Thomas and his memorial tablet statement that 'he forcibly feels her loss' is in marked contrast to the more restrained comments to his first wife's death. This memorial also includes a verse which seems to reflect the poems which previously had been reserved for his much loved sister Elizabeth and his mother:

> When Death unthought of, from his secret Stand
> Struck my Augusta his relentless Hand
> Markd her for Heav'n, but the envenom'd Dart,
> Thro' her has pierc'd, incurably, my Heart
> Incurably, is there no Saviour found
> To draw the Point and Poison from the Wound
> Yes: If submissive to the Will of God

---

[22] At this time occupied by the 3rd Duke of Portland, who became Prime Minister twice in the reign of George III.

[23] JCTSW II p.304

[24] ibid I p.32

Thro' Faith and Hope, I bless the chast'ning Rod:
With those I honoured most, and lov'd the best,
Not only here my mortal Part shall rest,
But rais'd Immortal we shall meet above
Where all is perfect Peace and perfect Love.

Her Will made bequests of three thousand pounds to a god-daughter and five hundred pounds to a cousin, and the rest of her estate went to Thomas Sedgwick. Curiously, it was drawn up on 18th May 1803, five days before her marriage and yet not signed and witnessed until four years later on 8th April 1807, six months before she died.

10.3 Augusta Whalley's memorial tablet, which joined the other two put in Burrington church by Thomas Sedgwick Whalley

After her death Thomas went to live with his sister and brother-in-law Mary and James Wickham in Frome, where he received a letter of condolence from Anna Seward dated 19th October.[25] Later, he went to Malvern Wells, then on to see his oldest friend, George Warrington, at Wrexham, whom he had first met at Cambridge (see Appendix 1), returning via Mrs Piozzi's house, Brynbella, at St Asaph.

In June 1808 Thomas made his way to Scotland, partly as a holiday but also to receive a Doctorate from the University of Edinburgh, which he did on July 10th. According to Hill Wickham, he had enlisted Sir Walter Scott to proffer the petition, believing that a DD from Edinburgh would be seen as more meritorious than one from Cambridge.[26] This is borne out by the letter of support addressed to 'Mr Scott', which was enclosed, unsealed, in a letter sent to Thomas Sedgwick by Anna Seward, dated May the 12th, which he received before he left for Scotland. In this she says that his wish must be hers, but she does also suggest that, like Handel, Thomas should decline to accept a doctorate.[27] It is also clear from what she quotes from an earlier letter that Walter Scott was extremely reluctant to help such literary gentlemen to 'profit by degrees'. Her letter the following month, in which she expresses her delight that this Scottish holiday has improved his health, also rebukes him roundly for accepting the doctorate, which she says served no purpose unless he is seeking to achieve further 'Church dignities'.[28]

It seems that, while on his way to Scotland, he stayed at Bowness with Robert Vans Agnew.[29] Perhaps in gratitude to

---

[25] JCTSW II pp.307-9.

[26] ibid I p.33

[27] ibid II pp.317-8

[28] ibid II p.323

this, or maybe inspired by his visit, Thomas dedicated *Kenneth and Fenella*, described by him as his 'trifling poem', to Agnew. This legendary tale, as he remarks himself, is connected with the tragedy of Macbeth and describes the murder of Kenneth II by Fenella, who according to legend was the grandmother or great aunt of Macbeth. The poem seems to have been written at the end of 1808 and published in 1809.[1]

In the winter of 1809 Thomas Sedgwick bought or rented a house in Baker Street;[31] this was close to where his friends Mr and Mrs Siddons lived in Upper Baker Street and not far away from Sir Walter and Lady James. For the next 4 years he lived mainly there. According to Hill Wickham, he entertained sumptuously, was a collector of paintings and had a weakness for items of expensive jewellery. They were purchased from Messrs Rundell and Bridge, the Royal Jewellers of Ludgate Hill whose work now sells for millions. It is not clear where this information comes from, how reliable it is, or who these were for, as they are not mentioned in his Will. Perhaps the answer lies in the suggestion made by Mrs Piozzi in April 1808.

> As to my expressed hope of hearing that you had made a third choice [of wife], I was perfectly serious there, conscious as I am that the comfort of your future days depends upon an event of that sort. You dote upon Mendip Lodge, and to make that little Eden indeed an Eden to you, it is necessary that you should have a partner in its delights, and that you should have friends around you to partake them also, and to receive from one dear to

---

[1] Whalley T.S., *Kenneth and Fenella – a legendary tale*. Hatchard J, London, 1809.
[31] JCTSW I p.33

you those attentions which neither the habits of your life, your health, nor spirits permit that you yourself should pay. There is a lady of whom, from your youthful days, you have thought most highly, the titled relict of a man of worth and honour; a lady suitable to you in every respect. Clarissa [Elizabeth Cornwallis, niece of the Marquis of Cornwallis, Bishop of Coventry and Lichfield 1781-1824] first suggested the idea to me; persuasion is in your accents[sic]; and we think it probable you would not sue in vain. You cannot, I think, mistake the person I allude to.[32]

Perhaps the lady suggested by Mrs Piozzi did not meet with his approval, or perhaps she could see no advantage in marrying a 62 year old in poor health, but such a pattern of providing gifts and then seeking something in return appears to be Thomas Sedgwick's means of getting his own way. This method had worked in getting Mrs Siddons to perform his play *Edwy and Edilda* at Drury Lane, but a later gift of 'the beauteous and magnificent sables' in 1802 failed to achieve its desired effect for another play.[33] On this occasion Mrs Siddons says 'I thank you for your kind offer of *Rosilda* but at present it is not in my power to get it up'.[34] There is no record of Thomas Sedgwick having written such a play but it seems clear that this is what it was. It is obvious that he was engaged writing several works at this time for his cousin Mrs Pennington (née Weston) thanks him for the 'beautiful and elegant poem' he had sent to her in 1809.[35]

[32] JCTSW I p.314

[33] ibid II p.223

[34] ibid II p.228

[35] ibid II p.332

CHAPTER 11
Cousin Penelope Sophia Weston (1751-1827) and Her Husband

Penelope Sophia Weston, Thomas Sedgwick's cousin by marriage, remained a friend and correspondent throughout his life, and each influenced the other's life. Rather than try to weave her story into the other chapters of the book, it seemed appropriate to write it as a separate account at this point. The readers can, if they wish, jump to Chapter 12 and return to read this account later.

Penelope Weston was born on 5th April 1751 in Worcester. In her first recorded letter to Thomas Sedgwick, from Tetley near Ludlow in May 1781, she refers to herself as his cousin but was in fact only a second cousin through his marriage to his first wife, the widow Elizabeth Sherwood née Jones.[1] In other words, Miss Weston shared one pair of great grandparents with Elizabeth.[2] Penelope's father was Edward Weston, a merchant from Worcester, and her mother, Mary Pryce, a Mercer's daughter from Ludlow whom he married in 1749.[3] Her parents moved to Worcester after their marriage, and Penelope and her mother only returned to Ludlow after the death of Edward in 1765. She had two brothers, Joseph and Gilbert, but only Penelope and Joseph,

---

[1] JCTSW I p.317

[2] Since the Jones were an ancient wealthy Welsh family, this would fit; Ludlow had been the centre of English/Welsh trade as well as the administrative centre of the Marches since the middle ages.

[3] "Mercer "– a dealer in textile fabrics esp silks and other costly materials (OED)

the 'good son', are mentioned in their father's will. The National Archives show that there was a sizeable marriage settlement made on Mary Pryce by her father William Pryce,[4] which in due course came to Penelope.[5]

Penelope must have got to know Thomas Sedgwick soon after his marriage to Elizabeth Sherwood in 1774 and was soon a member of his circle of correspondents. It is clear that by May 1781 Penelope had visited the Whalleys at Langford Court several times, describing the place as her 'terrestrial paradise'.[6] In a letter the following year, she explains to him how she has little in common with her mother.

> My mother is a very good woman but our minds are, unfortunately, cast in such different moulds – our pursuits and ideas on every occasion and every subject are likewise so – that it is of very little moment our speaking the same language. Our tête-a-têtes, therefore, you may suppose, are not much enlivened by the arts of conversation. Indeed, I see very little of her for she is either busied in domestic matters, praying, gardening or gossiping most part of the day; while I sit moping over the fire with a book or pen in my hand, without stirring (if the weather unfavourable) for weeks altogether without the cheerful face of a friend, and a single creature or circumstance intervening to enlighten my solitude, till my brains are perfectly addled, and my ideas so confused, that history, poetry,

4   See   http://www.nationalarchives.gov.uk/A2A/records.aspx?cat=166-mi1750&cid=-1#-1

5 See http://www.nationlaarchives.gov.uk/documentsonline / PROB 11/907

6 JCTSW I p.317

sentiment, morality and politics all swim in one incongruous and indistinguishable mass before me; and I am sometimes tempted to make an essay of my own voice merely to satisfy myself, that I am anything like the thing I was, and have not totally lost the power of articulation with my other faculties.[7]

Her first recorded letter to another mutual friend Anna Seward, the romantic poet and memorialist, is dated October 29th 1784,[8] and three years later she was being described by Anna as 'the leading spirit of a knot of ingenious and charming females in Ludlow'.[9]

By 1779 Penelope was indulging in a semi-platonic relationship with a doubtful character, Samuel Jackson Pratt, who was now residing in Bath. Although coming from a good family and having been ordained in to the church, Pratt soon abandoned his clerical profession to take up acting and writing. In 1772 he had eloped with Charlotte Melmoth;[10] whether they ever married is doubtful, and they eventually separated, she to pursue a successful acting career in America. How he met Thomas Sedgwick Whalley is unknown, although their ordained fathers may well have known each other in Huntingdon. Both Whalley and Pratt were would-be poets and playwrights, and in her letter of May 1781, Penelope says:

7 JCTSW I pp.361-2

8 Constable A (Ed) *Letters of Anna Seward, Written Between the Years 1784 and 1807,* Vol I., George Ramsay and Co., Edinburgh, 1811, p.7

9 TIL p.4

10 Variously descrbed as a 'farmers daughter' or a 'pretty boarding school miss'.

> I long to see Pratty's new poem and hope our dear
> Amelia will have the goodness to send it to me with
> some things I expect by the return of a family from
> Ludlow who are now at Bath. Poor Pratty! Most
> heartily do I wish him all and every degree of
> prosperity, but I fear for him from a thousand
> causes .[11]

Eventually, though, Penelope saw through him and declined his advances. Despite warnings from his friends,[12] Thomas Sedgwick continued to befriend the worthless Pratt (who also now went under the name of Courtney Melmoth) to the concern and disapproval of many. Matters came to a head when Pratt started circulating unfavourable comments about the 'meanness' of the Whalleys' close friend Mrs Sarah Siddons. This arose after the latter had asked Pratt for the repayment of a small short loan which she had made to him.[13] This Pratt objected to on the grounds that the now famous Mrs Siddons could well afford to overlook such a debt as she was getting 'a vast deal of money'. By August 1786 even Thomas Sedgwick had finally denounced him, though Pratt was still using various ruses to imply that he retained Thomas's friendship.[14]

Penelope Weston seems to have met the remarkable, recently widowed Mrs Thrale in April 1781, when she came to Bath. This was through Thomas Sedgwick, who knew Mrs Thrale through Lady Miller's Bath Easton poetry circle (see Chapter 3). This introduction, Mrs Piozzi later recorded with gratitude.[15] It was

---

[11] JCTSW I p.318

[12] ibid I p.317

[13] ibid I p.437

[14] ibid I p.492

[15] TPL III p.333

not surprising that the two ladies should get on so well, since both were descended from distinguished Welsh families. Penelope's lifelong correspondence with Mrs Thrale began in 1788, not long after the latter returned from an extended honeymoon on the continent with her second husband, Gabriel Piozzi, an Italian musician and singer. It was clear, though, that by this time Mrs Piozzi had already visited Penelope in Ludlow, whom she describes in a letter to Sophia Byron dated July 1788 as being sincere, of good humour and an excellent conversationalist.[16]

Penelope and her mother moved to Queen Square, London, in 1787.[17] Two years later, Penelope appears to be acting as governess in London to an uninspiring young lady, whom she declares is unaffected by the lively company she was now able to enjoy.[18] By this time the Piozzis were in London, living in Hanover Square, and they and the Siddons were in regular contact with the Westons.[19]

Some time after this, Penelope's brother Joseph seems to have got married. There is a record of a Joseph Weston marrying in May 1791 in east London. Shortly after this, despite warnings,[20] Penelope and her mother went to live with them, with catastrophic results. Penelope was persuaded to hand over her own inheritance to her brother to pay for his debts, and her mother likewise had to sell her house in Queen Square, London and was forced to take rooms for Penelope and herself at 14

---

[16] TPL I p.267

[17] TIL p.17

[18] JCTSW II pp.31-2

[19] ibid II p.20

[20] Constable A (Ed), *Letters of Anna Seward, Written Between the Years 1784 and 1807,* Vol, III., George Ramsay and Co., Edinburgh, 1811, p.85

James Street.[21] A year and a half later, Anna Seward recorded how matters stood in a letter to a Miss Stokes:

> After all the rashness of Miss --- [Weston's] unfounded trust in a dissipated brother; when it had, as you learnt from my last letter [sadly not recorded], reduced her to the dreariest prospect of want and dependence; when that delusive hope of matrimonial establishment, which had lead her to such a dangerous plan of expense, was vanished amid the gloom of descended penury, a miraculous fortunate reality of that sort intervenes, and snatches her from overwhelming darkness, to competence, to liberal competence, and to permanent peace. [22]

The miraculous intervention was that of William Pennington, who had heard of Penelope's predicament through their mutual friend Thomas Sedgwick Whalley. This was described in a letter from Thomas to his close friend Anna Seward, which she recounted a few months later in a letter to a Mrs Stokes dated November 1792.

> My friend ----- [Mr. Pennington] enquiring about Miss----- [Weston] a few weeks ago I related to him her hapless situation. He paused a few moments and then said 'Would to God she would accept of me as a comforter and protector, and command the little independence it is in my power to give

---

21 TIL p.64

22 Constable A (Ed), *Letters of Anna Seward, Written Between the Years 1784 and 1807,* Vol. III, George Ramsay and Co., Edinburgh, 1811, p.189-93

her' On this more than hint I spoke to her, business calling me to town. After much conversation and some hesitation, she consented to hear and see, though she would not bind herself to accept the noble minded being who wooed her, for the first time in the midst of want and distress. They had not met for near ten years, and, when is rarely the case, she found him, at their interview, full as agreeable in his person, and infinitely more so in his mind, that she had ever known him. All his oddities and eccentricities seemed done away by time, good sense, and the constant friction of good company; so that all his merits struck her with double force. Everything is settled... [22]

William Pennington

So, who was William Pennington? He was once thought to have been born in Culmstock, Devon in 1744 and to have joined the 66th Regiment of foot,[23] but this man has been proved to be a former weaver who was invalided out of the army in 1785.[24] Oswald Knapp, in his book *The Intimate Letters of Hester Piozzi and Penelope Pennington*, suggests that William came from a family of Bristol merchants, which is more likely.[25] Several members of the Pennington family existed in Bristol at the time, including the firm of Pennington and Biggs, listed in Bailey's directory of 1774 and 785 as Merchants of Orchard Street. There was also a James

[23] Crune, R., *James Pennington of New Brunswick and William Pennington of N. Carolina, Loyalists during the American Revolution,* Generations, 2005: 27 (1) 1-10
[24] British Army Service Records. 66th Regiment of Foot. Discharge Record, March 18th 1785
[25] TIL p.57

Pennington, born in Bristol in 1746, who was a Bristol Customs
Officer (1776-1800)[26] who took over this office from his father.
Such appointments were only achieved through the patronage of
a member of Parliament, and at the time Sir Joseph Pennington
MP (1718-1793) had been Commissioner of Customs since 1751,
and his father before him. James Pennington had a brother
William born in 1740, and this is probably our man.

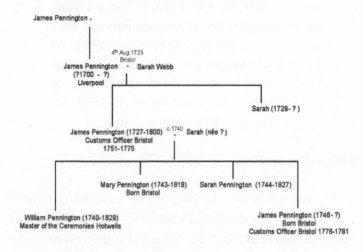

11.1 The probable family tree of William Pennington

The Will of Edward Jones of Langford Court, Thomas
Sedgwick's father in law, contained a bequest of £500 to 'Miss
Mary Pennington my Child's Companion and friend, Daughter
to Mr Penington [sic] Collector of Excise'. This could well have
been a sister of William Pennington, who was six years older
than Elizabeth Jones. Several Penningtons also appear in a lease
document for a property in Bath once owned by Sir Joseph

---

26 The Bristol Poll Book being a list of persons who voted at the Election 1781
District of St James.

Pennington's father-in-law, the apothecary John Moore. William may have held military rank, as being the eldest son, he would be likely to have gone into the army. Almost all the customs officers in the American colonies were officers of the army or navy at that time.[27] The fact that William served in March 1765 on the Board of Enquiry in N. Carolina into the death of a naval Lieutenant, Thomas Whitehurst, in a duel would tend to support this.[28] One later account gives him the rank of colonel.[29] However, his name as yet has not been found within either the Army or Navy lists, although the latter are incomplete for this period.

Whatever William's origins may have been, in 1764 the Treasury appointed him as comptroller of customs for the port of Brunswick, North Carolina's leading port.[30] As a customs officer William was paid £40 per annum but seems to have received another £100 a year in emoluments. He travelled out to America with William Tryon, a Lieutenant colonel in the 1st Regiment of Foot (the Scots Guards) who came from a landed family and had been appointed Lieutenant Governor of N. Carolina.[31] Tryon's wife, Margaret née Wake, came from a very wealthy family and was related to Lord Hillsborough, Lord of Trade and Plantations, and it is likely that Hillsborough was behind Tryon's appointment in 1764.[32] Margaret travelled out

27 Sabine, L., *Loyalists of the American Revolution*, Vols 1&2, Boston, 1864

28 Powell, W.S., Dictionary of N. Carolina, Vol. 5, N.Carolina Press, Chapel Hill, N.Carolina 1994, p.67-8

29 Marriage Announcement, Bristol Gazette and Public Advertiser, 3 January 1793

30 Warrant dated 11 May 1764, North Caroline State archives, Mars on line catalogue (http://mars.archives.ncdcr.gov)

31 Oxford Dictionary of National Biography, Oxford University Press, 2013

32 Haywood, M. de L., *Governor William Tryon and his administration in the Province of North Carolina 1765-1771*, Edwards Broughton and Co., Raleigh N. Carolina,1958

with him, as did her sister, who was reported as later having considerable influence on colonial affairs.[33] A year later, when Governor Arthur Dobbs died, Tryon was appointed Governor of the province and was soon appalled by the level of corruption that existed in the colony. Faced with a host of problems, he was to acquit himself well and clearly held Pennington in high regard.[34] The new governor was immediately confronted by a rebellion of N. Carolina colonists against the Stamp Act of 1765. In February the following year a delegation of colonists sought William Pennington at Tryon's house in connection with the implementation of the Act, but the Governor Tryon refused to let them take him. The next day, 400-500 men arrived to take Pennington by force. With no real alternative he agreed to go and signed an oath under duress that he would not implement the new Act. A month later, though, the Governor restored him to his post, having stated that any oath made under compulsion was not valid.[35]

This was the beginning of the "Regulator Movement", a North Carolina uprising lasting from 1765 to 1771 in which citizens took up arms against such issues as unequal taxation and unhappiness with local officials. Although unsuccessful, some historians consider it a catalyst to the American Revolutionary War. Tryon was sympathetic to some Regulator demands and was a personal friend of some of its leaders, but in 1768, following British instructions, he marched the militia to Hillsborough to put down Regulator demonstrations. In 1770 the Regulators arose again and broke up the superior court at Hillsborough, intimidating court officials and lawyers. They also burnt down

[33] Sabine, L., *Loyalists of the American Revolution*, Vol. 2, Boston, 1864, p.364-66
[34] Powell, W.S., *Dictionary of N. Carolina Biography*, Vol 5, N.Carolina Press, Chapel Hill, N.Carolina, 1994, p.67.
[35] ibid p.68

"Tryon's Palace", which has now been rebuilt. The ring leaders were convicted and outlawed, and in March 1771 Tryon inflicted a crushing defeat on 2,000 Regulators. In July Tryon left for New York, as he had succeeded Lord Dunmore as governor of that province. He gave the house which he had owned on the outskirts of New Brunswick to Pennington.[36] It seems that Pennington then remained at his post until February 1776, when he was driven from office and all Customs activity ceased as the American Revolution began. William fled to New York; one report says that he joined the loyal forces there but was captured by the Americans in or near New York on July 16th, 1781;[36] another says he returned to England via Cork in 1777. The British forces in New York held out against the colonists until the Battle of Yorktown in 1782, where they surrendered.[37] However, by 1780, convinced that the war could not be won, Tryon resigned his civil and military positions and returned to England and lived quietly there with his wife until his death.

Whenever William made his way to England, the events of that passage are recorded by Hill Wickham:

> His probity was strikingly evinced on his voyage
> from America. A fellow-passenger, a voluntary exile
> from the land of his birth, like himself, but who had
> amassed a considerable fortune, which he took with
> him, conceived a strong attachment to Mr.
> Pennington, and opened his mind on various
> subjects, and, among others, upon the little prospect
> of satisfaction he felt in tracing out his distant
> relatives in the land of his forefathers. The voyage

36 Powell, W.S., *Dictionary of N. Carolina Biography*, Vol 5, N.Carolina Press, Chapel Hill, N.Carolina, 1994, p.69

37 Fort Tryon Park still exists in Manhattan.

was long and after a time this gentleman became ill and was assiduously nursed by his new friend. He grew worse, and feeling he should not survive, made a Will, in which he left everything to Mr. Pennington, saying that he had received great kindness from him, and wished him to inherit his property in preference to his unknown relations. He died on the voyage, and on arriving in England, Mr. Pennington destroyed the Will, found out the relations, and put them in possession of all the property of the deceased.[38]

If William did have links with the Bristol firm of Isaac Pennington and Biggs, it is likely that as he journeyed home he thought of himself as returning to a wealthy family. This would perhaps explain his generosity to the family of the man who died on the voyage home. However, by then the trade with Bristol had been drastically affected when hostilities broke out in 1775; in addition, many British ships were lost to American privateers.[39,40] Whatever the causes, the firm of Pennington and Briggs had disappeared from the Bristol records by 1775. Interestingly, there was a claim lodged in Connecticut in 1795 by Thomas Pennington, who was described as the surviving partner of that company, to recover £7000 owed to it by Charles McEvers's Company of New York.[41] Thomas Pennington does not seem to be resident in Bristol by this time.

---

38 JCTSW I p.385 (Footnote)

39 Little, B., *The story of Bristol*, The Redcliff Press, Bristol, 1991, p.58.

40 Knowles, L.C.A., *The Indutsrial and Commercial Revolutions in Great Britain during the Nineteenth Century* George Routledge and Sons, London , 1941, p. 366

41 Roote, J., *Report of cases argued and determined in the Supreme Court of Errors in the State of Connecticut in the years June 1793 – January 1798*, Vol. 2, Hudson and Goodwin, Hartford Connecticut, 1802, p.233-238

Back in England there was strong public support for loyalists returning to the country, and a Loyalist Claims Commission was set up in London to recompense faithful Government servants. William, supported by Tryon, made a successful claim for his losses.[42] Palmer, in an updated version of Sabine's work, states that this was for £941 sterling, of which William was only awarded £150, but he also received a pension of £60 per annum.[43] William's pension continued at least until 1784.[44] The next mention we have of William is in a letter dated January 26th 1783 from Penelope Weston to Thomas Sedgwick Whalley, saying that she thinks Pennington and 'Coz [Edward] Somers' would feel themselves very comfortable in the same habitation.[45] Edward Somers would have been of a similar age to William and was a cousin of Penelope; he lived in Butcombe, close to Langford Court, until his early death in death in 1790.[46] Since Penelope's letter is in reply to an earlier one from Thomas Sedgwick Whalley that conveys this information, it confirms that William must have arrived back in Bristol no later than 1782 and had met up with Somers soon afterwards. More than one account describes William as being elegant and witty,[47] and it does seem that he was well educated, though he does not appear to have attended

[42] TPL I p.360-1 (Footnote 3).

[43] Palmer, G., *Biographical Sketches of Loyalists of the American Revolution*, Meckler Publishing., Westport, Conneticut, 1984, p.681

[44] Claim of William Pennington case 1152, dated 27th February 1784, in Fraser, A., *United Empire Loyalists, Second Report of the Bureau of Archives for the Province of Ontario*, p.1197 See also
http://archiver.rootsweb.ancestry.com/th/read/PENNINGTON/2003-03/1048785356

[45] JCTSW I p.385-6

[46] Somers, B.E., *The pedigree of the Somers family*, 1916

[47] Sabine, L, *Biographical Sketches of Loyalists of the American Revolution*. 2nd Ed. Little, Brown and Co., Boston, 1864, Vol. 2 p.165

University.[48] In a letter to Penelope dated 22nd May 1801, Mrs Piozzi includes her own poem on the victory of Abercrombie over the French at Alexandria and remarks 'Mr Pennington will see an allusion to an Epigram by Martial in the first stanza'.[49] A further letter suggests that he was familiar with the works of Dean Swift.[50] A letter from Anna Seward describes him as 'by birth a gentleman, whose situation, through his youth, had been unsettled, and his finances scanty'.[51]

Penelope's Marriage to William Pennington

Bloom and Bloom suggest that the first intimation of the marriage between Penelope and William Pennington is contained in a letter from Mrs Piozzi, dated between 9th and 15th August 1791.[52] A clearer indication is contained in another letter from her, to Penelope dated September 9th 1792.[53] By this time Penelope was 41 years of age and William 52 or 53 years old. As already mentioned, Thomas Sedgwick Whalley and Anna Seward were enthusiastic about the match, but Penelope, despite her precarious financial state, was much less certain about marriage. Mrs Piozzi appears almost irritated by her temporary lack of enthusiasm. In a letter to her, dated Saturday 29th September, she says:

---

[48] A search of the records of schools in Bristol have not identified him as being educated there, but Biggs and Pennington's office was close to the Bristol Grammar School.

[49] TIL p.217

[50] ibid pp.351-2

[51] Constable A (Ed), *Letters of Anna Seward, Written Between the Years 1784 and 1807*, Vol. III, George Ramsay and Co Edinburgh, 1811, pp.189-193

[52] TPL I pp.359-61

[53] TIL p.56

How can you be so cold to him? But 'tis illness which make you so; be well sweet friend and reject not heavens offer of temporal happiness in its natural form: that of a good husband.[54]

Two months later, though, Anna Seward is able to report a happy outcome to her friend Mrs Stokes, in a letter dated 15th November 1792:

This heart of mine can yet exult and glow in the prosperity of those I love, or whom I have ever loved; and I have news to tell you, in which you will, equally with myself rejoice. It met me in a letter from Mr Whalley, on my return home last night. After all the rashness of Miss --- [Weston]'s unfounded trust in a dissipated brother; when it had, as you learnt from my last letter, reduced her to the dreariest prospect of want and dependence; when that delusive hope of matrimonial establishment, which had lead her into such a dangerous plan of expense, was vanished amid the gloom of descended penury, a miraculous fortunate reality of that sort intervenes and snatches her from the overwhelming darkness, to competence, liberal competence, and peace.

For this she is indebted to a very old acquaintance – by birth a gentleman, whose situation, through his youth, had been unsettled, and his finances scanty. Some five years since, he was appointed

54 TIL p.61

master of the ceremonies at ----------. I saw him the summer before last; and, as I guess, his age is about forty five, – his figure tall and genteel, his face plain. He is allowed to be a man of sense and taste, but with laughable oddities, both of temper and understanding; yet of much exterior politeness, and of great goodness of heart. Ten years ago Miss ---[Weston] and he were much together at Mr Whalley's – but in the interim they have not met, and he was never suspected of glancing towards the fair Sophia*, with an eye of aspiring affection, or even marked admiration...

...Everything is settled, his generous friend Mrs -------, highly approves his choice- a very material point. [This must be Mrs Tryon, who was widowed in 1788 and who later left them money in her Will.] The bride elect comes down to us next week, and before Christmas I am to bless their union at the alter. Mrs ------- has quantity of elegant furniture, china, plate, and linen, and their income will be a clear £500 per annum with fair promise of yearly increase from the great increase of the buildings around the springs where he is universally beloved and esteemed.

You will not wonder dear Mrs Stokes that I have thought of little else but this welcome, this unlooked for good news, since I heard it. May the sunshine this union be permanent! – a wish to which, I am sure you will breathe, and very sincere amen![55]

---

[55] Constable, A. (Ed), *Letters of Anna Seward, Written Between the Years 1784 and*

* At about this time Miss Weston decided that she wished now to be known as Sophia rather than Penelope

Mrs Piozzi clearly approved of the match, and in her letter of November 1792, she says 'we are all in the right to love Mr Pennington' and asks to be 'the first to receive a letter signed PSP'.[56] Knapp observes:

> The match she was now contemplating was not brilliant, or even romantic, and probably her head was much more concerned in the decision than her heart. But the suitor, in spite of a somewhat scandalous story retailed to Sophia by her cousin Mrs. Whalley, was evidently an honourable man, and certainly his suit was not prompted by mercenary motives.[57]

Quite what the scandalous story was is not clear, but it may refer to him having owned slaves in N. Carolina at a time when all those in the Whalley circle were ardent abolitionists.

The couple were married in Bath in December 1792, with Thomas Sedgwick performing the blessing at the marriage.[58] The reception was at the Whalley's house in Royal Crescent.[59] This must have been before the 27th, by which time Mrs Piozzi was writing to Penelope, addressed as 'Mrs Pennington', at Royal

1807, Vol. III, George Ramsay and Co Edinburgh, 1811, pp.189-193

[56] TIL p.70

[57] ibid p.57

[58] Constable A (Ed), *Letters of Anna Seward, Written Between the Years 1784 and 1807*, Vol.III, George Ramsay and Co., Edinburgh, 1811, p.189-191

[59] ibid Vol.II p.85 (Note 1)

Crescent.[60] This suggests the couple stayed with the Whalleys for Christmas. The announcement of their marriages in the Bath Chronicle of 3rd January 1793 states 'William Pennington Esq; Master of the ceremonies at the Hotwells to Miss Weston of James Street Westminster', which were in fact her mother's rented rooms there.

Two weeks later, Mrs Piozzi adds 'How happy Mr Pennington must be in Mrs Tryon's admiration of his Sophia's qualities.' This confirms that the influential and wealthy Tryons have now met Penelope. She then goes on to say,

> These are the bright moments, the lucid spots of life, which those who never marry never see. Mr. Whalley's is really a lucky house, seldom have I seen it without a courting scene in the foreground.[61]

This seems to imply that William had proposed at Mendip Lodge. Soon the couple were living in Dowry Square, within a short walk of William's employment at the Hotwells.

The Bristol Hotwells

The hot springs of the Avon Gorge were described by William of Worcester in 1480 [62] but were reputedly known before this time for their beneficial properties by sailors visiting the port of Bristol. By 1661 these perceived medicinal properties were becoming widely known, and the Corporation of Bristol spent

---

60 JCTSW II p.78

61 TPL II p.85-6

62 *'Fons callidus emanat de profundo aquae Avyn, sicut est Bathoniae'*, William of Worcester, 1480

£100 improving the roadway so that they were accessible to horses and coaches. In 1691 Sir John Knight, the mayor of Bristol, endeavoured to enclose the spring at the Hotwells in a wall, to prevent the waters of the Avon from contaminating the spring at high tide, but with limited success.[63] (The spring was 10 feet above low water but 26 feet below high water.) Finally, in 1695 the Society of Merchant Venturers of Bristol, who were Lords of the Manor, leased the site to Sir Thomas Day Robert Yates and Thomas Callow,[64] and the latter, with Charles Jones, built Hotwell House and installed a pump, which overcame persisting problems of contamination from the river and provided attractive premises for those taking the waters. During the early eighteenth century the spa became a highly fashionable resort. The season began in early May and continued until late September.[65]

The Hotwells's heyday was 1760-1790, when visitors attended more for pleasure than their health. The Duke of York and the Duchess of Marlborough became regular visitors. Hundreds of people came during the season to "take the waters" but in reality to attend the balls, view the scenery and cross the Avon by ferry to picnic in Nightingale Wood or enjoy strawberries and cream in Long Ashton village.[66] Mathews described the facilities at the Hotwells in 1793 as follows:

> There are three sets of large, elegant public rooms;
> the first is called, the old, or upper long-room, kept
> by J. Barton: the second on the opposite side of

[63] Chilcot, J., *Chilcot's New Guide to Bristol Clifton and the Hotwells,* .J Chilcot, Bristol, 1826, pp.183-4

[64] Mathews, W., *A new history, survey and description of the city and suburbs of Bristol,* 1794 p. 99

[65] At which point many visitors would move on to enjoy the Bath season.

[66] Evans, J., *The picture of Bristol, or a guide to objects of curiosity and interst in Bristol, Clifton and the Hotwells and their vicinity,* W.Sheppard, Bristol 1814, p.133

the street, is called the lower or New Long Room, kept by J. Ferry. At these are public breakfasts during the season, every Monday and Thursday alternately, with cotillions and country dances, for which each person pays 1s. 6d. The Balls are on Tuesdays; subscription to which is one guinea at each room, and for walking in the rooms and gardens, and reading the papers 5s. Subscribers to the Balls are allowed two tickets, which admit two ladies: non-subscribers pay 5s. each ball.

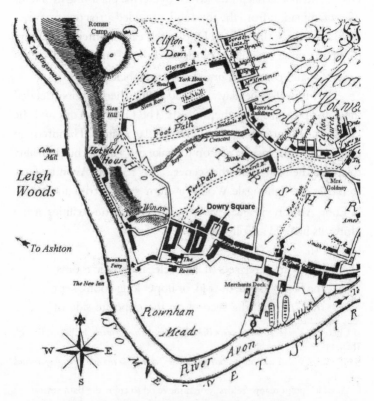

11.2 The Hotwells and Clifton, 1787 after Hill

11.3 Print of the Hotwells as it was drawn by G.W. Manby
probably in 1802, The colonnade built in 1796 is included.
From Manby. G.W., *The History and Beauties of Clifton Hotwel,*
Thomas Wilson, London, 1806

Other local attractions included the New Vauxhall Gardens,
Gabriel Goldney's Grotto, Mr Johnson's fossil collection in
Dowry Parade, and Mr Hippisly's theatre in Jacobs Wells, which
opened in 1729 and continued until the Theatre Royal opened in
1776.

Following various published accounts extolling the benefits
of Hotwells water, the number of invalids began to outnumber
the pleasure seekers. Bottled Hotwells water became widely
known, and by the mid 18th century London newspapers were
advertising the 'Famous Bristol Hotwell Water, fresh from the
well, delivered to any part of the Town for six shillings per dozen
bottles'. When Elizabeth Whalley travelled to India in 1775, she
took with her two cases of Hotwells water, each containing twelve
dozen bottles.[67] (See Chapter 4). Gradually, towards the end of
the 18th century, the Hotwells's reputation changed. It became

---

[67] JCTSW I p.284

known as the place where consumptives and the elderly sick came to die.

The Penningtons and the Hotwells

In 1785, in an effort to regain its reputation as a centre for entertainment, the Hotwells followed the example of Bath and appointed William Pennington as its Master of the Ceremonies.[68] A contemporary account states that he was inducted to this important office 'under the patronage of the Archbishop of Tuam [the senior cleric in Ireland] and the Bishop of Cloyne, and with the unanimous voice of a numerous circle of nobility and gentry'. It is clear that there was much local support for William's appointment. Many Americans as well as British had left the American colonies at the outbreak of the War of Independence and settled in Bristol, where they formed their own social circle based on College Green.[69] These included Thomas Hutchinson, the former Governor General of Massachusetts, and Henry Cruger, who, although born in New York, was elected as one of the MPs for Bristol 1774 -1778, where he served with Edmund Burke, who, like him, had strong American sympathies. The first American Consulate opened in Bristol in 1792, in defiance of the government in London, when the Bristol merchants invited Elias Vanderhorst to come from Boston to serve as American Consul for the city from 1792-1815. Later correspondence exists between Sophia Pennington and his daughter, so it is highly likely that she and William were part of their circle.[70]

---

[68] There appears to have been a Mr Hunt in post before this but his title and duties are unclear.

[69] Little, B., *The story of Bristol*, The Redcliff Press, Bristol, 1991, p.59

[70] See Letters dated 24 and 16 December 1823, Bristol Record Office, Bristol,

William wore a gold medallion on a blue ribbon to emphasize the dignity of his office, and it was his responsibility to organise balls and public breakfasts and other attractions for the visitors. One account says that the office of Master of Ceremonies was a paid one, but records held in the Bristol Records Office do not confirm this. Neither does the Merchant Venturers' Cash Book (1785-mid 1787) nor does the Beadle's cash book for 1787/9 contain any entry for a payment to William.[71] It is certainly the case that William received substantial tips. *Mathews's Guide of 1794* says, 'Every stranger who visits the Hotwells paid him an acknowledgement for his attention'.[72] This is confirmed by *Shiercliff's Guide of 1793*, which says 'His office, like that at Bath, is attended with emolument as well as honor; every stranger who visits the Hotwells paying him an emolument for his attention'.[73] With 300 people visiting the Hotwells at the height of its popularity, and each tipping him at least a guinea and probably more, he could be doing very well. Mrs Piozzi put his income at £400 a year.[74]

England, Ref: 8032 (84)

[71] The Beadle was responsible to the Merchant Venturers for collecting rents, and managing their estates generally

[72] Mathews, W. A. ,*New History of Bristol or the Complete Guide and Bristol Directory*, Bristol, 1794, pp.101-105

[73] Shiercliff, E., *The Bristol and Hotwell guide: containing an historical account of the ancient and present state of that opulent city; also of the Hotwell*, Bulgin and Rosser, Bristol, 1793

[74] TPL VI p.404

THE BATH ✦ CHRONICLE.
Printed by R. CRUTTWELL in S. JAMES's STREET.

To the NOBILITY and GENTRY frequenting BRISTOL HOTWELLS.

PERMIT me to return you my warmest and most sincere thanks for the very flattering instance of favour which I have received this Day, in having been unanimously elected MASTER of the CEREMONIES, on Mr. HUNT's resignation.

I deeply feel and gratefully acknowledge the polite and generous support I have met with from my first application to the present hour: My attention to the duties of my office, and my unremitted endeavours to fill it with propriety and to advance the interests of the place, will be a better proof, than any professions I can now make, of the zeal and gratitude with which I have the honour to be

Your most obliged,

Thursday Evening,   And very humble servant,

July 28, 1785.   WILLIAM PENNINGTON.

11.4 William Pennington's appointment in 1785

As in Bath, William presided over the Hotwells Assemblies and soon after his election directed that the following regulations for preserving the dignity of the public entertainments should be hung up in the rooms:

> 1st That a certain row of seats be set apart at the upper end of the room, for ladies of precedence, and foreigners of fashion.
>
> 2nd That every lady who has a right to precedence, deliver her card to the Master of the Ceremonies on her entering the room.
>
> 3rd That no gentleman appear with a sword or with spurs in these rooms, or on a ball night in boots.

259

4th That after a lady be called to a dance, her place in the next is at the bottom; and for the future it is to be understood that no lady of rank can avail herself of it, after the country dances are begun.

5th That on ball nights when minuets are danced, ladies who intend dancing there, will fit in a front row for the convenience of being taken out and returning to their places.

6th That on all occasions ladies are admitted to these rooms in hats, not excepting the balls given by the Master of Ceremonies.

7th That the subscription balls will begin as soon as possible after seven o'clock, and conclude at eleven, on account of the health of the company.

8th It is earnestly requested, that when a lady has gone down the dance, she will be so polite as to not retire till it is concluded.

But despite his appointment and efforts, the Hotwells continued to decline. In 1784 the original lease expired, and the Society of Merchant Venturers advertised for a new tenant at a greatly increased rent. There were initially no takers because the lessee was also required to spend at least £1000 undertaking repairs and improvements. Eventually, in 1790, after the Society had been forced to undertake these repairs, Samuel Powell became the new tenant, but the increased rental forced him to put up the charges to visitors.[75]

Shortly after William was appointed, a new hot spring, the Sion Spring, was discovered in Clifton by a Mr Morgan. This was

---

75 Waite, V., The *Bristol Hotwell*, The Hotwells and Clifton Community Association, Bristol, 1977 p.12

at a depth of 264 feet and was found when he was seeking a water supply for an intended house.[76] Soon the large Sion House was built on the site, with lodgings for visitors adjacent to the Pump Room, where water was raised by a 'fire engine'.[77]

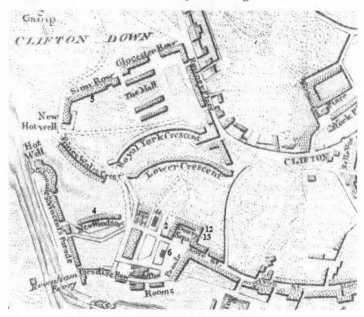

11.5 From Evans, *The picture of Bristol or a Guide to objects of curiosity and interest in Bristol Clifton and the Hotwells*, 1814, showing the growth in Clifton and Howells. 2,12,13 = Dowry Sq addresses of the Penningtons; 4 = Whalley's house in 1826; 5 = the house where Mrs Piozzi died; 6 = Dowry Chapel

[76] *Chilcotts New Guide to Clifton and the Hotwells*, J Chilcott, Bristol, 1826, p.206.
[77] Griffiths, L.M., *The reputation of the Hotwells (Bristol) as a health resort*, Reprinted from the Bristol Medical Chirurgical Society, JW Arrowsmith, Bristol, 1902, pp.24-5

Clifton was expanding rapidly at this time, and Sion House was modern, gave better views from its elevated site than the older accommodation in Hotwells, and was away from the smells and noise now coming from the Avon and its docks. The popular artists Rolinda Sharples and her brother were soon comfortably accommodated in Sion House, which also supplied visitors with a reading room and public library. This soon eclipsed the library and bookshop run by the personable Miss Yearsley, the 'milkmaid poetess', at the Lower Hotwells colonnade, though she would continue to run this until her death in 1809. Further libraries opened at 5 and 6 Sion Place, Gloucester Row, Clifton and, finally, in 1806 the new Upper Assembly Room in the Mall was completed as part of the Clifton Hotel (now the Clifton Club), with their own Master of Ceremonies. Now everything which had only been available at the Hotwells was replicated in Clifton.

These developments, and William Pennington's disabling attacks of gout which sometimes prevented him from carrying out his duties, became of increasing concern to his wife.[78] Despite this he would outlive her, though their financial worries continued to affect her, especially when in December 1802 her brother, whom she had once saved from bankruptcy, was dismissed from office and threatened with criminal charges, whereupon she lost what little remaining financial independence she had.[79, 80, 81] In 1802 she shared her fears of impending insolvency with Mrs Piozzi and, apparently, her friend Sarah Siddons, but the bankruptcy never came to pass.[82] This may have been through a

78 Letter 5th March 1793. John Rylands University Library of Manchester. Ref. 566.32
79 JCTSW II p.228
80 TPL III p.353
81 ibid III p.371 (Note 3)
82 ibid III pp.375-6

gift of £80 made by Mr Siddons at the request of his wife.[83] In November 1804 Mrs Piozzi was writing to inform Thomas Sedgwick that 'The storm, also, which threatened her [Sophia Pennington's] peace is passing away, and she is in high spirits at the sunshine. Mrs Tryon took her up to town and has not yet returned to the Hotwells'.[84]

In May 1809 Sophia wrote to Thomas Sedgwick, expressing her concern at the decline of the Hotwells, as follows:

> MY DEAR FRIEND,—
>
> It is quite impossible to express the joy and satisfaction which the sight of your well-known hand, and the contents of your kind letter, conveyed to my heart! Better days will, I hope, arrive, and none that we can look forward to with so much pleasure as the period of your kind invitation to Mendip Lodge, which must be in exquisite beauty at this delightful season, notwithstanding all the frosts and blights we have had, which have sadly disappointed the hopes of my dear little garden, the only thing I delight in. Pennington's Clifton Ball will be on the 25th of July, and probably his only ball this summer, for there is an end to everything like amusement below the Hill, and sorry I am to say that things have taken so unfavourable a turn at Clifton, that, instead of above one hundred subscribers at this season, as in former times, they can only muster thirty-one; and it is much feared that it will be found

---

83 JCTSW II p 228
84 ibid II p.258

impossible to support the ball, even there, through the season. They have been indefatigable in their plans for ruining this place, and have effectually succeeded. Could you think, they have even cut down the trees on that pretty walk leading to the Wells, and deprived the poor invalids of the only shade the place afforded, and me of the only walk I delighted in, and which I have often sought for an hour to refresh my weary spirits, but shall never do so with pleasure again? This is done under the pretence of making a towing-path, which they cannot use until they have taken down the Pump-room, and that, they say, they cannot afford to do for two or three years, if at all.[85] At the same time, they could, at a very moderate expense, have made a path for this necessary purpose on the other side the wall; but the Bristolians would make any sacrifice to their chief idol, gain....[86]

Nevertheless, William continued to officiate as Master of the Ceremonies until 1813, when he retired through illness at the age of 67. However, after a visit to Weymouth he recovered enough from his gout to resume the duties, as his successor had proved to be ineffective.[87] It would seem that in 1814, perhaps to supplement their income, they also took in a lodger at Dowry Square. Mrs Mary Hays, a supporter of Mary Wollstonecraft, maintained a prodigious correspondence from this address but seems to have despised and disliked her hostess.[88]

---

[85] When the old Hotwells was demolished in 1822, the replacement building was set back to allow a towpath to pass in front of it.
[86] JCTSW II pp.331-3
[87] TIL p.272

> ...Mrs Pennington possesses some talent but little real knowledge or mental culture...Vanity and commonplace ambition are her ruling passions, beauty, youth, fashion and style & wealth are her idols, & her regrets from having lost or missed some of these advantages are incessant and undisguised.

In a letter to Dr Whalley in December 1815, Mrs Pennington reports on the double burden of nursing her mother and her husband and states that in the summer she thought 'she had lost him'. However, following the death of her mother later that year and a short holiday in Weston Super Mare, William's health greatly improved.[89] He finally retired in March 1816.[90]

11.6 13 Dowry Square today

[88] Mary Hays to Mrs Henry Crabb; 26th November 1814., Bundle 6, XIII, Dr William's Library, London

[89] JCTSW II p.419.

[90] *Bath Chronicle,* 28th March 1816.

The Penningtons had lived in Dowry Square since their marriage, but their exact address is not known. By 1821 they are recorded in *Matthews's Bristol Directory* as living at 12 Dowry Square, then at 2 Dowry Square in 1824 and 1825, and finally 13 Dowry Square from 1826-28. During all this time the popularity of the Hotwells continued to decline. Mrs Piozzi recorded in 1820 how the area had deteriorated:

> The place is now deserted... and their [The Pennington's] house with 5 elegant rooms on a floor [This sounds very much like 13 Dowry Square] a perfect and positive incumbrance [sic] such as they can neither let nor sell.[91]

This does seem to confirm that Mary Hayes mentioned above was not the only lodger they took in once they were unable to let a whole floor of their house.

Mrs Piozzi died on 2nd May 1821 at 10 Sion Row, Clifton. Sophia, who had been in contact with her almost daily in her last two years, was greatly saddened by her death.[92] She was responsible for a moving obituary, which appeared in all the London papers.[93] With the loss of Mrs Piozzi's correspondence, there is less information about the Penningtons in their final years.

In her final recorded letter to Dr Whalley, dated October 1822, shortly after he returned to England, Sophia reports that 'Pennington is tolerably well'. She also expresses delight in an impending visit by Dr Whalley and his 'sweet niece', (which must mean Mrs Frances Boyle Sullivan). She regrets, though, that she

---

91 TPL VI p.404
92 TIL p.370
93 ibid p.371

no longer attends 'public places and Clifton parties', but states that she would have pleasure in attending whatever would give his niece pleasure.[94] She suggests that her house would be warmer than any other in the district in which Thomas might spend the winter and that 'her valuable old servant who had nursed her mother' would be available to assist him and his manservant John.

Sophia died on 8th August 1827, aged 75, and William Pennington soon followed in March 1829 (Powell says in his 91st year). It would seem by this time that none of his relations were living.[95] In his Will, drawn up immediately after his wife died, he left his entire estate to the spinster Sophia Wron, who looked after him in his final years.[96] He was buried in the vault of Dowry Chapel, Clifton, Bristol, within a few yards of his house.[97] This had been erected as a chapel of ease to St Andrew, Clifton in 1744, to serve the needs of those visiting the Hotwells. It was never consecrated, but in 1793 it was described as

> ...for the nobility and gentry resorting to a residency at the Hotwells was built and is supported by their voluntary subscriptions. This plain-laid building has within it columns of freestone which support the roof, a pulpit and benches for the audience. In the season the congregation is by far the most genteel and brilliant in the whole town. [98]

---

94 JCTSW II p.487

95 No Penningtons are recorded in Bristol in 1851. (*Mathew's Annual Bristol and Clifton Directory and Almanack*, Bristol, 1851)

96 The National Archives; Kew, England; *Prerogative Court of Canterbury and Related Probate Jurisdictions: Will Registers*; Class: *PROB 11*; Piece: *1756*.

97 Campbell, Mary V., *Parish Registry Transcripts St Andrews Clifton ,Gloucestershire 1538-1837,* Bristol Record Society, Bristol., 1987, p.47

There were once bronze plaques in the Dowry Chapel, recording the lives of William and his wife, but they were lost when the chapel was demolished and replaced by the church of St Andrews the Less[99] to cater for the increasing local population. This, too, was eventually demolished in the 1960s and is now the site of a very ugly block of flats.[100]

Nothing remains of the Hotwells today, except for part of the Colonnade, which used to house Ann Yearsley's library, and other small shops for the visitors. The original Hotwell buildings were demolished in 1826 and replaced by more modern facilities built by James Bolton, but these were never a real success and were demolished in 1867, at which time Hotwell point was blown up to improve navigation. This work partially disrupted the spring, but a free tap was installed in 1877 and remained there until removed in 1831. However, after much public agitation and the threat of legal action, a replacement pump was installed and remained until 1913, when the source was found to be polluted and the site closed on health grounds.[101]

---

[98] *The Bristol Directory 1793/4*, p.78

[99] Consecrated in 1873

[100] See http://www.churchcrawler.pwp.blueyonder.co.uk/andless.htm

[101] Waite, V., *The Bristol Hotwell*, Hotwells and Clifton Wood Community Association, Bristol, 1960.

11.7 The Colonnade today – the plaque put up to mark the site of Ann Yearsley's library is just visible

11.8 All that remains of the Hotwells today. The source was reinstated in 1877 at public request but later condemned and closed

CHAPTER 12
The Third Mrs Whalley

The first suggestion that the 67 year old Dr Whalley was intending to marry again came in a letter from Thomas to Mrs Piozzi, dated 16th June 1812.[1] Clearly, Mrs Horneck was well known to them both, but Thomas Sedgwick speaks in this of her talents and uncommon merits, which he had come to know over a period of 30 years of correspondence and 'confidential friendship'.

The widowed Mrs Fanny Horneck was the daughter of Nathaniel Gould, a sometime Lt Colonel who had married Frances Mary Buckworth in 1752. He had two children from this first marriage: Fanny, born 1755, and Bulkeley (Buckley), born 19th January 1753 in Westminster, who would later become mad. When his first wife died in 1759, Nathaniel Gould, now a Captain, immediately married Elizabeth Cochrane, the cousin of the diarist Boswell's mother. This is why we know something about him. Boswell had first met Nathaniel in 1762, and during the following months he often dined with the Goulds and enjoyed their company. Fanny, who according to Hill Wickham was known to be clever and well connected,[2] nevertheless married late in life. This was to Major Charles Horneck of the 62nd Regiment of Foot in 1790, when she was already 35 years old. She was Horneck's

---

1 TPL V p.154
2 JCTSW I p.33

second wife. His first marriage to Sarah Keppel in May 1773 did not last long. Within a year, Sarah had absconded with another officer, John Scawen. Charles petitioned for divorce, and the marriage was dissolved by Act of Parliament in 1776.[3] Charles's second marriage took place in Bath, and this seems to have been about the time that Thomas Sedgwick got to know Mrs Horneck, as by this time the Whalleys were entertaining lavishly at their house in Royal Crescent. We do not know where the Horneck's were living at this time, but by 1813, when Thomas married her, Fanny was living at 16 Queen Square, Bath.

Captain Charles Horneck had been a colourful character in his younger days and was known as the 'Military Macaroni'. The name came about when young men of the nobility and gentry returning from their Grand Tours adopted continental fashions and enjoyed the Italian dish first made fashionable in England through the "Macaroni Club".[4] The Macaronies were the foplings, fribbles or beaux of the day. Walpole refers to them as early as 1764, but their height was in the early 1770s. Many well-known names were found in their ranks, including Richard Cosway, who painted the miniature of Frances Sage.[5]

Charles Horneck bought his commission as Ensign in the 3rd Footguards in 1768. Later, as Captain he was based at St James barracks, where the guards had a reputation for parading in the nearby park in their finery and enjoying the attractions of London.

---

[3] Private Act, 16 George III, c. 85 HL/PO/PB/1/1776/16G3n147

[4] See Rauser, A.F., *Caricature unmasked: irony, authenticity and individualism in 18th century prints*, Associated Universities Presses, New Jersey, 2008

[5] This and the subsequent paragraph draws on the recent work of Moira Bonnington which is now contained in her unpublished MA thesis *The Military Macaroni: Charles Horneck and the nature of 'macaronidom' in the late eighteenth- century*, University of Leeds (submitted November 2013)and her account on the 'Soldiers and Soldiering' website http://redcoats.ning.com/profile/MoiraBonnington

The Macaronis were the subject of mockery, and doubt was cast on their masculinity, sexual preferences and general conduct. In 1789 Horneck, now a Lieutenant Colonel, transferred by exchange of commission with another officer to the 62nd Regiment of Foot.[6] When his new regiment went to Jamaica, he seems to have been able to delay joining them, finally arriving in Kingston in May 1793.[7] Four years later, he was serving with a small detachment in the Mediterranean, assisting Sir Gilbert Elliot in the evacuation of the short lived Anglo-Corsican Kingdom.

Capt.ᵗ H——, or the Military Macarone

1772

12.1 This plate faces the first page of *The Macaroni and Theatrical Magazine* of October 1772

A letter from Nelson, now Admiral of the Red and the senior officer in the Mediterranean, written off Cape Pallas and dated 1st May, 1797, states:

---

6 Boswell, J., *The Scots Magazine, 1789; 51: 311.*

7 *Royal Gazette*, Jamaica, May 25th 1793.

> I have the satisfaction to tell you, that all the Troops
> — except the Royals, who were always intended to
> be embarked in the Ships of War — are embarked
> in the Transports, with the exception of twenty, and
> General Horneck, who are in two Vessels loaded
> with wine.[8]

Mrs Horneck does not seem to have spent much time with her first husband or have any clear idea of his movements. In July 1799 she wrote to the Whalleys from Bath, saying that she had just heard from her husband 'by the fleet, which was a great relief to me, as there are now two packets due from Jamaica', which seems to suggests that she thought her husband was on the way home from Jamaica![9] In the same letter she asks for her compliments to be passed on to the Whalley's niece Mrs Mullins, though by this time she was divorced from William Mullins and had been married to the Reverend Robert Boyle Sullivan for three years! It is difficult to say from this how well she knew the Whalley family, as it is the only letter from her recorded by Hill Wickham.

General Horneck died on 8th April 1804, but his Will of 8th August 1802 left his entire estate to 'Henry Genean my faithful servant'. Mrs Horneck, who was still living in Bath at this time, would have received a military pension as his widow but seems to have been living beyond her means. She was now free to remarry and after 7 years of widowhood was approached by Dr Whalley. According to Hill Wickham, his friends had been urging him to remarry for some time, having 'no lady to preside at his

[8] Harrison, J., *The Life of the Right Honourable the Viscount Lord Nelson*, Vol. 1, Ranelagh Press, London, 1806, p.183.

[9] JCTSW II p.126

table'.[10] Thomas Sedgwick was now in his late sixties, and Mrs Horneck 10 years his junior.

In a letter to Hester Piozzi, dated April 18th 1812, seven months before his third marriage, he wrote:

> ...Mrs Lutwyche informed you of my fair prospect for the renewal of those domestic Comforts which I have, since I could observe, and reflect, valued above all others and without which the Life of Life, with me is gone — Your Lynx Eye and quick perception would enable you to distinguish Mrs Horneck's Talents and turn of mind, on a cursory acquaintance; but they could not give you the full knowledge of her various and uncommon merits, that I have after a confidential friendship and Correspondence with her of more than 30 years, — know she likes you, and I think I know you well enough to be confident that you like her; and when you know each other au fond, which I trust you will do , you will esteem and have sincere affection for each other.[11]

Her reply two weeks later goes as follows:

> Brynbella Monday 29th June 1812
> I direct to my Dear Doctor Whalley at Bath tho" I do believe this anxious evening sees him at London at the Theatre [this was at the farewell performance of Sarah Siddons at the Garrick]. You who never

---

[10] JCTSW I p.33
[11] TPL V p.154.

forget old friends will feel for our charming Siddons, tho' your heart is once more taking irrevocable Engagements may they be happy as I wish, and as you deserve. It is impossible to know Mrs Horneck and not to love her, equally impossible not to see that she loves you; I am glad that things are to end so, and pray divide my cordial congratulations between you ... [12]

Given all this, it is difficult to entirely believe the account by De Quincey, though there is considerable truth in it:

Finding himself in difficulties by the expenses of this villa [Mendip Lodge] going on concurrently with another large establishment, he [TSW] looked out for a good third marriage as the sole means within his reach of clearing off his embarrassments without proportionable curtailment of his expenses. It happened, unhappily for both parties, that he fell in with a widow lady who was cruising about the world with precisely the same views and in precisely the same difficulties. Each (or the friends of each) held out a false flag, magnifying their incomes respectively, and sinking the embarrassments. Mutually deceived they married, and one change immediately introduced at the splendid villa was the occupation of an entire wing by a lunatic brother of the lady's, the care of whom with a large allowance had been made to her by the Court of Chancery. This, of itself, shed a gloom over the place, which

---

[12] TPL p.155.

275

defeated the primary purpose of the Doctor (as explained by himself) in erecting it. Windows barred, maniacal howls, gloomy attendants from a lunatic hospital ranging about—these were the sad disturbances to the Doctor's rose-leaf system of life.[13]

12.2 This lithograph of a painting by Maxim Gauci is the only known portrait of Mrs Horneck Whalley. It probably dates from 1813-1814, after which point the couple separated.
© National Portrait Gallery, London

13 De Quincey, T., *The works of Thomas de Quincey Vol 11: Articles from Taits Magazine,* (North, J. Ed.), Pickering and Chatto, London, 2003, p.239.

The couple had married on 5th October 1813 and initially lived at 16 Queen Square Bath. This had at one time been General Horneck's address, though whether he rented or owned the property is not clear. As Thomas Sedgwick had sold his house in Bath after the death of his second wife, and as his marriage to Mrs Horneck took place at the beginning of the Bath season, this was a sensible arrangement. The following month, Mrs Siddons, now retired from the Garrick Theatre, read Macbeth to them at their house there.[14] According to Hill Wickham, his great uncle soon discovered that his third wife had debts of many thousands of pounds, which he now had to pay off.[15]

By July of the following year, the couple had moved to Thomas Sedgwick's usual summer residence of Mendip Lodge,[16] this time accompanied by the mad brother (Bulkeley Gould, 1753-1827), who the Court of Chancery had placed in the care of Mrs Horneck. This was too much for Thomas, for whom Mendip Lodge had always been his source of solace and joy. In a letter to Mrs Piozzi, dated 2nd July, he writes

> ...This once darling place is become a gilded millstone for me. As it would be a Folly and a Sin to keep at great Expense, what I can no longer hope to enjoy, I am looking out sharply, on all sides for a purchaser, of a Place and Property, highly attractive and eligible for a Person who has good Health fine Taste and a large Fortune. All the furniture is to be sold with the house etc...The Malady of my Chest, and, as wise Doctors say, of the bottom of

---

14 JCTSW II p.377 (Footnote)
15 ibid I p.34
16 ibid II p.372

my Wind pipe increases so much and made such a miserable Creature of me the whole of last Winter and Spring, that I have determined to... seek a milder and more settled climate somewhere in France... Mrs. Whalley cannot leave the Charge of her poor brother; nor indeed would she like the Journey and Voyage, or the accommodation and mode of living on the Continent. Her habits of Life and turn of Mind are peculiar, and new ones even with bonne Volonte, are not easily adopted, at 58 – Your old and true Friend, therefore is to become a wanderer at 68...[17,18]

Two days later, Mrs Piozzi replies:

Ah my Dear kind Friend my ever faithfully attached Doctor Whalley! And must we really part so without an well founded hope of meeting again in this World? Your sweet Letter would have taken my Breath quite away had not our beloved Siddons prepared me for its reception. Neither She nor I however can say a Word against your very rational Plan: Health is the first Thing to be considered, and as You say- our Lives are of Consequence to our Successors. I am glad I saw Mendip [Lodge] in its full Beauty and Glory – very glad. I have now seen the most beautiful place in England; under Possession of a Friend I must forever love and respect. [19]

17 TPL V p.283 (Footnote)
18 The Peace of Paris was signed in June 1814, and many now returned to the continent

To all but his closest friends, the reason for Dr Whalley's retreat to France was on the grounds of his health, but it is clear that the couple did not really get on. So he decided to leave for the continent alone; alone, that is, apart from his personal assistant Walter Amans, his servant John, his coachman and its two postillions! His dear niece, now Mrs Boyle Sullivan, and her husband had also decided to move to the continent some time after the signing of the first Treaty of Paris on 30th May 1814.

Mrs Lutwyche, a friend of Thomas Sedgwick as well as of Louis XVIII, had embarked for Paris soon after the Royal party returned to France at the end of June 1814. On September 7th she wrote to Dr Whalley from Calais to express her concern that he was now intending to move to France so late in the year,[20] but by October 10th he was in Orleans and planning to move south to Nevers shortly. Writing to his lifelong friend Arthur Anstey, he asks him to refer any person who might be interested in purchasing Mendip Lodge to his bailiff Mr Naish.[21] (John Naish would later lease Nash House, a Jacobean building in Lower Langford, from Thomas Sedgwick and would purchase it out-right in 1825, by which time Thomas Sedgwick was living in Windsor Terrace, Clifton.)[22] A two line footnote to the same letter states 'Amans is an unspeakable comfort to me in my very infirm health and dejected spirits'.

Thomas Sedgwick's relationship with Walter Slade Amons (Amans) is a curious one. He is described by Mrs Piozzi as a 'confidential servant',[23] but clearly he was treated far more

[19] TPL V p.282

[20] JCTSW II p.376

[21] ibid II p.384-5

[22] Dixon, J., *Every House Tells a Story*. (Fryer, J., et al., Eds), Langford History Group, Langford, 2006, pp.55-6.

generously by Thomas Sedgwick. According to his master, Walter Amans was of as good birth as himself but had been brought down by family circumstances. Apparently, his mother had refused to marry her cousin the Duke of Bolton and had instead married Mr Amans without her father's consent and been disinherited. Worse, her husband had proved to be both thoughtless and extravagant, which had reduced his son to servitude. In 1814 by various legacies including a handsome one from a Mr Slade of Marlborough buildings, Bath, Amans had become independent but had nonetheless agreed to accompany Thomas Sedgwick to France. However, soon after they reached France, Amans returned to England to be reunited with his family. At this point Mrs Piozzi and Hannah More seem to have got hold of the idea that Thomas Sedgwick had been deserted by his servant,[24,25] but this was not the case, and Thomas Sedgwick immediately corrected this misunderstanding.[26] The two remained firm friends until Thomas's death, and in his Will Amans was left a life interest in the dividends of Thomas's eight Somerset Coal Canal Shares.[27]

Thomas remained in Nevers over the winter of 1814/5. It is clear from Hannah More's letter to him there in February that his apartments were spacious and that his niece Mrs Boyle Sullivan was with him.[28] Here he enjoyed the company and hospitality of Count Coëtlosquet, the general of the district and a lively cultured man. The Count's military connections meant

23 TPL V pp.152-3

24 ibid V p.348

25 JCTSW II p.408

26 TPL V p.349 (Note 7)

27 The Will of Thomas Sedgwick Whalley, 25th June 1824

28 JCTSW II p.390-2. It is of significance that Hannah More refers to her as 'your fille', and it is true Frances had been like a daughter to him for many years, though never referred to like this anywhere else.

that he had early knowledge of Napoleon's escape from Elba at the end of February 1815, the start of his "one hundred days". The Count wrote immediately, urging Thomas Sedgwick to flee (*'Partez de suite et le plus tôt possible sera lent à retourner en Angleterre, sans vous arrêter'*).[29] He did not follow this advice but, confident in the abilities of the Duke of Wellington, retreated first to Mons, at the time an important allied base, and then to Leuven, 20 miles to the east of Brussels, which was within a few hours by fast coach from Antwerp should he need to make a hasty escape!

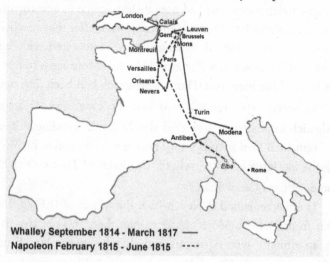

Whalley September 1814 - March 1817 ——
Napoleon February 1815 - June 1815 - - - -

12.3 Whalley's travels 1814-1817 and Napoleon's 100 days

Immediately after the Battle of Waterloo, Thomas wrote to his sister Mrs Wickham, giving a vivid account of his observations and experiences, a section of which is reproduced here. The whole, with the observations of his great nephew, indicates how fully informed Thomas was. It should be remembered that by

---

[29] JCTSW II p.393.

this time he was only accompanied by his servant John,[30] his friend Amans having returned to England:

> Though distant above thirty miles from the field [of battle], I distinctly heard the roar of artillery for twelve hours, and could perceive that it advanced and became louder on the left, where the Prussians were so far defeated as to fall considerably back. Night luckily came to their assistance, added to the extreme exhaustion of the French to whom some hours' repose became absolutely necessary...

> There was no affair on the 17th except between Blucher's rearguard and some French cavalry and light troops, Meanwhile, the Duke had reinforced his army with two of our best regiments of infantry cantoned between Brussels and Termond [sic] with nearly ten thousand of our matchless cavalry.....

> The field of battle being not more than five little leagues from Louvain, the thunder of artillery and musketry shook the windows at which I stood. From three to five the momentary roar of war grew louder; from five to seven it neither increased nor decreased ; from seven till half past nine it became, to my great joy fainter and fainter. But while I was reassuring the loyal and worthy family in whose house I lodged that the French were evidently beaten and retiring, various persons, some of them very intelligent and respectable, came in with

---

30 This was John Clarke. See Appendix 5, *The Will of Thomas Sedgwick Whalley*

haggard looks and confidently asserted that the Prussian Army was entirely routed, and that Lord Wellington was slowly retiring though disputing every inch of ground to Brussels...

I now began to think that my ear had greatly deceived me; and, as I could fly but not fight I had been foolhardy in placing such implicit confidence in the Duke of Wellington for my protection...

As necessity had no law, I threw myself humbly on the protection of the Almighty, and submitted with trembling to my fate. Fatigued, agitated and harassed, I was preparing to go to bed, when the post-horse master and another gentleman, kindly came to assure me that I might sleep and stay here in peace, as certain news had arrived that the great French army were [sic] defeated at all points and retreating in the greatest disorder...[31]

By April 1815 Mrs Horneck Whalley, for so she seemed now to be known,[32] had left both her house in Queen Square and Mendip Lodge, which was now in the sole care of Thomas Sedgwick's bailiff . According to Mrs Piozzi, she was living in a cottage 'within sight of the Mendip Lodge', forced to do so on financial grounds.[33] This does seem very curious, as she was still married to the relatively wealthy Thomas Sedgwick.

---

[31] JCTSW II p 401-3

[32] This seems to reflect the practice of including a mother's surname as part of a child's name, but a widow including a previous husband's name after a second marriage does not seem to have been commonplace.

[33] TPL V p.348

Thomas moved on to Leuven for three months, before travelling to Gand (Ghent) in September 1815. Then, in November he progressed to Brussels, where he stayed three months with William Mullins, William's third wife and their 18 year old heir, who William had so earnestly desired but whose second wife, Thomas Sedgwick's niece Frances, had failed to produce. Thomas has nothing but praise for his 'old and steady friend' and his family for their courtesy and charms.[34]

12.4 Rue Ducale, where Thomas stayed in 1815. Lord Byron lived in this house the following year

Despite being on the continent, the sale of Mendip Lodge was still very much on Thomas Sedgwick's mind. According to Hill Wickham, in December 1815 he wrote the following from Brussels to his legal adviser Arthur Anstey, son of Christopher Anstey:

---

[34] JCTSW II pp.412-3

Next summer a favourable offer may be made for Mendip Lodge, or, if not next year the following one. However straitened my income, I will contrive to live under it. I have been guilty of too much waste, and too many follies in money matters; but those who come after me, shall not have to reproach my memory for sacrificing their interest to the selfishness of selling, at a very inferior value, such a property as will one day not only sell for, but be well worth, the sum I now demand for it viz £30,000.[35]

Curiously, while Hill Wickham quotes this paragraph in Volume I, the letter itself is not included in Volume II, although there is a rather similar passage in a letter which Thomas Sedgwick had written in September 1815 from Gand.[36]

Thinking that Brussels would soon be too damp for his health, Thomas moved on to Chambéry. There he was joined by his old friend General Galateri, and they moved on together to Turin, arriving in September of 1816. He then travelled further south to Modena for the following winter and seems to have spent several months there. According to Hill Wickham, Thomas Sedgwick was now 'seized with a serious illness, during which he received the greatest kindness from the Duke and the Royal family, which insisted on sending him meat from their own kitchen and wine from their cellar'.[37] Thomas did not return to Turin until March of 1818 and seems to have already determined to return to England at once.[38]

---

[35] JCTSW I p.40

[36] ibid II p.411

[37] ibid I p.36

[38] TPL V p.543

By the end of March he was back in Bath and had purchased the central house (No 5) Portland Place.[39] This he furnished lavishly and elegantly, and when she viewed it on June 6th, Mrs Piozzi said she had seldom seen such splendid apartments.[40] Thomas Sedgwick's first recorded letter from his new address is to his great nephew and is dated July 1818. Hill Wickham was now aged 11 years and had just visited there. Thomas expresses the hope that he will be able to visit him again during the Christmas holidays.[41] Hill Wickham would write later that the house in Portland Place had been bought by his great uncle with every intention of his remaining there for the rest of his life. Sadly, this was soon to change.

12.5 Portland place today

[39] TPL VI pp.176-7
[40] ibid p.192
[41] JCTSW II p.442

A year later, in July 1819, Thomas finally sold Mendip Lodge to Benjamin Somers as he had always intended to do, but only three months later, Thomas's wife deserted him under a plea of ill treatment.[42] A letter from Mrs Piozzi to the actor Conway, dated 1st September 1819, reported 'old Whalley's wife running away from him and settling in Freshford'.[43] But in a slightly earlier letter to John Piozzi Salusbury,[44] Mrs Piozzi recounts that Mrs Whalley had long been wishing to part from her new husband and had now taken her mad brother and herself off while Thomas was away.[45] This event was soon well known in Bath and was reported by Mrs Piozzi in a letter dated 29th October 1819 to their mutual friend Mrs Pennington:

> Dr and Mrs Whalley seem to have been giving la comedie gratis here while the theatres are shut up. Incidents are certainly not wanting and the Catastrophe kept quite out of sight as Bayes recommends, for purpose of elevating and surprizing. Those who come to hear what I say on the subject go home disappointed for I say nothing and indeed have nothing to say.[46]

Various conjectures circulated as to her reason for so doing, but according to Hill Wickham, it was her accusation of cruelty

---

42 JCTSW I p.36

43 TIL p.285

44 This was a nephew by her marriage to her second husband. He had been so named in the hope that Mrs Piozzi would support her husband's brother's family. In the end, JSPS received her house, Brynbella, along with the rest of Mrs Piozzi's estates in Flint, Denbigh and Caernarvonshire, thus becoming one of the foremost landowners in Wales.

45 TPL VI p.317

46 TIL p.279

which forced Thomas Sedgwick to seek a legal separation.[47] Mrs Whalley subsequently attempted to correspond with him, but Hill Wickham says he 'never again addressed her'. While the grounds for separation were incompatibility, it would seem that Thomas made efforts to prove his wife was now as mad as her brother Bulkeley (1753-1727) and her mother had been before her.

After they separated, their friends were divided in their allegiances. Most sided with Thomas, but the influential Mrs Lutwyche and a few others sided with Mrs Whalley, and this group seem to have had no further contact with Thomas Sedgwick.[48] He, on the other hand, seems to have soon settled down to a comfortable life in the house of his sister and brother-in-law at Frome. In November 1820 Mrs Piozzi writes from Penzance to their mutual friend Mrs Sophia Pennington that 'Dr Whalley is playing Whist with his just Admirer Miss Hudson – so he will do well enough these 20 years'.[49] This would seem to suggest that she is observing him in Penzance, but a later letter shows she is merely passing on gossip.[50]

At the time of her second marriage, Mrs Horneck had not been well off, for she had been excluded from the Will of her first husband, General Horneck, who left all his estate to 'his faithful servant and approved friend Henry Genean'. This may be the reason why Whalley, after their marriage, found himself having to pay off her debts. Her own Will shows that, at the time of her death, she had a small income from commercial property in London. However, as part of a 'comfortable settlement', Mrs Horneck Whalley gained a large house at 2 Catherine Place, just

---

[47] JCTSW I p.36

[48] ibid II p.470 and footnote

[49] TPL IV p.460

[50] ibid p.496

north of Royal Crescent and south of Portland Place.[51] According to Hill Wickham, Mrs Whalley was thereafter known in Bath
for her 'handsome parties'.[52] One of these, held in September
1824, was at her 'mansion' in Queen Square (see below). This
might suggest that she had sold her Catherine Place house in
order to return to her old address in fashionable Queen Square,
where she had lived before her marriage to Whalley. However,
an advertisement placed shortly before her death, in the Belve-
dere on 16th September 1832, advertised an auction of her effects
from 2 Catherine Place, which she must have somehow retained
until that time.[53, 54]

> On Tuesday Mrs. Whalley gave a Private
> Concert at her mansion in Queen Square, consisting
> of an admirable selection of vocal and instrumental
> music from the works of Handel, Haydn, Mozart,
> Rossini, &c. The Concert was under the direction
> of Mr. C. W. Manners, who displayed great taste in
> the arrangements. In the course of the evening a
> beautiful original concerted piece, written by Mrs.
> Whalley, and composed by Mr. Manners, was twice
> performed : it is very effective, and was received
> with enthusiastic delight : the subject of the piece
> is an elegant tribute of friendship to the Duc
> D'Angouleme.

12.6 From the Bath Journal of 14 September 1824

After his separation from his third wife, Thomas let his
house in Portland Place, as he did not wish to live any longer in
Bath, where he was the subject of public ridicule. His finances

---

[51] JCTSW I p.36

[52] *Bath Chronicle and Weekly Gazette*, 13th August, 1829

[53] ibid 19th April, 1832

[54] ibid 20th September, 1832

now became stretched, as in 1822 he was compelled to buy back Mendip Lodge from Benjamin Somers, who had found himself unable to keep up the mortgage payments (see Chapter 13).

Seen from the 21st century, the status of a woman legally separated from her husband at this time was anomalous. This will be clear from the following insight. In the summer of 1822, while Mrs Whalley was living at Freshford, both she and Thomas Sedgwick's lifelong friend Sir Walter James were burgled. The miscreant was caught, and Mrs Whalley bounded over to prosecute him. She wished to involve Sir Walter, whose property had been returned prior to the arrest, in a joint action to reduce costs.[55] He refused to have anything to do with the action as, if successful, it would be likely to lead to the death of the individual:

> ...though I would punish the offence in question
> as it may deserve, yet as no blood of ours has
> been shed, nor any act of brutality been experi-
> enced, I cannot, nor will I either seek the death
> of the parties myself, or lend my aid or assistance
> to others who may be seeking thus the destruc-
> tion of their fellow creatures.

The prisoner, Richard French, was tried before Mr Justice Borrough at the summer assizes and found guilty. He duly hanged in the summer of 1822. The judge, in passing sentence on him, thought it proper to reserve the question of ownership of the recovered property for deliberation by the Twelve Common Law Judges. At that time the Twelve Judges operated as an advisory body on matters referred to them from County Courts.[56] These

---

55 JCTSW II p.483

56 Oldham, J., *Informal Law-Making in England by the Twelve Judges in the Late 18th and Early 19th Centuries*, Law and History Review, Paper 361, Georgetown Law

judgments were both informal and private, and the results of their deliberations were not regularly made public, but in this case they were.[57] Who did Mrs Whalley's earrings belong to? On the one hand they had been bought by Mrs Whalley with her own money and stolen from a house which she rented herself with her own money and which her estranged husband had never set foot in. Nevertheless, the Twelve Judges ruled that the house was not the wife's because by law she could have no property; it could therefore only be her estranged husband's. Thus, the earrings stolen from it also belonged to him! Sir James must have been aware of the likelihood of this ruling, for in his letter he goes on to say:

> In the indictment it is called your house and some
> of the articles are in law called yours. She is
> herself called yours; but I suppose you will not
> claim your rights or seize your lady.

It is odd that Sir James uses the term 'seize your lady' as by this time Thomas was legally separated from her, and it must have been obvious to all his friends that he did not want to have any more to do with her!

Faculty Publications, 2011
57 Russell, W.O., Ryan, E.. *Rex vs Richard French*. in Twelve Judges of England 1799-1824, Lincolns in Fields, London, 1839

CHAPTER 13
Thomas's Final Years

Almost immediately after Mrs Horneck Whalley 'ran off' to Freshford in the late summer of 1819, Thomas abandoned public life in Bath and viewed his 'gala days' as now being over.[1] He let out the house he had only recently purchased in Portland Place, and he went to lodge with his sister and brother-in-law in Frome,[2] there setting about obtaining a legal separation from his third wife.

In July 1819 he had been confident that Mendip Lodge, which had become a burden to him, had been sold to Benjamin Somers, 'to his great content.'[3] The contentment was because he had always felt unhappy about the breaking of the entail which was started by his first wife's first husband, John Sherwood, and which had denied the Somers family ownership of Langford Court after the death of Elizabeth Whalley (née Jones).

---

[1] JCTSW I p.470

[2] The house was eventually sold in February 1834 after a Decree of the Court of Chancery following an action taken by Augusta Edgell against Wickham. (See Chapter 14)

[3] JCTSW II p.462

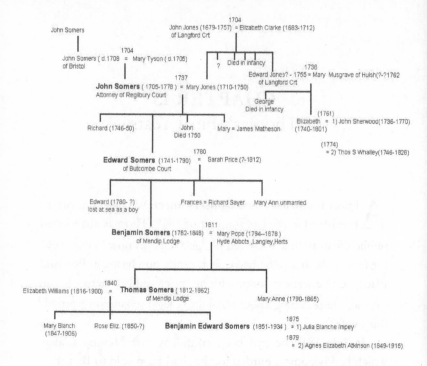

13.1 The Somers family and its relationship to Elizabeth Whalley née Jones

Despite the footnote in Hill Wickham's book which says the sale was never completed,[4] there is no doubt that it took place and the house and estate was purchased by Benjamin Somers on 14th June 1819 for £22,500, though subject to a mortgage of £15,000 to Arthur Anstey Calvert, Thomas Sedgwick's legal adviser.[5,6]

[4] JCTSW II p.462 (Footnote)

[5] Papers of the late Commander M. Lawder, Somerset Heritage Centre, Taunton. Unlisted collection, ref A/CHZ Acc M/1386. Box 8 Deeds 4 page 583 and Deeds 2 page 268

[6] Arthur Anstey (Calvert) was an attorney and son of Christopher Anstey, author of the New Bath Guide.

And so in April 1820, free of both his third wife and the burden of Mendip Lodge, Thomas Sedgwick set sail for France to visit his adored niece Frances Sullivan (née Sage). After a rough crossing from Brighton to Dieppe, he made his way to La Flèche via Rouen, Bernay, Alençon and Le Mans, accompanied by his ever faithful manservant John. On May 29th 1820 he is able to write to his great nephew:

> La Flèche is rather a pretty town in a pleasant and fertile country. There is a famous extensive and handsome college here [This was the famous National Military Academy], where languages, mathematics, military sciences etc. are taught under the best preceptors, and which is governed by a general and a colonel. The latter (besides several other gentlemen) has visited me, and is a noble looking, well bred and agreeable man. Mrs. Sullivan, my niece and your cousin was overjoyed to see me. The house she has engaged for me is one of the best in the town. I have a handsome drawing room, a large saloon opening into it, a dining parlour on the other side of a vestibule, a large kitchen, and other offices and a large and beautiful bed chamber, with a dressing room for myself and a good bedchamber for John (his manservant) and an inferior one for a French servant. My best apartments look in to a pretty flower garden full now with various sorts of roses in full bloom, and the house standing within a court, is shut up at night. I am as quiet here as if I was twenty miles from a town. I shall have a very select and agreeable society who will come to me

> four or five times a week, to chat or play whist and
> a game called Boston. [7]

It will be recalled that Frances and her second husband, the Reverend Robert Boyle Sullivan, had moved there from England sometime after the signing of the second Treaty of Paris in November 1815, but this was Thomas's first visit to La Flèche. It is clear from this letter that the Sullivans lived comfortably in France, but there is no clue as to how their life was financed or whether the Reverend Robert Boyle Sullivan was employed as an Anglican priest while living there. In fact there is no mention whatsoever of Robert Sullivan on any page of the two volumes edited by Hill Wickham.[8] During that summer of 1820 Thomas became very well established in La Flèche and a respected member of the local community. This is not surprising; he spoke fluent French (though we are told with a terrible accent) and was a royalist who was already well connected with French society from his earlier visits to the continent.

About this time rumours began to circulate that Mendip Lodge was to be bought by the Duchess of York. There must have been some hope that this would happen, as the main bedroom at the rear of the house had by this time become known as the Duchess of York's bedroom. A press report in the 1950s describes the Lodge as being 'almost bought by Queen Caroline'.[9] This seems to be a repeat of the claim by Coyshe et al.

---

[7] JCTSW II p.476

[8] Nor have I been able to discover anything else about his life after he left the curacy of Bradford on Avon - CDS

[9] 'Ruin in the Mendips – The end of an Eighteenth-century Castle in the Air', *The Times*, October 9th 1958

> The state bedroom, like the dining-room, is at the
> back, and was fitted up with much magnificence
> in expectation of its being occupied by the late
> Duchess of York on an intended visit to this spot.[10]

This would have been Caroline of Brunswick, who had separated from her husband almost immediately after their marriage and since 1814 had been living rather scandalously on the continent. On the death of George III in 1820, her husband became king and she returned to England, where she had always been very popular, unlike her husband George IV, who was now trying to divorce her. He forbad her from attending the coronation, but she nonetheless attempted to do so but was barred at the doors of the Abbey. While the timing of her return to England might well suggest that she could have had an interest in purchasing Mendip Lodge and indeed may have met Thomas Sedgwick in France, it is hardly likely that he, now in his mid 70s, would have wished to get involved in a very public dispute between the new king and his queen. Whatever the truth of the matter, a public denial reached the press in 1821. This was published in the Bristol Gazette and reprinted in the Morning Post of July 16th. It would seem that the owner at this time was still Dr Benjamin Somers, as a report of a coach accident involving him and a Mr Ricketts at Froxfield in December 1822 refers to him as the owner of Mendip Lodge.[11]

When and why Thomas returned to England is not clear. Hill Wickham is rather confused about this period, which is not surprising when he himself was away at school.[12] As a

---

10 Coyshe, A.W., Mason, E.J., Waite, V. *The Mendips,* Robert Hale Ltd, London, 1954, p.130

11 *London Gazette,* 9th December, 1822

12 At the end of 1819 he transferred from Southampton to Warminster –

consequence, there are few letters recorded by him at this time. He states that 'with the exception of the winter of 1823, which he [TSW] spent with his niece Mrs Sullivan, he visited among his relatives until 1825'.[13] But we have seen that by the summer of 1820 Thomas was already living in La Flèche. It is likely that while there he was visited by his other niece Frances Stafford (née Whalley), who lived only a few miles away. The two cousins had been good friends since childhood, and by this time both their fathers had died – Colonel Francis Whalley in 1813 and Isaac Sage in 1818 – thus Thomas Sedgwick Whalley was their only surviving relative of his generation. It is also significant that the last child of John and Frances Stafford, who had been born in August 1828 shortly after Robert Boyle Sullivan's death, was named Boyle Torriano Stafford.[14]

Sometime early in 1822, Thomas returned to England. This is likely to have been because of the concerns of his solicitor and executor James Anthony Wickham or perhaps a letter from Benjamin Somers himself, who had found he was unable to keep up the mortgage payments on Mendip Lodge. As a result, Whalley bought the house, its original contents and the estate back on 10th May 1822 for £5000 less that he had sold it for.[4] By July 1822 Thomas Sedgwick was back in North Hill Frome, the Wickhams'

---

probably to Lord Weymouth's Grammar School, established 1707, whose pupils had included Thomas Arnold, later Head Master of Rugby, and Samuel Squire, Bishop of St Davids, who might well have been related to Thomas Sedgwick on his mothers side.

13 JCTSW I p.36

14 A Mr Torriano also attended Thomas Sedgwick Whalley's funeral in La Flèche, who is described by Hill Wickham as being 'the son of one of his oldest and most intimate friends' (JCTSW I p.38). In fact this was probably a grandson of Charles Stafford born in Wells in 1716 but who does not seem to be mentioned in any letter of the two Hill Wickham volumes and died in Bath in 1791. A Major Torriano, perhaps his father, is described as having been killed at Toulon when it was taken by Napoleon in 1793 (JCTSW I p.247).

family home. His old friend Sir Walter James wrote to him there about the forthcoming trial which followed the burglary of his and Mrs Whalley's houses[15] (see also Chapter 12). Thomas Sedgwick remained at North Hill Frome with this nephew and his family until at least October of that year. This was a large house which had regularly accommodated him ever since his sister Mary married James Wickham, the father of James Anthony Wickham and grandfather of Hill Dawe Wickham, in 1763.

One might have expected Somers to have moved out and Thomas Sedgwick to have reoccupied the house after he bought it back in May 1822, but this does not seem to have happened. It is quite possible that he allowed Somers to continue living there as a tenant, which would account for him still being identified as the owner in December 1822.

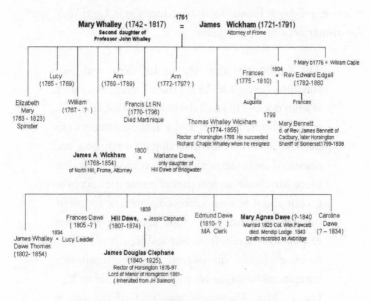

13.2 The Wickham family tree

15 JCTSW II pp.482-5

It seems, then, that at the invitation of his cousin Penelope Pennington, which Thomas received while at North Hill, he spent a comfortable winter of 1822/3 with the Penningtons in Dowry Square, Clifton, arriving there in November 1822.[16] Penelope's original invitation had extended to Mrs Sullivan, but it is not clear if she joined them there. By May 1823 Thomas was back in London, staying at his friend Aman's new house, which he found greatly to his liking,[17] but was soon back in France, staying in Versailles with Frances for the summer. Their address at this time is the finest; the avenue de Sceaux is one of three roads that radiate from the Place d'Armes in front of the Palace of Versailles. Once again there is no mention of her husband, Robert Boyle Sullivan, who was to die only a year later.

Thomas wrote from Versailles to his great nephew, who was now on holiday at Frome from his education at Lord Weymouth's Grammar School, Warminster:

> The summer is drawing to its close with less sunshine (except in 1816) than I ever remember. Within doors I have all the comforts that spacious, commodious, pleasant and warm apartments can bestow, added to the affectionate attentions and animated and entertaining conversation of my dear niece Mrs. Sullivan who never leaves me except to go out about housekeeping concerns, or to call on our few acquaintances. One agreeable and very respectable family from Shropshire named Owen I have lately discovered to be temporary inhabitants of this noble town. The mother of Mrs. Owen, Mrs. Cummins, was one of my oldest

16 JCTSW II p.487
17 ibid p.490

friends... My weak health has prevented me from going to Paris to visit several noble families, and particularly Count Coëtlosquet who is, and who merits to be, high in the King's favour and is director general with the war with Spain. He is reckoned to be one of the cleverest, and is certainly one of the best-bred and most agreeable men in France. But as I cannot go to him, overwhelmed as he is with the most important affairs, he has very kindly promised to come and dine with me and Mrs. Sullivan at Versailles next Sunday se'nnight....[18]

Thomas returned to England, as he had intended to, in October 1823. He was still nominally the owner of Mendip Lodge, but there is no evidence he ever lived there again after his separation from Mrs Horneck Whalley in 1818.

Perhaps remembering his pleasant stay with the Penningtons two years before, Thomas Sedgwick now purchased the lease of 4, Windsor Terrace, Clifton, at its spectacular location above the Avon Gorge. This was only a few hundred yards from his cousin Penelope Pennington's house in Dowry Square and close to the house in Clifton where his lifelong friend Mrs Piozzi frequently stayed. Windsor Terrace had been completed in 1820 by William Watts. He had made a fortune from discovering how to make perfectly round lead shot, then almost bankrupted himself in building the terrace. Thomas's first letter from his new house is to his great nephew, dated November 1825. He writes in response to his 'darling Oxford Scholar's...affectionate and entertaining letter'.[19]

18 JCTSW II p.493
19 ibid II p.494

13.3 Thomas's house in Windsor Terrace Clifton (arrowed), viewed from the Cumberland Basin Swing Bridge over the River Avon

13.4 4 Windsor Terrace, later given to Hannah Moore

Hill Dawe Wickham was by this time an Oxford undergraduate, having gone up to Exeter College in 1824. He would eventually follow his great uncle into holy orders.

One event in 1825 which greatly pleased Thomas Sedgwick was the marriage in September of another great niece, the beautiful Mary Agnes Dawe Wickham.[20] She was the second youngest daughter of his executor James A Wickham and the younger sister of Hill Wickham. Her husband, Major (later Colonel) William Fawcett, was a member of a distinguished military family. Both his father and grandfather Sir William Fawcett KB had been generals.

A letter which Thomas received at Frome from his old friend the Marquise de la Pierre, dated March 28th 1826, shows that, only a few months after he had leased it, his new Clifton house in Windsor Terrace did not suit him and that he was recovering from yet another illness.[21] Hill Wickham says that his great uncle had imagined that the fogs of the Avon were the cause. Fogs in the Avon Gorge are not a very frequent feature of today's winter, but at that time the River Avon had become the main sewage outlet for a city of 60,000 people and was its major shipping route. This may have partly contributed to the decline in popularity of the Hotwells Pump Room at the river's edge directly below Windsor Terrace.

It would seem that by now Thomas Sedgwick had realised he did not have very long to live, and he set about trying to put his affairs in order. He gave up his 13th Coombe Prebendary of Wells. His resignation is dated 23rd January 1826, and his great niece Mary Dawe Fawcett née Wickham and her elder brother, Edmund Dawe Wickham, witnessed the resignation document. Thomas

---

20 TSW II pp.498-9

21 ibid II p.496

was now eighty years old and far from well, as his shaky signature demonstrates.[22] He was still making efforts to sell Mendip Lodge and set about making the property more attractive by building a new drive through the Park, with two entrance Lodges where it joined the West Harptree Turnpike (see Chapter 6).

13.5 Thomas Sedgwick's shaky signature in 1827

In 1827 we find him trying to retrieve the interest, if not the capital sum owing to him, from William Mullins, who had been Frances Sullivan's first husband. William had now become the second Lord Ventry and inherited the long awaited fortune from his very long-lived father. It has already been pointed out in Chapter 8 that Frances Mullin's divorce from William had been convenient to both parties, and the evidence to enable the Church Court to agree to the divorce was probably carefully engineered by her father, Isaac Sage. After the divorce it was not surprising that Thomas remained on very good terms with William, who in 1815 he described as 'my old and steady friend Mr Mullins'.[23] This may well explain why Thomas Sedgwick, who had already advanced half the money for Frances dowry in 1790, was prepared to advance further money to Frances's former husband.[24] The loan appears to have been made on the

---

[22] *Registers of the Bishops of Bath and Wells*, Somerset Heritage Centre, Taunton, Somerset Ref D/D/B Reg 34 f.31v

[23] JCTSW II p.412

[24] At one point, Thomas describes the first Lord Ventry as 'a mean old skinflint', and this meanness might well have contributed to the break-up of the marriage,

understanding that it would be repaid on Mullins succeeding to the title, which happened on 11 Jan. 1824. However, after three years the interest was not up to date, nor was their any likelihood of the capital sum being repaid immediately.

The letter below, which Thomas Sedgwick addressed to Wm Bromley Esq, Grays Inn Square, Holborn, London, was written from the Frome house of his brother-in-law, who was not only his executor but a lawyer. It is reproduced here in full:

North Hill Frome April 27th 1827

My Dear Sir,

As you wrote me that Mr Bateman thought the debenture for the good purpose of paying Lord Ventry's numerous creditors,[25] of course by instalments, would be sent to them about Easter, I wish to know whether they have been or when they are likely to be sent. If a debenture should not be sent to me stipulating for payment in fair proportion to my just, and may I add paramount claim, on Lord Ventry I will cast aside all further regard and indulgence towards a noble man who has grossly violated every principle of honour friendship and gratitude in return for the many efforts and sacrifices I have made to serve him.

As usual he has not answered my last letter; therefore, as soon as I know that he and his privy

---

since Frances never became a mistress of a house in England.

[25] This would have been the first Lord Ventry, who had many debts.

counsellors have not done for me what they have done for their other creditors I will consult with you as to the measures it would be most eligible for me to adopt, in order to compel them to do me justice. I am too old and too near my grave to neglect a stake of such importance. I informed you that I had found a letter, from Lord Ventry, which tho' torn in pieces a sudden presentiment that it might prove of some consequence to my interest had withheld me from burning. I therefore carefully pasted every piece of the letter together and will copy the material content of it for your inspection. It was written by Lord Ventry from Boulogne a short time, perhaps a fortnight before Mr Simpson called on me at Amans's, where you met him and aided in discussing with him my claim on Lord Ventry and when he offered me as you must remember six per cent on that part of the debt due to me on the Deed sign'd by his Lordship; while I contended for the minor interest specified in such deed of 500£ per ann. (something less than 7 percent from the date of the Deed up to the time of the old Lords death) – a very moderate remuneration for the risk I ran of losing the whole debt in case the present Lord V'y died before his father who lived above seven years from the date of the deed.

I am dear sir your faithful obedient servant,

Thos Whalley

The obvious resentment is surprising, since Thomas Sedgwick had spent the winter of 1815-16 in the Mullins' house in Brussels and wrote cordially of his gratitude for the kindness of his host.[26] Thomas's obvious anxiety may have arisen because of the death of Frances's second husband in 1826, which may well have reduced her income. Whatever Robert Boyle Sullivan's circumstances might have been, Frances was soon in financial difficulties, and Thomas was referring to 'the pressure of pecuniary obligations on her mind'.[27]

The following is from the second Lord Ventry's undated letter which Thomas refers to above:

> The Rev'd Dr Whalley
> No 32 Connaught Terrace
> New Road [Now Euston Road]
> London
>
> Dear Dr Whalley,
>
> I am sorry to inform you that I fear I shall have great difficulty in settling my affairs although I hope in time to accomplish it. I would willingly allow you annuity interest if I could find the wherewithal to answer the numerous demands against me but you cannot imagine how harassed I am. In my opinion the fair and straight forward [sic] is to put it into the hands of our respective solicitors and abide by their decision, that I am willing to do and to pay when and as soon as I can

---

26 JCTSW II p.413
27 ibid II p.507

but promising to do what is impossible is foolish; I shall write to Mr Simpson when I hear of his arrival. I regret extremely that you were detained in town in consequence of this business I can't see the necessity of your remaining. I should think that your friend and mine would arrange it as well absent as present by giving them the particulars, the delay at present cannot be long Believe me

Yours sincerely

Ventry

Finally, there is an addendum from Thomas Sedgwick, written the following day:

Saturday April 28th

Such are the most material contents of Lord Ventry's loosely worded and incorrect letter. He detests writing so much that when compelled to it hurries over the detested task. Proper stops, clearness of expression and even grammar being frequently neglected. Dates he despises but his signature will prove that the letter in question was written after his father's death as will its direction and contents that I recv'd it at Mr. Amans while waiting there week after week for Mr. Simpson's arrival in town.

According to Lord Vy's proposal you as my solicitor's agent met Mr. Simpson at his Lordship's at Mr. Aman's on purpose to arrange the business and specify all my just Claim. Mr Simpson's subsequent and shuffling behaviour I need not to you enlarge. Lord Vy's aberrance of his being willing if he could find the wherewithal to allow me annuity interest (by which I know he means ten percent) can only allude to the Deed signed by him. For his note of hand for 600£ several years after engages him expressly to pay interest on it of 5 per cent. And the various smaller sums acknowledged by his signature at Boulogne to be due to me have nothing to do with annuity interest.[28]

Five hundred pounds I have agreed to take on the debt ascertained in the Deed signed by Lord Vy year by year till his father's death who bequeathed freehold estates to his eldest son, the net Rents of which amount to more than 20 times 500£ per ann. The old peer's whole property be it remembered was in Ireland and all in land.

Pray favour me soon with a few lines that I may know whether ap… [this is probably 'appropriate' but is obscured by a tear] steps have been taken reflecting Lord Vy creditors etc.

Quite apart from the delay due to the chaotic state of the finances of his father, the 1st Lord Ventry, there were other

---

[28] It would seem from the bequests made in TSW's Will that the total sum owing was at least £2200.

complications.[29] The recently elevated second Lord Ventry may already have been seriously ill by this time, as he died six months later on 5th October 1827 at his residence, Château de la Cocherie, near Boulogne. Because his son had predeceased him, the title and estate now passed to William's cousin, making recovery of the debt even more unlikely. It is possible that the Whalley estate never recovered this sum, although there were clear instructions in Thomas Sedgwick's Will that this sum was still owing, and James Wickham, Thomas' executor, would have pursued this claim. Almost certainly, Frances Sullivan's financial embarrassment was because her £1000 a year divorce settlement, which was supposed to be continued by William Mullins's 'heirs and assigns' for the rest of her life, had ceased at his death.

During the winter of 1827/8 Thomas Sedgwick had been far from well. In December he was living with his elder brother at Winscombe Court, from where he wrote to his nephew, who was about to take his final degree examinations at Oxford, saying that he expected to spend Christmas in bed.[30] In April, though, he was sufficiently well to return to Clifton, where he says in a further letter to his nephew that he had bid a last, sad farewell to Hannah More:

> Yesterday I went to bid a last sad adieu to my dear admirable old friend Mrs. H. More. I sat two hours with her, and, ye gods! we talked – how we did talk![31]

---

[29] It may also be relevant to the financial difficulties which William Mullins was having at this time that a Mrs Mullins, one assumes his third wife, was one of the names on the list of creditors of Marsh Sibbald & Co, the Regent Street bank which failed following the crash of 1824.

[30] JCTSW II p.504

[31] ibid II pp.505-6

This must have been at 4 Windsor Terrace, which by then he had made over to Hannah. She had turned to Thomas and John Harford for advice when she discovered that her servants at her house Barley Wood, near ~~Winford~~, were stealing from her. They suggested that she should move into Thomas's house in Windsor Terrace, where she would be close to her friends. The dramatic account of her departure from ~~Winford~~ is vividly described by Reverend Thompson in his *The Life of Hannah More*.[32] This author, who was the Curate of Wrington, also records that after Thomas's death his executor, James A Wickham, continued to show 'the most assiduous attention to her comfort'. That would have pleased his uncle. There is now a plaque on the house in Windsor Terrace, recording Hannah More's occupation (incorrectly given as being from 1829). She lived there contentedly until her death in 1833. Sadly, there is no plaque recording her friend and benefactor who had made this occupation possible.

By July 1828, or perhaps earlier, Thomas had decided to go to France to rescue his beloved niece from her financial difficulties. On the 14th of that month, while in London, he made a final modification to his Will and then wrote to his great nephew to tell him of his decision:

> My choice therefore lay, especially after knowing of Mrs. Sullivan's distress, between La Flèche and Exeter and all the circumstances impartially considered, none of my English friends can wonder at my preferment of the former to the latter, for my residence next autumn, winter and spring. Beyond the latter I dare not extend my views though should I be so fortunate as to sell

32 Thompson, H., *The Life of Hannah More,* Blackwood and Sons, Edinburgh, 1838, pp.313-21

beautiful Mendip Lodge this year and my life be prolonged by wintering in a warmer climate I would do the utmost to engage Mrs. Sullivan to accompany me back to England and live in some snug and pleasant house in Devonshire.[33]

He assured him that he was now in rather better health and would make the journey by several stages in his easy running coach, taking 4 or 6 stops per day, and so no one should have any fear for him. He anticipated arriving on or shortly after the 28th July, but the exact date is not known. When he did arrive, he probably learnt of the death of William Mullins and the fact that the annuity to Frances of £1000 p.a. had ceased. This may be the reason why he added the following to his Will on 11th August:

I Thomas Sedgwick Whalley DD do hereby acknowledge to you the Executor of my last Will and Testament that I owe my niece Mrs Frances Elizabeth Sullivan otherwise Sage widow of the late Revd. Boyle Sullivan residing at La Flèche Department of the Sarthe in France the sum of one thousand and fifty two pounds sterling which she lent to me and which I am bound to repay her as follows Viz four hundred and fifty two pounds sterling on the twenty fifth day of December one thousand eight hundred and twenty eight and six hundred pounds sterling on the twenty fifth day of June one thousand eight hundred and twenty nine I order you the Executor of my last Will and testament in case my death should take place

[33] JCTSW II p.507

before the payment of the abovementioned Debt
to pay my niece Mrs Frances Elizabeth Sullivan
the aforesaid sum of One thousand and fifty two
pounds sterling out of my property before any
Legacy or other sum of money whatsoever.

It may, on the other hand, have been to pay off the mortgage for
a new house, as on 6th August 1828 Thomas Sedgwick made
arrangements to buy a house at Six rue Vernevelle, La Flèche for
Frances. This is one of the most magnificent houses in the town.
Built in the early 18th century for Louis Huger de la Molière, it is
now a listed National Monument and currently houses a centre
for the contemporary arts and is known as Hôtel Huger. At the
time of purchase the main house consisted of the following:

Ground floor
A large hall with the main staircase, two reception rooms,
two dining rooms, a kitchen, a pantry.

First floor,
Seven bedrooms, two small dressing rooms.

Attic
Four rooms with access from the main staircase and two
side staircases.

13.6 Frances's new house at 6 Rue Vernevelle La Flèche as it is today

Why did he buy this large house for a 59-year-old, English widow? Perhaps it was felt by both of them that it was a wise investment, and owning such a house would mean Frances was no longer liable for any rent she might have otherwise have had to pay out of her reduced income. Up to this time Frances had been living nearby in the suburb of Saint-Jacques, but whether she owned or rented a property is not known.

The new house cost 24,000 F at the time (about $4350 or just under £1000) and was originally the property of the Mother Superior of the Convent of Notre Dame of La Flèche. It had been bequeathed to the Convent on her death in 1818, but the following year it was sold to Charles Côme Rivière, a barrister, to pay off the Convent's debts. Frances's purchase was transacted by a mortgage with a deposit of 6000F; other payments were due on 25th June 1829, with a final payment no later than 21st November 1829. The sale was completed on 27th October 1829. Rivière had made a handsome profit thereby, since he had bought the property in 1819 for only 17600F. In the documentation of the sale *'Dette Walley* [sic] *et recu Rivière'*. *Docteur Walley* (sic) undertook to pay Rivière 6045.85F on the following Christmas Day, by which time he had died, and this could explain the sums mentioned in the French Codicil to his Will.

Thomas Sedgwick died peacefully in his armchair in Mrs Sullivan's house at Faubourg Saint-Jacques on 4th September 1828.[34] The codicil was subsequently translated and added to his Will in London on 4th February 1829. This was then proved on the 7th, with James Anthony Wickham, Thomas's nephew, the sole executor. Such a codicil was a wise measure, since most of Thomas Sedgwick's estate capital was tied up in Mendip Lodge, which had so far failed to sell.

The fact that the Staffords and the Sullivans were living only 30 miles apart in France explains why General Stafford, doubtless accompanied by his wife, Frances's cousin, was able to attend the funeral. The only other attendee mentioned by Hill Wickham was Mr Torriano, the son of one of Thomas's oldest friends Major Torriano. An Anglican clergyman came out from Nantes to officiate.[35] Thomas had made a great impression on La Flèche society when he stayed there during a previous extended visit from the summer of 1820 until late in 1822. Thus, the wishes of visiting Anglicans were over-ruled by the local residents, and Thomas was buried at La Flèche in the burial ground of the Roman Catholic church of St Thomas. His final resting place was initially railed off, but these railings have since been lost. The tomb, however, is still there.

---

[34] Hill Wickham says the 3rd, but the death certificate says the 4th at 'trois heures du soir'.

[35] JCTSW I p.38

13.7 Dr Thomas Sedgwick's tomb in the
cemetery of St Thomas, La Flèche

The inscription is as shown below, which is curiously not quite
the same as set out in Hill Wickham's book, from which one must
conclude that he never visited the grave of his great uncle. It looks
rather as if what had been written in England by Thomas's
executor was modified on site by the person who supervised the
engraving.

THOMAE SEDGWICK WHALLEY SANCTAE
THEOLOGIIAE DOCTORIS
EX COMITATU SOMERSETTIAE, CUI MAGISTRATUS
PRAERAT
IN ANGLIA
ECCLESIAE CATHEDRALIS WELLENSIAE
PRAEBENDARII

VIGEBANT IN EO BENEVOLENTIA ERGA DEUM
PIETAS
BENEVOLENTIA ERGA HOMINES VERE CHRISTIANA
LIBERALITAS ERGA EGENOS EFFUSA
HUMANITATEM VILLAE FORMOSISSIMAE SUAE
MENDIP VICINIAE
TESTANTUR
AMORE ITAQUE QUEM PER LONGAM VITAM
INGENII EXCELLENTIA ET MOREM SUAVITATE
CONCILIARAT
MORTE TANDEM IN DESIDERIUM ACERRIMUM
COMMUTATO
ONIMBUS CHARUS SUIS CHARISSIMUS
OBIT TERIO DIE SEP. A.D. MDCCCXXVIII
AETATIS SUAE LXXXIII

It should perhaps be added that De Quincey's widely quoted contention that Whalley died 'in a common lodging house…in all things the very antithesis of that splendid abode which he had planned for the consolation of his melancholy and the gay beguilement of his old age' has not the slightest foundation in truth.[36] Whether De Quincey was misled or added this out of pure spite can only be guessed at, but it is clear from this and earlier accounts that De Quincey, who as a boy had lived close to the Whalleys in Bath, disliked Thomas Sedgwick and his lifestyle.

The news of Thomas's death reached England very quickly and was in the newspapers within two weeks. [37] It is possible that Frances herself would have undertaken to take the news and

[36] Coysh, A.W., Mason, E.J., Waite. V., *The Mendips*, Robert Hale Ltd, London, 1954, p.132
[37] *Bath Chronicle*, 15 September 1828

Thomas's Will to England, or it could have been his faithful servant John Clark, who in any case would have had to return to England, taking Thomas's personal effects and his carriage. Perhaps she travelled with him. Under the terms of the Will, Thomas's executor, James Wickham, took over the ownership of Mendip Lodge, and John Clarke received one year's full wages, fifty guineas, plus a further sum of two hundred and twenty pounds. By the following year Rutter in his book was describing Mendip Lodge as 'The seat of the late Dr. Whalley and property of James Anthony Wickham of North Hill Frome'.[38]

So what happened to Frances? One popular belief is that she lived on quietly in France in poverty recalling her days as "Queen of Bath", but this is quite untrue.[39] One must assume from the purchase of the house at 6 Rue Vernevelle, which Thomas had paid for, that Frances had intended to continue to live on in France, and yet two years later, on 3rd September 1830, she sold the house to Edouard Le Monnier de Lorrière and his wife for 26000F. This change of mind was probably precipitated by the unrest in France which preceded the abdication of Charles X. There had been three poor harvests, 1826-1829, and food was now in short supply in France. Perhaps the trigger for Frances was the riot of March 24, 1830 in Merdrignac, only 100 miles from La Flèche,[40] but by 26th July there was full revolution against the Bourbons in Paris, followed by the abdication of Charles X on 2nd August.[41]

---

[38] Rutter,J.,*Delineations of the North Western Division of the County of Somerset and of its antediluvian Bone Caverns,* Longman Rees and Co., London, 1829, pp.112-3

[39] Lowndes, W., *They came to Bath,* Redcliffe Press, Bristol, 1982, p. 90

[40] Tilley, C., *The political process in revolutionary France 1830-1832,* University of Michigan, 1973

[41] For a full account of these events, see Latimer E.W., *France in the 19th Century 1830-1890,* Bibliobazaar Books, Charleston, 2006

Where Frances then went is unknown, but she probably came directly to Bath. While its hey-day was past, it was still a fashionable place to be, but rather than being the haunt of East Indiamen seeking eligible young brides, it was becoming the home of retired elderly gentry. Sir Isaac Pitman, the inventor of shorthand, who came to Bath in 1839, wrote, 'Of the many beautiful cities in this fair country, Bath is unquestionably the most beautiful'.[42] He would later retire to the Royal Crescent. Frances was in Bath by 1841, by which time the Great Western Railway had arrived. The census of that year records her as living in Gloucester Place with her 30 year old servant Nancy Price. This was a district consisting largely of lodging houses. Although the Gloucester Place houses were unnumbered in the Census, they were located adjacent to Burlington Street, and the house was run by a female lodging house keeper, Mary Roberts. There were four other female inhabitants and one male occupant. Gloucester Place was severely damaged in the Bath Baedecker raids of World War II but had been described in Egan's Guide of 1819 as being of no particular architectural merit.[43] On the Ordnance Survey map of 1952, the same site is named Gloucester Place, but it is shown as ruins. This corresponds to the City's bomb damage maps, which show the site as being so badly damaged that demolition was necessary. Later planning records show applications to build on the site in 1979, 1983 and 1985. When rebuilding finally took place, the houses on it were renumbered as 1-4 Burlington Street.

Why did Frances choose to live in such a location? It was close to Thomas Sedgwick's old house in Royal Crescent, but it is unlikely that anyone she knew would still be living there. More likely it was because it was in reach of the church she had attended and where she had been first married. By 1851 Frances had

[42] Lowndes, W., *The Royal Crescent in Bath*. Redcliffe Press, Bristol, 1981, pp.81-2
[43] Egan, P., *Walks through Bath*, Meyler and Son, Bath,1819. pp.139-40

moved to more desirable rooms at 2 Paragon Buildings. Perhaps she was able to do so following the final settling of Thomas Sedgwick's estate. This house was nearer to her church of St Swithin's, which could now be reached on the level. The 1851 census describes three households as living there: Thomas Peggs, the lodging keeper, with his wife, daughter and niece, the last two being described as dressmakers; this family also had one servant; then CA Morewood, PhD,[44] aged 70, who seems to have been a physician; and Frances Sullivan, with her 40 year old servant Sarah Mercer from Chew Stoke. The census entry states Frances as being aged 75 years, though in fact she was 81 years old!

So it would seem that her annuity extended to supporting one servant, and one might suppose she occupied one floor of the three story building. Her living costs therefore would not have been much more than £300 a year at the time. Her annuity must have come partly from the sale of her house in France, which raised F26000 in 1830 and had given her about £1000 Sterling, but the 5% interest rates applicable to the UK at the time would only have provided Frances with £50 p.a., so she must have had other sources. These could have been other sums from the sale of her jewellery, and her income may have been supplemented by her cousin James A Wickham, Thomas Sedgwick Whalley's executor, who lived until 1854. It is possible that until 1834, when it was sold, Frances benefited from the rent of Whalley's old house Portland Place. Clearly, had her divorce settlement of '£1000 per year for life' not ceased with the death of her first husband, she would have been living in considerable luxury. As it was, it seems she had enough for her rent, living expenses and one servant.

Frances died of bronchitis on 5th February 1857, but her 1851 Will was not proved until May 1857 in London. This contained

---

[44] Was this perhaps an abbreviation for Doctor of Physick, as a PhD at this time to one of his age would be very unusual?

a significant bequest to her servant Sarah Mercer, of one years wages plus all her clothes and linen, provided she was still in Frances's employ at the time of her death. This may not have been the case, as the death certificate was witnessed by Ann Peggs, the lodging-keeper's illiterate daughter, who could only make her mark on it. There were further bequests in the Will, of £300 to be shared among the children of her cousin Frances Maria Stafford and £100 to her cousin Elizabeth Mary Salmon, the youngest daughter of the Rev Francis Edwards Whalley. James Dawe Whalley Wickham Esquire, the eldest son of her cousin Frances Anthony Wickham, who was one of her executors, received £50, and her residuary estate went to her other executor, his younger brother and Thomas Sedgwick's biographer, the Reverend Hill Dawe Wickham. Maybe this he used to assist him in the publications of his great uncle's 'Memoirs and Correspondence'.

Frances was buried, as she had requested, in the new cemetery for the Parish of St Peter and St Paul just below Prior Park (Section II, A.9.10.). Her plain grave overlooks Bath and Royal Crescent and bears the following inscription:

𝖘𝖆𝖈𝖗𝖊𝖉

TO THE MEMORY OF
FRANCES ELIZABETH
ONLY DAUGHTER OF THE LATE
ISAAC SAGE ESQr
OF THORN HILL DORSET
(FORMERLY HIGH SHERIFF
OF THAT COUNTY)
AND RELICT OF THE
REVD. ROBERT BOYLE SULLIVAN
SHE DIED 5TH FEB 1857
AGED 86 YEARS

13.8 The grave of Frances Sullivan (née Sage)

13.9 The view from Frances's grave

It is intriguing to ponder how Frances passed her time in Bath. Fanny Burney, later Mrs D'Arblay, returned to Bath towards the end of her life and died there in January 1840. She had known Dr Whalley and had first met Frances as an 11 year old at his house in Bath 1780 (see Chapter 5). Was Frances back in Bath before 1840, and did they meet again? The D'Arblays were buried in Walcot cemetery, where Frances Sage had been married, and so Frances may have been at Fanny D'Arblay's funeral. There was much to occupy a widow in Bath at this time, all of which would have been accessible by Sedan chair. The Theatre Royal still operated during Frances's later life there, and although ticket sales declined in the early 19th century and it was threatened with closure several times, it remained open until 1862, when it was destroyed by fire. The Pump Room Orchestra, too, continued to operate. The Bath Literary and Scientific Institution was established 1825, the new premises being opened under the patronage of the Duke of York and the Marquis of Lansdown. By 1843 ladies were admitted as members. Papers were presented on a wide variety of topics. Such was the level of interest that The British Association met in Bath in 1864. All this would have kept the well educated Frances Sullivan amused.

CHAPTER 14
The Last Days of Mendip Lodge

The Will of Thomas Sedgwick Whalley is complex and runs to 16,000 words. In it he leaves Mendip Lodge, its contents and estate, and other properties in the parishes of Churchill and Burrington to his executor and his heirs, with the added requirement that these should be sold as soon as possible after his death

> for such price or prices or sum or sums of Money
> as to the said James Anthony Wickham his heirs
> executors administrators and assigns shall seem
> reasonable. [See Appendix 5]

But there was, however, a let out clause, which stated 'unless such sale or disposition within such period shall in his or their judgement be impracticable or manifestly inexpedient and disadvantageous'.

Thomas had left money to all his nephews and nieces, but in the case of his niece Frances Wickham, who had married the Reverend Edward Edgell, this was left to her daughters, Augusta and Frances, as their mother had died in 1810. By the time of Thomas Sedgwick's death they had reached marriageable age, and perhaps they or their father wished to acquire dowries. It was Augusta's legal action which forced Wickham to sell Thomas Sedgwick's other house, 5 Portland Place, Bath in 1834.[1]

---

[1] Edgell v Wickham, *London Gazette*, 27 December. 1831, p8; 24 January 1834,

Mendip Lodge was also held by his executor James Anthony Wickham, who seems to have made no serious efforts to sell it. This may have been quite deliberate. It will be remembered that, shortly before Thomas Sedgwick's death, James Anthony Wickham's daughter the beautiful Mary Agnes Dawe Wickham had married Major William Fawcett.[2] Thomas seems to have had a hand in arranging the marriage and greatly approved of the match. Sometime between then and his death, the couple moved into Mendip Lodge and through the delay in sale continued to live there and bring up their family until Mary's death in 1840.[3] The census of 1841 gives the household as being made up of the following:

William Fawcett	50 years	Head of Household
Selina Fawcett	10 years	Daughter
Theodore Fawcett	9 years	Son
Emmeline Fawcett	3 years	Daughter
Margaret Ambler	30 years	Governess
Charles Clothier	35 years	Manservant
Rachel Powell	42 years	Female Servant
Mary Bridgemore	30 years	Female Servant
Rebecca James	25 years	Female Servant
Susan Green	17 years	Female Servant

Perhaps up until Mrs Fawcett's death, relatives who were due to benefit from its sale were reluctant to evict her and her family in order to obtain their bequests. On the other hand, James Anthony Wickham, Thomas Sedgwick's executor, was an attor-

---

p.12

[2] JCTSW II pp.498-9

[3] It seems very likely, given that he had taken over the ownership of Mendip Lodge on his uncle's death, that James A Wickham should choose to let his daughter and her husband live there while the house was in Chancery.

ney of some ability. He was the secretary to both the West Harptree Turnpike Trust and the Somerset Coal Canal Companies and could have used his abilities to delay the sale until Benjamin Somers was in a position to buy it back again as his uncle had wished. Whatever the reasons for the delay, matters were brought to a head by a second action led by Augusta and Frances Edgell,[4] and in 1844 the Court of Chancery insisted that Mendip Lodge and its estate be 'peremptorily sold', and it was advertised for sale in the national and local press several times between 1844 and 1845.[5]

BETWEEN Augusta Edgell, Frances Edgell, and James Whalley Dawe Thomas Wickham, on behalf of themselves and all other the unsatisfied Legatees named in the Will and Codicil of Thomas Sedgwick Whalley, late of Bath, in the County of Somerset, Dr. in Divinity, deceased, who shall come in and seek the benefit and contribute to the expenses of this suit . . . . *Plaintiffs.*

AND

James Anthony Wickham, Frances Sullivan, and Hyde Salmon Whalley Tooker, late called Hyde Salmon Whalley . . . . *Defendants.*

SOMERSETSHIRE.

Particulars and Conditions of Sale
OF A VERY DESIRABLE

FREEHOLD ESTATE,
CONSISTING OF

MENDIP LODGE,
A CAPITAL MANSION,
TOGETHER WITH

EXTENSIVE PLANTATIONS, SHRUBBERIES,

4.1 The enforced sale of Mendip Lodge July 1844

In the intervening years between 1822 and 1844, Benjamin Somers had been energetically and successfully pursuing his mining and smelting interests on Mendip and in the Tamar

---

[4] Edgell and others v Wickham and others, *London Gazette*, 22nd February 1859, p.40

[5] *The London Gazette*, 7 May 1844; 31 Jan. 1845; 11 March 1845

Valley, and on 8th August 1846 he was able to buy back Mendip Lodge for £16000.[6] His family now moved in to the Lodge from Langford Place, where they had been living. Benjamin continued to re-work the Roman lead slag at Priddy.[7] He also undertook ochre mining at East Harptree, but sadly in 1848, two years after he purchased Mendip Lodge, he died, leaving the house to his wife, Mary. His son Thomas Somers (1813-1862), who by now was married to Elizabeth (née Williams), inherited Langford Place, which his father had bought in 1841. He too carried on lead smelting and silver extraction on Mendip. Two years later, the couple exchanged properties with his mother by mutual consent, and so their son Benjamin Edward (1851-1934) was born at Mendip Lodge. According to him, it was his parents who restored Mendip Lodge and its garden to their former glory and built the upper stables.[8] Before this horses were kept at the foot of Stoney Lane, then known as "The Old Road". The house was also modernised by its later occupants. Dwerryhouse reports that both hot water radiators and electricity were installed.[9] Benjamin Edward, after he was called to the bar, also undertook mining on Mendip and had coal pits at Ubley. He prospected for iron and ochre on Mendip with little success.[10]

[6] Benjamin qualified MD at St Andrews and soon afterwards, in 1811, married Mary Pope, who he had met while practicing in Hertfordshire. She was the heiress to Childwicke Estate, owned by her uncle. Shortly after they married, the estate was sold for £20,000, and the couple moved to Wrington. In 1820 Benjamin seems to have given up medicine and taken to life as a miner and smelter.

[7] See Foord J., *The story of Benjamin Somers MD.; Gough J.W., The Mines of Mendip, Clarendon Press,* Oxford, 1930

[8] Somers, B.E., *Pedigree of the family of Somers of Mendip Lodge,* 1916, p.16

[9] Dwerryhouse, R,M., '£60,000 Mendip Mansion to be demolished',. *The Weston Mercury and Somersetshire Herald,* 17 September 1954, p.4.

[10] Clarke, M., Gregory, N., Gray, A., *Earth colours – Mendip and Bristol Mining,* The Creative Edge, Radstock,,2012, pp.128-130.

The 1851 National Census shows that Thomas and Elizabeth employed 8 servants, a coachman and a groom. In 1862 Thomas died at Mendip lodge, but Elizabeth Somers and her three children continued to live there with her mother-in-law, who was still the legal owner of Mendip Lodge until her death in 1878. It was reported that the widowed Mrs Mary Somers would later have number of lady visitors staying with her at the Lodge. One account says that among these was Mrs Henry Wood, who wrote part of her famous novel *East Lynne* there.[11] This was published in 1861 by Bentley, who two years later would publish Hill Wickham's *Journals and Correspondence of the Reverend Thomas Sedgwick Whalley DD*. Mrs Wood had worked for *Bentley's Miscellany* in the 1850s. *East Lynne*, her most successful novel, had been written in 1860 and serialised in Bentley's *New Monthly Magazine*. This was at a time when Mrs Wood was ill and had been advised by her doctors to seek a change of air. She certainly visited Worcester and several other places during this time, but it has not been possible to verify that she came to Mendip Lodge.

In January 1875 Benjamin Edward Somers, now a barrister at law aged 24 years, married Julia Blanch Impey Lovibond. The marriage did not last long, as in September 1876 she eloped with a Mr Millward. Benjamin obtained a divorce absolute from her, which was granted in November 1877. In the meanwhile, in June 1877 Julia produced a son. Twenty years later, in April 1900, a Mr Benjamin Edwin Somers (formerly Benjamin Edward Millard) appeared on the scene, claiming to be Benjamin Edward Somers's legitimate heir. If so proved, then he, as the first born, would be entitled for a share of his father's estate. However, the case was soon dismissed.[12]

---

11 'Ruin in the Mendips', *The Times,* 9 October 1958, p.12

12 Bristol Mercury, 7 April,1900, p.8

In 1879, after his divorce, Benjamin Edward had married Agnes Elizabeth Atkinson and moved back to Langford Place,[13] leaving his mother to live at Mendip Lodge with various lady companions. In 1900, having inherited the Mendip Lodge estate on the death of his mother, Benjamin Edward commissioned a full mineral exploration of his land. This was undertaken by a Mr McMurtrie of Radstock, who reported in 1902 that there was nothing really worth exploiting. All the old lead waste had been reprocessed by his father and grandfather, and the ochre had been largely worked out, while the bottom had dropped out of the calamine market some years earlier. Benjamin then discovered that the mineral rights on his estate were owned by the church anyway,[14] as they still are today. Benjamin returned to being a solicitor/barrister at law, and the estate and house were put up for sale in 1903. Two farms, Paywell Farm and Ubley Warren Farm, were sold separately for £925 to Messrs Cathorn Hill and Eustace Hill in that year, and the remaining estate of £608 acres was eventually sold in January 1907 to RA Naylor. At that time the timber on the estate was valued at £3390, and the shooting rights had been let with a limit of 230 pheasant and 1600 rabbits.[15]

Two years later, the estate was sold on again, to Vernon Tickell Hill of Bath, with 604 acres of land for £16500. In 1919 Vernon Hill sold Mendip Lodge to John Beardsall Leigh, with some fields being sold separately to Samuel Baber of Grange farm.

In 1938 Vera Wills paid £3500 for Mendip Lodge and 116 acres, and this became part of the Coombe Lodge Estate, which

---

[13] The couple produced two children: Mary Ann Elizabeth (1883)and John (1885).

[14] Gough, J.W., *Mines of Mendip,* Clarendon Press, Oxford, 1930, p.244

[15] Hampsons Sale Catalogue 1903, Somerset Heritage Centre, DD\OB\15

was the Wills' family home.[16] With the outbreak of war in 1939, Mendip Lodge was requisitioned to allow Dr Fox's mental patients to be relocated from Brislington House Bristol, believed to have been the first purpose-built mental asylum in Britain, if not the world. It had been built by his ancestor the Cornish Quaker Dr Edward Long Fox and was opened in 1804. 'Dr. Fox's', as it became known, continued to be run by several generations of the Fox family. After the War the asylum (described elsewhere as a 'home for spastics') returned to Brislington House and finally closed in September 1950. The remaining patients were then dispersed elsewhere, presumably under the provisions of the new NHS.

At some time the Mendip Lodge Estate became part of the Langford Court Estate, which by now Sir (George) Peter Vernon Wills owned. When he died in April 1945, the Mansion and the remaining 101 acres were valued at £3035. At that time the house was still being rented at £75 per annum by Dr Fox, with two years left on his lease.[17] After Dr Fox departed, the Mendip Lodge remained unoccupied, although the coach house was still lived in by the Lever family until the 1960s. The Pepperpot entrance lodges were occupied by the family of Mr Frank Wookey, who ran a decorating business, until the family moved away, and later a fire made the Lodges uninhabitable.

In September 1950 the land, which included Dolebury Camp, was sold to a firm of timber merchants, and in November tree felling began.[18] By 1955 Mendip Lodge was described as 'derelict',

---

[16] The £60,000 which De Quincey claimed the house and gardens had cost to build would have been worth £166,000 in 1945 or £45M in 2012.

[17] *Notes on the Valuation of Sir Peter Vernon Wills Estate.* Charles Tricks and Son Valuers, Bristol, 1945

[18] Churchill Parish Council Minutes, 6 September 1950

and proposals were made for it to be used for Civil Defence Training; this was the time of the Cold War when there was the threat of nuclear warfare. As part of this it was agreed that the drive would be re-laid, with 75% costs being borne by the Home Office and the remainder by Somerset County Council. Six months later, this training had begun there.[19]

14.2 The rear of the now derelict Mendip Lodge in September 1954 (Picture courtesy of Weston Mercury)
Compare with the 1906 view of figure 6.13, page 131

In the 1950s a number of newspaper articles raised local awareness of the state of the house,[9,10] as did the book *The Mendips*, first published in 1954, which gave a brief history and description of the house at that time.[20]

---

[19] ibid 7 December 1955; 7 March 1956

[20] Coysh, A.W., Mason, E.J., Waite, V., *The Mendips*, Robert Hale Ltd, London, 1954, pp.129-32

It was shortly after discovering the whole of this strange story of Dr. Whalley and his Mendip Lodge that I went to explore the house itself. Although the little twin lodges on either side of the gates facing the main road are in ruins and the fine drive which winds through the trees is rutted and overgrown, yet the house itself looks in what gardeners call 'reasonably good heart'. It is therefore all the more astonishing to find on drawing nearer that its front assumes first the blank appearance of an empty house and then finally the desolation of a derelict ruin. Surely never did a house hide its dilapidation more successfully at a distance.

14.3 'Never did a house hide its dilapidation more successfully at a distance'.[21] Pat Wilson and Mendip Lodge in the 1950s

---

331

The stables are still occupied, but the house has fallen into a sorry state of decay. The paths are strangled by weeds and overhanging bushes; windows are smashed; the roof is stripped; and damp has rotted the woodwork. A rusty gate screeches on its hinges as it opens on to the lower verandah tangled with the wilderness of brambles now covering the slopes which were once smooth green lawns. Inside the house there is destruction, decay and an uneasy stillness. I opened a shutter to let a shaft of sunlight into one end of Dr. Whalley's "long suite of rooms"; there were still mirrors on the inside of the shutters, but paper hung down in festoons from the ceiling and floorboards had been ripped up. The walls of the "painted rooms" had been stripped, and the wisteria [sic] outside the Duchess of York's bedroom had run amok, pushed its way between the window sashes and was clambering across floor and up the walls. Only the view from the upper verandah remained unspoilt – a superb view of landscape spread out below, shining in that clear light which a northerly vista always seems to give.

As I passed out of this chill, mouldering, empty shell of Dr. Whalley's "architectural luxury" and left its shuttered ruined rooms once more to the throng of silent ghosts who must have been waiting to emerge from their shadowy hiding-places, I could not help thinking with what sardonic relish De Quincey would have viewed this pathetic ruin as a fulfilment of his prophecy that Mendip Lodge was a monument to the vanity of human wishes and a melancholy comment upon the blindness of human foresight.

In the late 1950s the house was partially demolished after much of the wood had been removed. One of the shutters was reputedly later used as a counter for a local Churchill shop. There are reports that charges were used by engineers of the Territorial Army to demolish some of the stonework, and certainly much of the house had been demolished by the 1970s.

14.4 Mendip Lodge, partially demolished, in 1956

14.5 Mendip Lodge being demolished in 1956. The shutters
referred to in the text are stacked in the foreground

Current State of the Site

Little remains today of the house except a large pile of brick and
masonry within its magical setting. Until recently part of the
front wall of the Mansion and much of the kitchen block and
stables remained, giving a very good idea of how the house must
have looked.

14.6 The front of the mansion in 1990

Sadly, further demolition of the house took place in July 2010, as there was considered to be a danger from falling masonry to pedestrians using the public footpath which passes in front of the house. The stable yard and its adjacent buildings have been similarly bulldozed to increase the parking area for the local shooting syndicate.

Only the Lookout is much as it must have been when Anna Seward and her host laid out their work 'which we carry thither in a morning', but the yew trees are now huge and in danger of further damaging the surrounding retaining bank. This has recently been restored by members of the SW England Dry Stone Walling Association. The Woodland Trust, which now owns the land, have been persuaded to fell a few trees to restore the view out to the northwest, to the Severn Estuary and Welsh Hills, which is much as it must have been two hundred years ago, but to the north and east the view is almost totally obscured by yew trees.

The location of the Lookout, now the only remaining example of Dr. Whalley's 52 follies, and its name are shrouded in mystery. It is sited just over the brow of the hill to the west of Mendip Lodge. It is therefore out of site of the Lodge and on its windward side. Had it been built slightly closer to the house, the view of the surrounding landscape would have been better without it being any more exposed. Its name first appears on the 1881 map, but we know from Anna Seward's account quoted above that is was already there in 1791, but she does not call it by this name. It has been suggested that the Lookout was built on an earlier Iron Age structure.[22] There is indeed evidence of what seems to be an early sheep enclosure above it and to the south west. It has also been pointed out that from the Dolebury hill fort the view to the east was obscured by the rising ground towards Pen Hill. Early warning of any impending Iron Age attack from this direction could have been obtained from the Lookout, since this would have given a view all the way to the hill fort at Lansdown to the north of Bath.

So ends the story of Mendip Lodge; only 'The Lookout' now remains to be wondered at, and although not listed, it would seem to be safe within the guardianship of the Woodland Trust and its local volunteer group. Thomas Sedgwick, its builder, was considered by his biographer and great nephew Hill Wickham as being representative of a type of English gentleman who by the middle of the 19th century had already disappeared from England. Despite Thomas Sedgwick's obvious personal extravagances, the evidence of his life, and the instructions of his Will, bear witness

---

[22] Tricks, C., *Personal Communication,* 2007

to his kindliness and generosity to others, particularly his relatives, including those acquired by marriage. (See Appendix 5).

14.7a The remains of the house today

14.7b The now demolished stables

APPENDIX 1
Friends of Thomas Sedgwick Whalley,
Who Are Recorded in His Correspondence

TSW = Thomas Sedgwick Whalley

Mr John Hiley Addington (1759-1818)
The younger brother of Prime Minister Henry, later Viscount, Sidmouth. He became an MP for Truro in 1787 and rented Langford Court from TSW in 1797 before buying it from him in 1804. He became Lord of the Treasury in 1800 under Pitt, and Paymaster to the Forces and a member of the Privy Council in 1803. He was a friend of Hannah More but curiously took the side of the Reverend Beare in the Blagdon Controversy. He had a serious accident in 1808 and died at Langford Court in 1818, whereupon the estate passed to his elder son, Haviland John Addington, and on his death to his younger son Henry Unwin Addington.

See JCTSW II p.161; 127-9; 315,319

William Walter Slade Amans (Amons) (c1770-1830).
A man befriended by TSW. He would have inherited a large estate from his grandfather Mr Slade, who was related to Lord Bolton, but for his mother marrying against her father's will. William's father, Mr Amans, soon proved to be a worthless spendthrift, leaving William in straightened circumstances. He appears to have acted as a personal servant-cum-secretary and is described as dining at Thomas's own table. It is not clear how long he lived

with TSW. The earliest mention of his name is in a letter from Anna Seward, dated January 1792, in which she speaks of 'good Mr Amons'. In 1814 a relative left Amans enough money for him to become independent. He moved to London, where he lived at No 7 Connaught Terrace, Edgware Road, which had briefly been the residence of Princess Caroline, daughter of the Princess of Wales. TSW visited him there and greatly approved of the house, which overlooked Hyde Park.

See Chapter 12 and JCTSW II p.385,408

Arthur Anstey, known also as Arthur Anstey Calvert (1756-1827)

Legal adviser to TSW. He was the son of Christopher Anstey (see below), who had married Mary Calvert. Arthur Anstey was articled to a lawyer in London in 1784 and became an authority on taxation. He lived in Kingsbury Regis, Somerset, before moving to London.

See JCTSW I. p.40

Christopher Anstey (1724-1805)

The son of a wealthy, ordained landowner of Cambridge who was a family friend of Whalley's parents. He was made famous by the publication of his satirical *New Bath Guide* in 1766 and became a neighbour of TSW in Royal Crescent. TSW officiated in the marriage of his 3rd daughter, Caroline, to his friend Henry Bosanquet.

See JCTSW I. p.311, 312 (Footnote)

The Duke d'Arenberg (1750-1820) and his daughter Princess Pauline d'Arenberg (1774-1810)

The Whalleys made the acquaintance of the blind Duke D'Arenberg and his daughter during the winter of 1786/7 in Brussels, where they had been joined by their niece Frances Sage.

The Princess and Frances remained close friends, being of the same age,[1] until the Princess's tragic death in 1810.

See Chapter 5 and JCTSW I p.20

Bishop Beadon (1737-1824)

A relative of TSW on his mother's side. Like him, Richard had attended St John's, Cambridge, gaining his MA in 1761 and his BD, with TSW, in 1769, which is probably how they became good friends. He was clearly very able. In 1778 he married the daughter of the Prebend of Ely John Gooch, who was the grandson of the Bishop of Ely. Richard in turn became Archdeacon of London (1775–1789), Master of Jesus College (1781–1789), Bishop of Gloucester (1789–1802) and finally Bishop of Bath and Wells (1802–1824).

See JCTSW II p.35

Henry Bosanquet (1760-1817)

A friend and a Barrister at Law to whom TSW let Langford Court when he and his wife went to the Continent in 1784. Thomas officiated when Henry married Christopher Anstey's daughter Caroline at Walcot Church on 3rd May 1790.

Count Coëtlosquet (1783-1837)

TSW met General Count Coëtlosquet, the military governor of Nevers, in the winter of 1813/4, and thereafter they became firm friends. TSW had only just returned to the continent, the Peace of Paris having been signed in May 1813. It was the Count who, nine months later, advised TSW to flee, following the news of Napoleon's landing from Elba in March 1st, 1814. The Count fought on the Royalist side during the "100 days". After Napoleon's defeat at Waterloo and the restoration of the Bourbons, he was appointed Deputy General Major of the Royal

---

[1] While Hill Wickham states this, it appears that the Princess was five years older that Frances.

Guard and awarded the Legion d'Honneur, later becoming Commander of the 7th Division and, later still, Acting Minister of War in 1823. Despite this he visited TSW at Versailles in August of that year, as TSW was too weak to make the journey to Paris.

See JCTSW I p.34 and JCTSW II pp. 390,392,453,492

Baron de Châtillon (1726-1817)

Baron Joseph de Châtillon Rambert was President of the Savoy Senate, and it seems that he and Thomas Sedgwick must have met during TSW's Grand Tour in 1769-1771. They met again in 1783 at the beginning of the Whalleys' European tour, when he described the Baron as 'my beloved amiable friend'. While Mrs Whalley remained at the castle, the Baron and Whalley toured Savoy. Sadly, it appears that the Baron died at the end of his third tour, Hill Wickham thinks through sunstroke.[2] Subsequent correspondence must have been with his son. It seems likely that they met again after TSW separated from his third wife and escaped to the continent in 1814. Curiously, only one letter is included by Hill Wickham, dated September 1816, in which the Baron regrets not being able to spend another three months in TSW's company.

See JCTSW I. p.43 and JCTSW II pp.434-7

Erasmus Darwin (1731-1802)

Darwin was a polymath and a highly successful physician who practised for more than fifty years in Lichfield and so became a close friend of Anna Seward and through her knew TSW. George III invited Darwin to be Royal Physician, but he declined. He was a member of the Lunar Society, wrote poetry and developed his system of evolution, later to be developed by his grandson Charles Darwin. Anna Seward states that is was her poem which gave him the idea of writing his own notable poetical work *The Botanic*

---

[2] JCTSW I p.167

Garden in 1772. This was a popular account of Linnaeus' works, which he had translated from the original Latin. It is not clear how well TSW knew him. One account says that Darwin stayed at Mendip Lodge. It was also through either Anna Seward or Darwin that TSW came to know Lovell Edgeworth and Thomas Day, although there is no recorded correspondence between them.

Thomas Erskine, 1st Baron Erskine (1750-1823)

Erskine was the third and youngest surviving son of Henry Erskine, 10th Earl of Buchan, who despite his title was not rich. Thomas was born in a tenement in Edinburgh and educated by his mother, the daughter of a solicitor general for Scotland. In an astonishing career Eskine served in the Navy and the Army. He then attended Trinity College, Cambridge, becoming first a highly successful barrister then Lord Chancellor (1806-7). He was much admired by TSW for his mastery of several professions. They met quite by chance in Brussels in 1786/7

JCTSW I p.21

The Reverend Sir Abraham Elton (1755-1842)

The 5th Baronet of Clevedon Court. His antecedents and his father in law had been Mayors of Bristol. He was a graduate of Queen's College, Oxford and Perpetual Curate of West Bromwich. His only correspondence with TSW relates to their joint support for Hannah More during the Blagdon Controversy. The one letter recorded by Hill Wickham does not suggest any close association.

See Chapter 9 and JCTSW II pp.197-8

Count D. Gabrielle Galateri de Genola (1761-1844)

The three page account by Hill Wickham into the eventful life of this remarkable soldier is well worth reading.[3] There is also an account in the *Italian Dictionary of National Biography (Dizionario*

---

[3] JCTSW I pp.16-19

Biografico degli Italiani - Volume 51). He and TSW first met in 1784 during the Whalley's continental tour with his wife. Galateri was then a young Piedmontese officer. They maintained their friendship and correspondence for the next 40 years, during which time Galateri served royalist causes in France, Russia and Turkey. When the monarchy was restored in France, Galateri became Governor of Nice and then Commandant of Alessandria. It was there that Hill Wickham met him shortly after TSW's death. He relates how he was received by the Count with great kindness. He also records that a large bundle of letters to TSW from Galateri and Baron Chatillon and other foreign correspondents had been 'inconsiderately destroyed' some years previously.

General (1750 –1804) and Mrs Horneck (1755-1832)
Mrs Horneck was the second wife and widow of Charles Horneck, whom she had married in 1790. She married TSW in 1813, but the couple soon separated.

See Chapter 13

The Reverend George Inman (c1720-1795)
Graduated from Clare College Cambridge and became perpetual curate of Burrington from 1744 until his death in 1795. He seems to have been held in high regard by TSW, as one of the three seats on the Mendip Lodge Estate described by Thompson in his *Life of Hannah More* was dedicated to him. Burrington was the local church for Mendip Lodge and is where the two memorials to TSW's wives are to be found, as well as many other memorials to occupants of Langford Court.

Mrs GG Jackson (?1761-?1798)
In a letter of August 1791, Ann Seward describes Mrs Jackson as 'a women of first rate abilities and virtues'.[4] While she signs herself as Mrs G.G. Jackson in her two letters to TSW, it is clear that she

---

4 Constable A (Ed), *Letters of Anna Seward, Written Between the Years 1784 and 1807* Vol. III, George Ramsey and Company, 1811, p.103

was known publicly as Mrs John Jackson of Turville Court, Oxfordshire, the author of *Dialogues on the doctrines and duties of Christianity; intended for the instruction of the young* (2 vols, Rivington, London 1806). In a letter to Mrs Jackson, dated 3rd June 1806, Anna Seward says that TSW has just brought her this long awaited volume. In a review of this work in the Anti Jacobin Review (Vol. XXVI pp.13-17) it is described as 'highly creditable to the respected author'. It seems from this and references by Anna Seward in later letters that Mrs Jackson was also a playwright, although none of her works have been identified. Apart from this, very little is known, except that she visited Mendip Lodge with her children in 1780 and was well enough known to the Whalleys and Anna Seward for the latter to discuss in detail the distress which Mrs Mullins's downfall has caused them.[5]

See JCTSW II pp.37,38

Dr Samuel Johnson (1709-1784)

Dr Johnson's name occurs frequently in the Whalley correspondence published by Hill Wickham, though as far as can be made out neither wrote directly to the other. Dr Johnson was a close friend of Mr and Mrs Thrale, and he seems to have used their house at Streatham as his base. When Mr Thrale died, Mrs Thrale married the Roman Catholic Gabriel Mario Piozzi and proposed to sell her Streatham house. Johnson was greatly put out, though whether from the impending loss of Mrs Thrale's company or use of the Thrales' former house is not clear. He seems then to have roused public attacks on Mrs Piozzi's marriage. Hill Wickham says that TSW used to speak of Johnson's conduct in this matters as unwarrantable and ungrateful.[6]

---

[5] Constable A (Ed), *Letters of Anna Seward, Written Between the Years 1784 and 1807* Vol. IV, George Ramsey and Company, 1811, p.50

[6] JCTSW I pp.10-11.

Sir Walter James (1759-1829)

Both Sir Walter and his wife Lady Jane were very close friends of TSW for more than thirty years. Sir Walter was born Walter James Head, the son of Sir Thomas Head. He was a graduate of Trinity College Oxford, achieving a doctorate of civil law in 1788. He married the Honourable Miss Jane Pratt, the youngest daughter of Lord Campden, whose younger brother was MP for Bath. The family seat was Langley Park, Berkshire, where his father was High Sheriff of Berkshire. Sir Walter assumed the family estates on the death of his brother and immediately took the name and arms of James by Act of Parliament. He became Warden of the Royal Mint (1806-1813), a post which had been occupied by Sir Isaac Newton, and was technically responsible for the country's coinage. He had a house in Lansdowne Crescent but spent the summer at his Manor House at Freshford. His descendants became Lords Northbourne. It is likely he and TSW met through personal or mutual contacts, as Thomas's niece Frances Sage had an uncle who was Assayer to the Royal Mint.

See JCTSW II p.267, 270, 387, 432, 433

Count and Countess de Lagondie of Le Mans

These are described by Hill Wickham as old friends of TSW who he met again shortly before he died.[7] Noel Andre de Guilhen Count de Lagondie was Lieutenant General of the King's Armies and Commander of the Royal and Military Order of Saint Louis of La Flèche. It is possible that this was the reason why his niece Frances chose to live in La Flèche. No correspondence is recorded by Hill Wickham between Frances and either the Count or Countess de Lagondie.

Mrs E Lambert

Wife and later widow of General Lambert and sister of Sir Philip Jennings. In later life she lived in Clifton, Bristol.

---

[7] JCTSW I p.3

See JCTSW II pp. 383,462

Very Reverend Charles Peter Layard (1749-1803)

A near contemporary of TSW, and their time at St John's, Cambridge overlapped. He and TSW remained lifelong friends. The two seem to have held each other in very high regard. Layard was ordained in 1771 and was Vicar of Kewstoke, only 10 miles from Langford, until he became Dean of Bristol (1800-1803). Perhaps through his time in Ceylon, he became a member of the Society of Antiquaries, a Fellow of the Royal Society and their Foreign Secretary (1784-90). There is a monument in Bristol Cathedral, following his early death, which describes him as a man of great learning and amiable manners. He was one of the first to see that Samuel Pratt was a man of straw. He also wrote to TSW in October 1782 to ask if Mrs Siddons was worthy of support following her move to London.

See JCTSW I pp.316-7, 376-7

Mr Lehman

A neighbour of TSW in Royal Crescent and played whist with him one evening a week for one half guinea a point during the winter season. Lehman was also a friend of Mrs Lutwyche's and travelled on the continent.

See JCTSW II p.379

Mrs Mary Lutwyche (1748-1845)

A prominent figure in Bath in the late eighteenth century. Hill Wickham states that 'none ranked higher than Mr and Mrs Lutwyche' amongst the leading people of that city. She was the only daughter of Sir Noah Thomas, Baronet, physician to George III. She married William Lutwyche of Lutwyche Hall (d.1818), a Captain in the Guards and wealthy Shropshire gentleman. She was a friend of Duchess d'Angouleme and the Bishop of Cloyne and was amongst those who played host to the exiled King of

347

France Louis XVIII, in Bath at her house in Marlborough Buildings. Consequently, she had many friends amongst the French nobility. The French king himself entertained the Lutwyches in Paris after his restoration in 1814. Mary died in 1845 at the age of ninety-three.

See JCTSW II p.375,379

Marquis and Marquise de La Pierre
TSW maintained a correspondence with the Marquise from 1803-1827, by which time she was living in Hampton Court. He had met the English Marquise by chance in June 1784 while on his second tour. The Marquis, a Royalist, emigrated to England when the French Revolution took place, and as a result he lost property in France. Initially, the couple lived at Hampton Wick, but by 1824 they were enjoying a Grace and Favour accommodation in Hampton Court.

See JCTSW I p.98; JCTSW II p.250

Mrs (Lady) Anne Miller (1741-1781)
Soon after he arrived in Bath, TSW was introduced to Mrs Miller's poetry circle, which met weekly at their Bath Easton house during the Bath season until just before her death. He was already a member of this group by 1780. In 1775 the first selection of these poems had been published and proved extremely popular. This and three later volumes were sold in aid of the Millers' charity, the Bath Casualty Hospital, which later merged with the Bath City Dispensary and Infirmary to become the Royal United Hospital Bath, which still exists today.

See Chapter 3
See also:

Egan P. *Walks through Bath*. Meyler and Son, Bath 1819, pages 304-5

Sturge, M., *Mrs. Miller* at:
http://www.bath.ac.uk/lmf/fileinfo/37757

Miss Hannah More (1745-1833) and her sisters

Hannah was born in Stapleton near Bristol in 1745. Her father, Jacob More, was the headmaster of a school in Fishponds. She was the fourth and most able of five sisters. Hannah was a lively, quick witted and charming young woman. She met and became engaged to Edward Turner, owner of a large estate close to Bristol. Turner kept postponing the marriage and in the end settled an annuity of £200 per year on her as a way of extricating himself from the engagement. This made her independent enough to make her way through writing. She had been writing poetry for some time and now turned to writing for the professional stage. Through her theatrical activities, Hannah More had also developed friendships with David Garrick and his wife and often stayed in their house. Through them, she met with other literary figures who soon held her in high regard. After the deaths of Garrick, her father and Dr Johnson and other members of her London circle, she became influenced by the Clapham Sect (so named because many of its members lived close to Clapham), which was an influential but informal group of wealthy evangelicals who sought to reinvigorate the Church of England with what could be described as a modified form of Methodism. Its members included William Wilberforce (1759-1833). After they first met in Bath in 1786, Wilberforce became a regular visitor to the sisters' new cottage at Cowslip Green, to where they had moved in 1785. Out of their discussions Hannah set up a Sunday School in Cheddar at his expense and subsequently opened more than a dozen such schools in neighbouring villages.

It is not clear how well Thomas Sedgwick Whalley knew her before his involvement in the Blagdon Controversy in 1800-2, but thereafter they were close friends. Hannah and her sisters moved to a house they had had built for them near Wrington, called Barley Wood, where they lived happily for many years, but by 1819 Hannah was alone. For some years she suffered poor health. She was rarely out of her bedroom, and when in 1826 she discovered her servants were cheating her, she sought Thomas Sedgwick's advice. He persuaded her to move to his house at 4 Windsor Terrace, Clifton, which he had found unsuitable, but where she lived contentedly for the remainder of her life.

Hannah More

See Chapter 9

Further reading: Thompson, H., *The life of Hannah More with notices of her sisters* .W Blackwood and Sons Edinburgh, 1838.

Charles Moss (1763-1811)

The son of Charles Moss (1711-1802) who was Bishop of Bath and Wells and subsequently Bishop of Oxford. Charles Moss Junior, also an Anglican clergyman, served as Bishop of St

David's from 1766 to 1774 and then as Bishop of Bath and Wells from 1774 to 1802, succeeding his father as Bishop of Oxford in 1807. As TSW's Bishop the two knew each other well, but the only correspondence between them concerns the Blagdon controversy.

See JCTSW pp. II 166-167

William Pennington (1744-1829) and Penelope Sophia Pennington (née Weston) (1751-1827)

William Pennington was a British Customs Officer in America before returning to Bristol and becoming Master of the Ceremonies at the Hotwells. He married TSW's cousin Penelope Sophia Weston in 1792.

See Chapter 11

Mrs Piozzi (1741-1821). Formerly Mrs Thrale; née Hester Lynch

The life of this remarkable lady is well documented. According to Hill Wickham, Mrs Thrale made the acquaintance of Thomas Sedgwick and his wife on her first arrival in Bath after the death of her first husband in 1781. Mrs Thrale by this time had been the focus of an intellectual literary group centred on her house in Streatham. She met Dr Johnson there in January 1765, two years after her marriage, and despite almost continuous pregnancies and acting as nursemaid to the demanding Johnson, her literary output was considerable.

The death of her first husband in 1781 gave her freedom to lead her own life and an income of £2000 per annum. Her second marriage, to the Italian musician Gabriel Mario Piozzi (1740–1809), three years later aroused considerable public and family protest but was to secure her happiness. It also caused her estrangement from Samuel Johnson, who appears to have seen himself as Mr Thrale's successor. Mrs Thrale remained a close friend of TSW and Mrs Pennington (née Weston), who was with her when she died in Clifton.

See JCTSW II p.468 ; also Bloom, E.A., Bloom, L.D., *The Piozzi Letters*, Vols I-VI, Associated University Presses, London, 1999

Mrs Thrale aged 40, as she would have appeared when Whalley first met her

Very Reverend Dr. Beilby Porteous (1720-1809)

Dr. Porteous supported Hannah More, William Wilberforce and the Clapham Sect in their efforts to abolish slavery and promote education for the poor. He was appointed Bishop of Chester in 1776 and translated to the Bishopric of London in 1787 on the advice of William Pitt the Younger. He was a close friend of Hannah More and acknowledged the excellent support which TSW had provided for her.

See JCTSW II p.169

Samuel Jackson Pratt (1749-1814)

Otherwise known as Courtney Melmoth, this able but shallow man was a prolific poet and playwright. He was ordained as a Church of England clergyman and was initially a popular preacher before entering into a sham marriage with a farmer's daughter with whom he ran off to become an actor, adopting the stage name of Courtney Melmoth. The couple initially toured together but were always in financial difficulty, borrowing money from many people, including Mrs Siddons and Benjamin Franklin. In 1781 the couple separated. Charlotte Melmoth became a well known actress in America. Pratt seems to have entered the Whalley circle through either Mrs Miller's poetry circle (his name first occurs in a letter from her to TSW in October 1779) or Mrs Siddons, who befriended him when he made guest appearances in three plays at the Theatre Royal Bath in 1778/9, while the Siddons were still members of the company. During the same season Hannah More's play *The Fatal Falsehood* was performed for the first time, so she would have met him at this time also. For a while Pratt lived with the Whalleys at Langford Court. He opened a bookshop in Bath and courted Miss Weston, but one by one his friends saw through him, TSW being the last to abandon him.

Miss Anna Seward (1747 -1809)

Anna Seward, also known as the Swan of Lichfield, was the daughter of the Reverend Thomas Seward – a graduate of St

Johns Cambridge and tutor to Lord Charles Fitzroy, whom he accompanied on his Grand Tour in 1739. Through this connection, Thomas Seward gained initial preferment to the living at Eyam in Derbyshire, where Anna was born. In 1755 her father was appointed Prebend, and the family moved to Lichfield. Despite her father's death in 1790, Anna continued to live in the Bishop's Palace there until her death. She became known through Mrs Miller's Poetry Circle and through it met TSW and many others. Sir Walter Scott later edited her poetical works.

Her letters reveal the breadth of her interests and the strength of her literary criticism. She counted many eminent figures among her correspondents, including James Boswell and Walter Scott. A six-volume selection of her letters first appeared in 1811 and cover the period 1784-1807.

See Lucas, E.V., *A Swan and her friends*. Methuen and Company, London, 1907.

Anna Seward

Mrs Sarah Siddons (1755-1831) and William Siddons (1744-1808)

Sarah Siddons née Kemble came from a Welsh theatrical family and rose to become the leading tragic actress of the 18th century. Much has been written about her remarkable life. She began as a lady's maid to Lady Greathead. At age 18 she married William, an actor, and soon gave birth to the first of seven children, but she outlived all but two of them. She and her husband became close friends of both Thomas Sedgwick and his first wife, who met her after they bought their house in Bath. Through them she became an early friend of Fanny Sage. By 1781 Sarah and the Whalleys were in regular correspondence, and by 1787 Thomas was referring to Sarah as his 'dearest friend'. TSW became godfather to her daughter Cecilia and was very fond of her and her brother 'little hercules' (this was probably the infant George) who stayed with the Whalleys at Mendip Lodge. Hill Wickham includes several of Sarah's letters and notes and recalls seeing an endorsement on one of these by TSW, regretting that many others had been lost or destroyed [8]

Her correspondence with Thomas Sedgwick continued until she became too ill to write, whereupon it was continued on her behalf by her daughter and her son George. Hill Wickham records that he accompanied his great uncle when he and Sarah met for the last time, in 1824 at her house in Upper Baker Street, London.

Frances Sage (1769-1857)

Frances was the beautiful and talented daughter of Isaac Sage and Elizabeth (née Whalley). She married William Mullins in 1790 but was divorced from him by Act of Parliament in 1796. She then immediately married the Reverend Robert Boyle Sullivan. The couple lived in France from 1818, but Frances returned to Bath, probably in 1830, after Robert's death. TSW remained devoted to her despite her fall from grace in 1796 and rescued her financially in 1828.

---

[8] JCTSW I p.8-9

See Chapters 8 and 13

Isaac Sage (1741-1778)

Isaac entered the East India Company's employ in 1762 and returned to England six years later a rich man looking for a wife. He married TSW's sister Elizabeth in 1769, and they became the parents of Frances, who, after her mother's death in 1778, spent a great deal of time with TSW and his wife in Bath.

See Chapter 4

Joseph Sage (1748-1821)

Frances Sage's Uncle Joseph was Assayer to the Royal Mint (1779-1820) and lived at Reading, where she spent some time when very young.

Major General John Stafford

Major General John Stafford married the daughter of Francis Whalley in 1808. His brother Hugh had married Robert Boyle Sullivan's sister Thomasine, which is perhaps how the Rev Robert Boyle Sullivan met and later married Frances Mullins (née Sage). Both the Staffords and the Sullivans moved to France in about 1818.

See Chapter 8

Reverend Robert Boyle (O') Sullivan (1762?-1826)

Robert was the second husband of Frances Sage, whom he married in 1796. He was a graduate of Dublin and for a short while was Curate of Winscombe before being dismissed for neglecting his duties. He and Frances moved to France in about 1818.

See Entry for Frances Sage above and Chapters 8 and 13

William Tryon (1729-1788)

William was commissioned in the 1st Regiment of Foot Guards in 1751 and by 1758 had achieved the army rank of Lieutenant-Colonel. In 1764 he was appointed Lieutenant Governor of North Carolina and went out to America, accompanied by William Pennington, who had been appointed its Customs Officer in the same year. They seem to have had a high regard for each other and remained good friends until Tryon's death in 1788. It was Tryon's pleading which gained William Pennington his pension when they were both forced to leave America during the War of Independence.

In 1757 Tryon had married Margaret Wake, a London heiress with a dowry of £30,000 who came to have a high opinion of Sophie Pennington (née Weston) and left her money in her Will.

See Chapter 9

Reverend George Warrington (1744-1831)

George was the 5th son of George Warrington of Stanton Hall, Lancashire, and Mary Thornhill, his wife. Through his mother he was related to the Dukes of Rutland. He and TSW had matriculated at St John's College, Cambridge in the same term and remained friends throughout their lives. Unlike Thomas, George Warrington junior immediately took up holy orders on leaving Cambridge in 1768 and married Mary, the only daughter of Henry Strudwick (1718-1772). Both the Thornhills and the Strudwicks were wealthy estate owners in Jamaica at the time. A letter from George to TSW in October 1773 refers to the sale of the estates he had inherited there through his wife. There are several letters referring to him included by Hill Wickham, the last letter being written by George within a year of TSW's death, which he opens with 'My Dear Old Friend'.

See JCTSW II p.278

Miss Penelope Sophia Weston (1751-1827)

Penelope was a cousin by marriage to TSW through his first wife, the widowed Elizabeth Sherwood (née Jones). She eventually married William Pennington (1744-1829), who was a former British Customs Officer in America before returning to Bristol and becoming Master of the Ceremonies at the Hotwells.

See Chapter 11

William Wilberforce (1759-1833)

Son of William Pitt's physician, Wilberforce became a politician, philanthropist and a leader of the movement to abolish the slave trade. While the majority of his friends during his early dissipated life as a Cambridge undergraduate, went into the church, he resolved to go into politics, eventually becoming Member of Parliament for Yorkshire (1784-1812). In 1785 he became an evangelical Christian and a member of what would become the Clapham Sect, through which he met Hannah More, who was to become one of his greatest friends. His biographer John Scandrett Harford was also a close friend of TSW's brother the Reverend Richard Whalley, and Wilberforce had certainly met TSW by 1794 and probably stayed with him at Mendip Lodge in 1813, when he gave his description of TSW as 'the true picture of a sensible, well informed, and educated, polished, old, well-beneficed, nobleman's and gentleman's house-frequenting literary and chess playing divine'

See Hague, W., *William Wilberforce*. Harper Press, London, 2008, pp.212-4

Rev. J.T. Wylde (1795-1831)

There is a mystery surrounding this name, which occurs in connection with the Blagdon controversy, where the 'Rev Wylde' is given as the Vicar of Burrington.[9] There is one letter from him to Thomas Sedgwick included by Hill Wickham, dated 1800,

---

[9] JCTSW II p.145

signed Rev J.T.Wylde,[10] yet the Vicar of Burrington at this time was Sydenham Teast Wylde (1795-1831), who was also Rector of nearby Ubley (1805-1826) and briefly curate of Rowberrow (1799). According to the Database of the Clergy of the Church of England, there were two Rev J. Wyldes during this period, but both were clergy in Worcestershire. So one must assume this was an error on the part of Hill Wickham in deciphering the signature of Sydenham Teast Wylde and interpreting S.T as J.T.

10 JCTSW II p.153

APPENDIX 2

The Poetry and Plays of Thomas Sedgwick Whalley

Edwy and Edilda (1778)

Whalley first published this poem under the pseudonym 'A beautiful young lady'. This was a not unusual practice in this era.[1] When he met Anna Seward, she discovered that he was the author and encouraged him to publish it under his own name. This he did in 1783 as *Edwy and Edilda. A Gothic tale. In five parts. By the author of The old English baron.*[2] It remained Anna Seward's favourite work, though she did express her criticism of it.[3] The reference to the Old English Baron is a curious one. The usual claim is that this poem was written by Clara Reeve (1729-1807) in imitation of, or rivalry to, *The Castle of Otranto* by Horace Walpole (1765). The Reeve novel was clearly influenced by Mary Shelley's *Frankenstein*. One has to assume in the days before copyright many versions of popular works were published, though, as far as can be determined, no surviving copy of Whalley's first edition exists.

The legendary history of Eadwig (Edwy) became known to a wider public in the second half of the eighteenth century, inspiring artists and providing material for a number of plays based loosely on the king's amorous affairs.[4] Whalley's poem was

1 Feldman, P.R., *Women Poets and Anonymity in the Romantic Era*. New Literary History, 2002; 33, 279-289

2 Whalley, T.S., Edwy and Edilda : a Gothic tale. In five parts. By the author of The old English baron. S. Colbert, Dublin, 1783

3 JCTSW I pp.355-6

4 Smollet T., A Complete History of England, 2nd Ed, Vol 1, James Rivington

followed by Thomas Warwick's *Edwy: a Dramatic Poem* (1784) and Frances Burney's *Edwy and Elgiva* (1788). In 1794 Whalley published a second edition with six engravings by a young lady (i.e. the daughter of Lady Langham).

The Fatal Kiss 1st Edition (1781); 2nd Ed R. Baldwin and T. Becket, 1782 - 47 pages
The nine hundred lines of rhyming couplets recounting a girl's seduction and downfall are written as if by the girl herself. The introduction reads:

> A poem Written in the last stage of an atrophy, by a beautiful and unfortunate young lady; The singular and melancholy Circumstances of whose Life may, perhaps, be one Day offered the Public, to the Confusion and Disgrace of one whose Fortune and Rank would not have Power to shield him from the Censure and Detestation of every one who has true Principles of Honour and Humanity.

Verses addressed to Mrs Siddons (1782)
These appeared after Mrs Siddons returned to Drury Lane in 1781, following her successes in Bath. They were perhaps written as an act of flattery.

Astarte (1785?)
This is referred to only once, in a letter from Mrs Siddons written on September 1785 in great anguish:

> My Dear Friend,
>
> I feel at this moment in the most painful situation I ever experienced. I tremble to offend you, to disappoint your expectations. But have you not conjured me to be sincere? and shall I not obey

and James Fletcher, London, 1758, pp.289-292

you? Yes was that conjuration necessary? No; for to you I ever have, and always will, lay open my whole heart. I am aware what danger I should incur in the present instance with any living creature but yourself; but you are noble-minded, and will not love me less for my honesty, and the agonising proof I now give you of my at present torturing affection for you. It is impossible for you to conceive, though you may a little guess, by the length of this (to me) dreadful preface how difficult it is to say – how shall I say it? 'Astarte' will not do as you and I would have it do! Thanks God! 'tis over. This has been so bitter a sentence for me to pronounce, that it has wrung drops of sorry from the bottom of my heart[5]

No other trace of this exists so perhaps it was never published by TSW. Indeed he may have taken the view before showing it to Mrs Siddons that to do so would encourage others to write their own versions, as had been the case with *Edwy and Edilda*.

Mont Blanc – an irregular lyric poem J.Marsh, Bath, 1788
TSW was much impressed with the mountain, which he visited in August 1784. At the time he believed it to be the highest mountain in the world, and it had yet to be climbed.[6] The Whalleys returned to England in the early summer of 1787. In April of that year Anna Seward records that TSW and another of her acquaintances 'took to the literary field. much to the honour of both',[7] which can only refer to the publication of *Mont Blanc*. In that month a savage attack on the poem appeared in *The Gentleman's Magazine*.[8] The following month, Anna , who believed

---

[5] JCTSW I p.443

[6] This was true at the time but not by the time the poem was published as it had been in 1787.

[7] *Letters of Anna Seward, Written Between the Years 1784 and 1807,* (Constable, A., Ed), Vol II, George Ramsay and Co Edinburgh, 1811, p.85

this was inserted by the influence Samuel Pratt,[9] mounted a counter attack on Thomas Sedgewick's behalf and received what amounted to a grudging retraction (pp. 437-8). In her letter of June 19th, Anna is able to report that his four friends Hannah More, Mrs Piozzi, Christopher Anstey and a Mr Potter have applauded his efforts.

The Castle of Montval (1791; 2nd ed 1799)

Baker says that the play, a tragedy written in blank verse, owed its story to 'The Parricide Punished' which appeared in *La Nouvelle Bibliothéque de Société*,[10] however this is unlikely as this collection was published in 1782. The original version had appeared anonymously in 1799 (see The Oxford Book of Gothic Tales, Baldick, C. (Ed), Oxford University Press,.Oxford, 1992). There seems to have been some doubt as to whether Whalley's play would ever appear. Mr Siddons wrote to Thomas Sedgwick on December 15th 1797, describing a rival version of the play by Matthew (Monk) Lewis, which appeared under the title of *The Castle Spectre*. Whalley's *The Castle of Montval* was finally opened at Drury Lane on 23rd April 1799, with Mrs Siddons as the Countess. There were 8 performances, the last being on May 22nd. Baker et al. state that it was 'tolerably well received', perhaps because Anna Seward had made every effort to ensure all the influential members of Society were present. However, the critics were not favourably impressed, and the play was never put on again.

Various accounts exist of how it was received, some kinder than others:

> I congratulate you on the success of your play.
> Many of my acquaintances have spoken to me of
> it as charming.[11]

8 Gentleman's Magazine, Vol. 58 part 1 April 1788, pp 146-7; 329-300; 437-438
9 JCTSW II p.26
10 Baker, D.E., Reed, I.,Jones, S., Biographica dramatica Vol II, Longman et al, London, 1812, p.89

Dear Mr Whalley's play... has been more favourably received by the Public than was expected, I fancy due to charming Siddons great exertions[12]

Dr. Whalley must then needs press a tragedy of his own upon her [Mrs Siddons], "The Castle of Montval," which was yawned at for three nights [In fact it ran in total for 9 nights, which was an average run for most plays at Drury Lane]. It is said that when the author went down to Mr. Peake, the treasurer, to know what benefit might have accrued to him, it amounted to nothing. "I have been," said the doctor, an old picquet-player, "piqued and re-piqued"; and so he re-tired from the scene of his discomfiture to Bath where he plumed himself on the fact of "having run for three nights"[13]

Poems and Translations (1797)
This is assigned to him, with several of the other publications given above, in *Literary Memoires of Authors of Great Britain* by Rivers, published in London in 1798, to which is added the comment that his poetry is not of the first order. Nothing else is known.

Rosilda (?1802)
There is a single mention of this work in a footnote of a letter from Mrs Siddons in Dublin to TSW, dated 24th December 1802: 'I thank you for your kind offer of 'Rosilda' but at present it is not in my power to get it up'.[14]

---

[11] *Letters of Anna Seward, Written Between the Years 1797 and 1801,* (Constable, A., Ed), Vol V, George Ramsay and Co Edinburgh, 1811, p.239

[12] Letter held by the John Rylands Library, University of Manchester Ref 567.81

[13] Kennard NA, *Mrs Siddons,* Roberts Brothers, Boston 1887, p 214

[14] JCTSW II p.228

It does not appear that it was ever published. Hill Wickham says TSW left some plays in manuscript, and maybe these included *Rosilda* and *Estarte*.[15]

Kenneth & Fenella – a legendary tale J.Hatchard, London, 1809 p.55

This poem was dedicated to the Reverend Robert Vans Agnew, with whom Thomas had lodged on his way to receive his Doctorate from Edinburgh in 1808. He points out that Fenella was either the grandmother or great aunt of Macbeth and that the murder of Duncan, who was Kenneth's great grandson, was a consequence of the perpetuating feud between the two families.

The *British Critic* commented

> The murder of Kenneth II by Fenella is circumstantially related by Guthrie, and in the opinion of the author exhibits a fine subject for a tragedy or legendary tale. To the former, he modestly observes, he found himself unequal; the latter he had attempted, with some variation from the printed story. It may be read with amusement and some degree of interest; and it may be presumed that the author cannot be ambitious of higher commendation.[16]

Smollet, in the *Critical Review*, quotes verbatim from TSW's introduction:

> … To the former I have found myself unequal; the latter I have attempted – and of my attempt the public must be the judge. It is the best effort of one whose imagination is clouded, and whose ardour is cooled buy old age and infirmities

---

[15] JCTSW I p.23
[16] British Critic, Vol. 33, 1809, p.629

Smollet then adds cruelly: 'Length of years must, we suppose, plead the Doctor's excuse for the want of poetic fire'.

Other poetry

TSW was a regular contributor to Lady Miller's *Poetical Amusements at a Villa near Bath*, which was published in four volumes. Only the last volume acknowledged the names of the poets. A number are quoted as examples by Hill Wickham but seem to have been drawn at random from the published volumes rather than being those written by TSW.[17] The following are known to have been written by TSW himself:

LINES ADDRESSED TO MRS WHALLEY BY HER HUSBAND
6th JANUARY 1775, THE FIRST ANNIVERSARY OF THEIR WEDDING DAY[18]

All hail to thee, bright ruler of the day!
May every cloud fleet from thy fervent ray,
And may thy course triumphant, on this morn.
Make glad the earth, and heaven itself adorn!
Far be remov'd each sorrowing sigh, and far
Each jealous scowl and frown, each brow of care.
Nor thou, dreaded Anger, show thy scarlet face,
Nor Doubt, nor Envy, dare pollute this place.
But Mirth and Joy, and Confidence and Peace,
Be ye all present on a day like this!
Thus love invokes; and let it be they care,
O honour'd Hymen! To indulge the prayer;
Since on a sister day, and sister hour,
Parent of chaste desires, thy fav'ring power
First pointed out the certain path to rest,
Beguil'd my pains and calmed my tortur'd breast.
For whilom, in my bosom pallid Care,

17 JCTSW I pp.235-24
18 ibid. I pp.231-4

And languid Sickness, beckoned to Despair;
Thought, lost in pensiveness, there held her sway,
And jealous doubtings drank my life away,
Disease triumphant totter'd in the van,
With constant Anguish, squalid, spare, and wan;
From her swoln eye still dropped the scalding tear:
Weakness was at her side, and in the rear
Sat Watchfulness and Woe; from off his stand,
The horrid dart pois'd in his wither'd hand,
In act to strike, appear'd the monster Death,
And grimly smil'd upon his prey beneath ;
But smil'd in vain: Eliza saw my need,
And new to save me with an angel's speed;
Kindly she spake; Despair conceal'd his head,
And every jealous fear and doubting fled:
Before her soothings Sorrow sank away,
And with her smiles my soul rehail'd the day.
Sick as I was, she took me to her breast,
Hush'd every sigh, and lull'd my cares to rest:
No more my mind sat brooding o'er its woe,
No more my heart all comfort would forego;
Peace once again outspread her balmy wing-,
And jocund Pleasure put forth buds of spring;
Soft Sleep his downy pinions light spread o'er
The bed, where Watchfulness had toss'd before;
And streaks of ruddy health began to break
Through the sad pale, that sallow'd my sunk cheek.
Death fled appall'd at that detested sight,
And with him fled the gloomy shades of night.
O thou! whose generous unexampled love,
Did all these evils and far more remove,
How shall my heart speak on that happy morn,
In which my blessings seem to be re-born!
From thy dear hand I date my life; from thee
My health, my peace, my independency!
0 blest, most blest above the sons of men!

In which my blessings seem to be re-born!
From thy dear hand I date my life; from thee
My health, my peace, my independency!
O blest, most blest above the sons of men!
How shall my feelings breathe along my pen,
When my full soul its gratitude would speak,
Or tell thy virtues ? Language is too weak,
To give the one or other equal fire,
Poor is my pen, but potent my desire!
Yet to be dumb, when gratitude, when love,
When every generous impulse that can move
The throbbing heart, demand the debt of praise,
Would speak that heart still colder than my lays;
And such I know is thy humility,
That still the wish to please, will pleasure thee.
Grace, then, with smiles, this tribute of my pen,
Since love, and love alone, indites the strain !
O dearer, than the dearest terms of life,
My cheerful kind companion, friend, and wife !
Thy converse sweet this spark of life endears,
And smoothes my passage through this vale of tears.
Sweet is thy temper, sweeter far thy mind; -
To every softness, every grace inclin'd.
Complacent, humble, tender, meek, and good,
By thee no wiles were ever understood;
On thy dear brow enthron'd we always see,
Mild sense, chaste mirth, and sweet simplicity;
The govern'd passions, and the tempered smile,
And all the serpent's wit - without his guile.
Still candid, gentle, generous are thy ways,
Still kind, still prudent, past the words of praise !
Still is thy heart alive to every woe;
Still has thine eye the tear humane to flow;
Transcendent still thou art, in earthly love, '
Transcendent still thy faith in God above.
O may that Being, whose almighty will

Best pleased thou art at all times to fulfil,
Long, long, preserve thy precious life, and please
Thy health, thy joys, thy comforts to increase!
Oft may'st thou hail this blest returning morn,
And may thy virtues long the earth adorn !
And when shall come, as sure will come, the day
That frees thy spirit from surrounding clay,
Grant, O All Merciful! that from its bands,
Its passage may be easy to thy hands!
O my Eliza! best of womankind,
Pardon, if here my fond, my faltering mind,
Sickens, and weakly turns, distrest, aside
At that dread thought, which Faith and Hope deride.
And well may they deride; since souls so fine,
So free from every spot and stain as thine,
Look far beyond this world for happiness,
And in the realms above expect their bliss.
Ah ! happiest far of all, that hour of fate
When souls like thine no more their freedom wait!
Glowing with fervent love, and hope, and faith,
How will thy spirit scorn the bed of death!
How will she pant for that immortal joy,
Which ne'er will perish, and can never cloy !
How joyful will she seek her blest abode!
For pure she is, and meet to dwell with God.

VERSES ON THE COMPANY ASSEMBLED AT LANGFORD
IN THE TIME OF THE HEAVY SNOW IN 1776.

[Preface by Mrs Torriano to the copy she wrote
from memory in 1829.]

'During the confinement of a large party at
Langford Court for several days in
consequence of a deep snow, Miss Luders

made a pen for Mr. S. Whalley, and insisted
on his writing her a copy of verses with it. He
immediately complied, supposing the pen to
speak.'[19]

LUCRETIA has made me, and now in despite,
She vows I shall pluck up my courage and write.
But what can I say ? For the weather's so chill,
That it freezes my wit, and dispirits my will.
Say anything, nothing, as long as you write.
Then let it be what you shall please to indite;
And if, like yourself, I protest and declare,
The theme will be pleasing and subject full fair.
Pooh, pooh ! that sha'n't serve you, so e'en set about,
The task I insist on; of what is without,
Or within you may write, it matters not what,
So the subject be merry and measure is pat.
Without or within you may write; why without,
There's nothing but snow, whisking each way about.
In such a cold cause, it is past all dispute,
My genius must languish, both barren and mute.
Or, should she bring forth, you would see in a trice,
Her offspring transformed into morsels of ice;
And surely, my mistress, pray think me not bold,
Can never approve of an offspring so cold.
Within then, perforce, I my subject must find;
I have it! 'tis suited exact to my mind.
And first my fair maker shall furnish a theme,
Bright as poets e'er fancied, and poets can dream;
But a fig for their dreams; Lucretia was made
As fair as her namesake, but not half so sad.
Far distant from pouting, and making a pother,
'Bout I scarce can tell what, and calling in brother,
And father, and husband, to hear an oration

[19] JCTSW I pp.246-254

For the loss of a bauble, not worth the relation.
Then, changing her curling-tongs into a sword,
And ripping her breast for the love of her Lord,
Our Lucy takes care no such slip shall undo her,
So keeps at arm's distance each buxom young wooer;
Yet smiles upon all, and, in spite of their wills,
Still murders in mirth, and subdues with her smiles.
All jaunty and tasty in manner and dress,
Full of English affection and French politesse,
Coquetting and rioting, gambling and flirting,
To the next I'll proceed, and on her drop the curtain.
Behold her co-equal in spirit and mirth,
Mad Hester, whose star jigged about at her birth,
As ne'er star jigged before ; for fuller of fun,
No jolly soul ever lived under the sun.
Merry Momus stood by at the font with his darling,
And answered, as God-Dad, while Gravity, snarling,
Bit her nails out of madness; and starch Prudery
Found her gizzard in dole; such a dread enemy
She knew there was born to her squint; and, fy, fy !
But Comus, and Venus, and Euphrosyne
Joined Momus and giggled that christ'ning to see;
And swore, since their Godheads were honour'd on earth,
They ne'er were so pleased as at La Faussille's birth.
But why, in the legend of Humour and Laughter,
Should tight little Wickham come hobbling' after ?
Since first, 'midst the foremost she ever will be,
In each scene of cheerfulness, frolic, and glee;
Her motions all spirit, her looks are all fun;
Those looks speak her mind, and her smart flippant
    tongue
To her mind or her eyes never does any wrong.
Such a trio never lived since old Momus had birth,
And with Comus and Venus enlivened the earth;
And Venus her Wickham has blest with good store
Of her charms and her graces, and, what is still more,

Tho' at variance in common, yet here Madame Die,
That Goddess so stupid, so cold, and so shy,
Relenting, has lent without scruple her aid,
With Venus, to Wickham, as wife and as maid:
As one, all her virtue and modesty gear
She lent her; as t'other,- attend and you'll hear,--
Tho' nine times invoked, with loud squalls and a
        pother,
To dub Madame Dapper with title of mother,
Still, cautious has been to preserve her from harms,
And has helped to re-touch and awaken her charms.
But enough of these flippants ; a number of faces,
I yet spy around me who all demand places.
Stand by; clear the way ; first approaching, I see
A lady of merit and high quality.
Your Ladyship's humble ; how does Lady Mary?
To tell you the truth, I am in a quandary,
For my fingers with cold, you may see, are quite dead,
And the frost is got into my stomach and head.
Alas! my dear lady, the matter is sad ;
But ne'er regard trifles; e'en let us be glad,
That we've got a sound roof hanging over our heads,
And can bid frost defiance with mirth and warm beds.
For while we are up, we will keep warm with laughing,
And strengthen our stomachs with eating and quaffing;
So I trust you'll do well, for a worthier dame
Never lived, I declare, in the annals of fame.
But what says fair Jenkyns to all this bad weather ?
And why are her placid brows wrinkled together ?
Indeed, Gaffer Care, you are somewhat too rude,
In a party so jovial as ours to intrude;
Tho' husbands are precious, yet husbands awhile
May be trusted to Heav'n; then let us beguile
The moments with mirth; and leave till to-morrow
Each murmuring sigh, and each symptom of sorrow,
Tho' gentle and civil, and kind and composed,

Yet still at the bottom full archly disposed.
I know the fair Jenkyns; and know sans all doubt
That a jest she can merrily bandy about;
Then clear let her brow be, and jocund her heart,
For merry we met, and in mirth let us part.
Ah, wags! t'espy you, a couple you are
Of as social spirits as e'er breathed the air.
There's Madam, the hostess of this company,
Will laugh and will jest till she scarcely can see;
And Sanford, though sometimes so grave and demure,
Each frolic will mend and each joke will secure,
And add of her own, too, at pleasure (none better),
A cargo of wit, in a legible letter.
To honour, good humour, and friendship, and sense,
No pair now alive can make better pretence;
Allied as in blood, so in manners and mind
I would not disjoin, who so aptly are joined.
Behold, Madam Susan, to bring up the rear,
So easy, an' please ye, so plump and sincere;
So hearty she laughs, that it does one's heart good,
And her song charms the ear, and enlivens the blood.
Pass on, my sleek Susan, and sing while ye can;
Short is life, and 'tis wise to enliven the span.
So much for the 'belles'; but pray where are the ' beaux?'
Oh ! not far behind them, as you may suppose;
And first (as 'tis fitting he should be) the chief,
See, bowing, the gallant Monsieur Zenovief.
What mortal can wonder we make no small fuss,
To see French politeness, engrafted on Russ;
And the Great Chamberlain of Russia's Majesty,
Appearing to grace such poor rustics as we ?
But silence there! Silence! not a word nor a squeak,
For Monsieur the Russian is going to speak.
(Votre humble, Madame, Ma'mselle Ludres; tres votre;
Madame Week, très agréable; and you be, vous autres,
De fort jolies Anglaises.' Oh, Monsieur, Monsieur!

Your most humble servant! I cannot endure,
To be tongue-tied so vilely. Miss Luders, explain
My good wishes to Monsieur, and say with disdain,
I hold the embargo that's laid on my tongue,
Which does my esteem for the Count so much wrong.
Lucretia interprets; and like a sly elf,
Says one word for Wicky, and two for herself;
While Monsieur, the Chamberlain, capers and chatters,
Salutes their soft hands, sighs, and ogles, and flatters;
Now talks broken English, now puts on the droll;
First plays like a monkey, then looks like a fool;
Acts the sot and the sick man, with each merry trick,
Making laughter re-echo, and gravity sick.
Agreeable, sensible, easy, polite;
The gentlemen's envy, and ladies' delight;
With the strength of a Samson, and humour of Foote;
A Mercury active, and loving to boot;
Can any one wonder, this gallant young Buss,
Has power our fair ones to charm and amuse ?
But should they at any time put on their rude airs,
Behold at his elbow, his 'aide de camp,' Luders;
Than whom upon earth, either sober or mellow,
There lives not, I swear, a more sprack little fellow.
Gay as youth can proclaim him, and jocund as day;
Full of mirth and good humour, and laughter and play;
A better companion can never be found,
To make a dull season run merrily round.
This Hetty can witness, whose lips seldom fail,
The effects of his raptures and prowess to tell;
But surely you 'll think me a fool or a sot,
Should Wickham, so courteous and calm, be forgot,
Whose carriage so gentle, and manners so easy,
Can't fail, if you know what is pleasing, to please ye.
With a soul full of goodness, and kindness, and spirit,
As loved for good humour, as honoured for merit;
Sense, tempered with candour, resides in his breast,

And mirth fills his bosom, in soberness drest;
When aces and faces skim over the green,
And the conflict grows hot, betwixt knave, king and
      queen,
'Midst the din of the battle, who better can wield,
Of the mighty god Whist, or the sword or the shield
Yet vanquished or victor, while tumults increase,
Unmov'd he is conquer'd, and conquers in peace.
But who, says Lucretia, pray who must appear,
In so social a party, to bring up the rear ?
Can you ask, my sweet Lucy ? why, maugre all doubt,
Who conducted them in, ought to wait on them out.
Behold, then, their host , as alert as a bee,
As 't is proper he should be, in such company;
Tho' skinny and lank, yet he 'll laugh with the best,
And never be guilty of marring a jest.
Full of joy, hospitality, peace, and good-will,
From the crown of his head, to the tip of his heel;
And when you reflect that he's tall as a steeple,
You will fancy his portion is large, my good people;
But think once again, that he's slender as tall,
And then you may fancy his portion is small.
Be that as it may, a more social party-
More jolly, more frolicsome, free, or more hearty,
Ne'er met since Don Sancho embraced his dear Dapple,
Since Israel danced hornpipes, or Eve ate the apple.
So met and so suited, each wind may blow round;
Bain rattle, frost chill, and snow whiten the ground,

On themselves and their mirth, they repose full reliance,
And to winter, and all his assaults, bid defiance.

Patronage
TSW and many of his circle was among the several hundred
patrons of the book of poems which Helen Maria Williams
(1761-1827), the novelist poet and translator, published in 1786,

but there is nothing to suggest that he knew her personally or her protagonist, the non-conformist minister Andrew Kippis, whom she had met in 1781. However, it may have been that TSW was recruited through his much respected near neighbour the Reverend Charles Layard, who like Kippis was a member of the Antiquarian Society. Several other members of that Society also subscribed.

LIST OF SUBSCRIBERS

The Right Rev the Bishop of Bath and Wells TSW's Bishop
Mrs Billingsley of Ashwick Grove, Somersetshire.
Henry Bosanquet, Esq. The man TSW let Langford Court to
Richard Cosway, Esq. One of the painters patronised by TSW
Mrs. Garrick Wife of David Garrick
Mrs. T. S. Jackson Friend of Anna Seward and TSW
Mrs. Hannah More
S. J. Pratt, Esq. The infamous Count Melmoth
Sir Joshua Reynolds One of the painters patronised by TSW
George Romney, Esq. One of the painters patronised by TSW
Miss Seward Lichfield Anna Seward
William Seward, Esq. Anna's Father
William Siddons, Esq. Husband of Sarah Siddons
Mrs. Siddons Sarah Siddons
Miss Weston Ludlow. TSWs cousin by marriage
Miss Wilberforce Hull. William Wilberfoce's sister, who also wrote poetry

APPENDIX 3
Paintings Associated with Thomas Sedgwick Whalley

Hill Wickham says that his great uncle considered himself to be an amateur judge of painting (he uses the word dilettante) and that he made a collection of some of the old masters as well as liberally patronising living artists of the time. He particularly mentions Thomas Barker (1769-1847), who painted landscapes but also became well known for his theatrical portraits and scenes from plays and illustrations of poems. Hill Wickham says that Barker's well known picture of 'The Woodman' was painted for Thomas Sedgwick (see below). Other landscapes painted by Barker, now held in the Tate Gallery, would have been very much to Thomas Sedgwick's liking, but no link has been established between him and the donors.

Romney painted the portrait of Elizabeth Whalley which Thomas kept with him all his life. The year before he died, he asked his great nephew to take the portrait to his framer and gilder, Mr Wakefield of Bath, to get the frame regilded. It was from this original that the engraving by Joseph Brown, from which the print in the front of JCTSW Vol. II was derived, was made. One can safely assume that the original of Frances Sage by Cosway, from which the engraving of her (which appears in JCTSW Vol. I opposing page 480) was made, was also commissioned by Thomas Sedgwick (see below).

According to Whalley's Will, those pictures remaining at the time of his death were to be divided equally between James Anthony Wickham and Richard Thomas Whalley. Sadly, none are listed, nor is there any indication of the number which were hung at Mendip Lodge. The only one definitely known to have existed there was the full length portrait of Mrs Siddons in the character of Hill's Zara, painted by Hamilton (see below). There was, however, a painting of the Vatican at Rome in a gilded frame left to his nephew Reverend Thomas Whalley, and two miniatures left to Eleanora Lewis.

Sir Joshua Reynolds RA (1723-1792)
This notable artist painted many in the Whalley circle, including Thomas Sedgwick himself, a work from which was made the engraving by Joseph Brown which appears at the front of JCTSW Vol. I.

Other Whalley acquaintances and contemporaries painted by Reynolds include:

Samuel Johnson
David Garrick
James Boswell
Horace Walpole
Hester Lynch Piozzi
Mrs Siddons
Oliver Goldsmith
Richard Brinsley Sheridan
Mrs Thrale *with her Daughter Hester Maria*
Warren Hastings
William Beckford

George Romney (1734-1802)
As mentioned above, the portrait of Mrs Sage (Elizabeth Whalley) was later the subject of an engraving by Joseph Brown. Hill Wickham also says that, about the same time as Cosway painted a miniature of Frances Sage, Romney painted a full length portrait of her.

Maxim Gauci (1774–1854)

A lithograph of Mrs Horneck Whalley, printed by Engelmann & Co and published by E. Collings, is held in the National Portait Gallery. This is likely to have been made in 1813, at the time of her marriage to Thomas Sedgwick. The background could well be that of Mendip Lodge.

Richard Cosway RA (1742-1821)

Although remembered primarily as a miniaturist, Cosway also painted oil portraits. Born in Tiverton, Devon he was a child prodigy. He came to London in 1754. He painted Mrs Siddons, then aged 27, in 1782, a work from which the engraving by Joseph Brown was made (this appears opposite page 136 in JCTSW Vol II). There are several letters at this time from Mrs Siddons to both Thomas and his wife, but none mention a sitting for any painting, though she had several by all the well known artists of the time.

Frances Sage was painted by Cosway, aged about 13-16 years; later, an engraving was made from this by Joseph Brown (it appears opposite page 480 in JCTSW Vol. I). The Cosway original could well have been the portrait which was sold in London in July 1987 for £220,000, but despite help from Mr Julian Gascoigne of Sotheby's, the current owner has not responded to enable this to be confirmed. The painting was paid for by TSW and cost £50. At the time Cosway's studio was just round the corner from Isaac Sage's house in Albermarle Street, St James's, London.

William Hamilton RA (1751-1801)

A full length portrait of Mrs Siddons in the role of Zara was commissioned by Whalley from this artist. (The play *The Tragedy of Zara* was written by Aaron Hill in 1735 and was an adaptation of Voltaire's *Zaïre*.) The exact date of the original painting is unknown, but the engraving made from it by Caldwell is dated 1789. Caldwell had made an earlier engraving, dated 1785, from

Hamilton's painting of Siddons in her role of Isabella. This may have been the spur for Thomas Sedgwick's commission.

Thomas Barker (1769-1847)

Hill Wickham credits his great uncle with commissioning the 'well known painting of the Woodman'. Several Barker paintings of this general title exist, examples including 'The Woodman in a Storm', held at the Tate Gallery, and 'The Woodman and his Dog', in the Pontypool Museum, for which a preparatory drawing exists in the British Museum. Another version, dated to 1789, is 'The Woodman Returning', which was exhibited in 1846 in a bid to raise money and support for Barker.

APPENDIX 4
The Character of Thomas Sedgwick Whalley

A fulsome account of Thomas Sedgwick's character comes from his great nephew and is repeated below in full. Despite the fact that he had reason to be grateful to his great uncle, the account does seem to be a fair and objective appraisal.

> In reviewing the character of Dr. Whalley, we see a type of English gentleman which has now passed away. The more tranquil political times, in which we happily live, the great increase in the numbers of the educated classes, the constant running to and fro by the agency of steam, tend much to raise the calibre of men's minds to the same standard. Great talkers are not tolerated in the present day; if anyone thinks he knows more than his fellows, he must let them have it on paper, not viva voce. Not so in the last century: Dr. Johnson' society was not cultivated because he had written the dictionary, nor George Selwyn's because he was a man of fashion, nor Burke's because he was a great statesman, but because they all talked well. Such were the powers for which, in a less degree, Dr. Whalley was best known. But for Miss Seward's eulogiums, few even of his contemporaries would have heard of his 'Edwy and Edilda', now long since passed into oblivion; but his large acquaintance with the

world, his extensive and varied information, his easy and yet powerful flow of language, and his elegant manners, obtained him the distinction of the literary friends, whose correspondence is now published, and a general reputation in society, which made him a welcome guest in so many good houses.[1]

Mr Wilberforce, in 1813, described him as:

the true picture of a sensible, well-informed, and educated, polished, old, well-beneficed, nobleman's and gentleman's house-frequenting, literary and chess-playing divine—of the best sort (not adulatory) — I hope beginning to be serious.[2]

As a dilettante, Thomas Sedgwick Whalley considered himself a judge of painting. He made a collection of some of the old masters and liberally patronised living artists, especially Barker of Bath, whose well-known picture of *The Woodman* was painted for Dr Whalley. He was passionately fond of music played on the piano and was so powerfully affected by a good military band that, when listening to it, he wept like a child. In politics he had an extensive correspondence with well-informed persons, and he considered himself an authority. He did not easily brook contradiction, as may be seen by his letter to Miss Seward defending Pitt's conduct in the war, which she returned to him.[3] Though possessed of a handsome income through his marriages, he could not confine his expenditure within its limits; much money was wasted in extravagance and vanity, which caused him much regret at the close of life. By then it was his great desire to arrange his affairs by selling Mendip Lodge in order that his relatives might benefit from him after his death (see Appendix

---

[1] JCTSW I p.38-9

[2] Sadly Hill Wickham gives no reference for this quote

[3] JCTSW II pp. 296-304

5). In a letter from Brussels to Mr Anstey Calvert, his friend and legal adviser, in December 1815, he says:

> Next summer a favourable offer may be made for Mendip Lodge, or, if not next year, the following one. However straitened in my income, I will contrive to live under it. I have been guilty of too much waste, and too many follies in money matters; but those who come after me, shall not have to reproach my memory for sacrificing their interest to the selfishness of selling, at a very inferior value, such a property as will one day not only sell for, but be well worth, the sum I now demand for it, viz. £30,000.

At about this time Whalley met Thomas De Quincey, who was visiting his mother at West Hay, Wrington, within a mile of Hannah More's house at Barley Wood. (It was through her that De Quincy met Mrs Siddons.) De Quincey also implies, from the age of Whalley when he says he met him, that this was also the occasion when he visited Mendip Lodge.[4] He then described the 68 year old Thomas Sedgwick as follows:

> The Doctor was a querulous old man, enormously tall and enormously bilious; so that he had a spectral appearance when pacing through the false gaieties of his glittering villa. He was a man of letters, and had known Dr Johnson, whom he admired prodigiously; and had himself been in earlier days the author of a poem now forgotten. He belonged at one period to the coterie of Miss Seward, Dr Darwin, Day and Mr Edgeworth etc., consequently he might have been an agreeable companion, having so

---

[4] De Quincey T., *The works of Thomas de Quincey Vol 11: Articles from Taits Magazine*, North J (Ed), Pickering and Chatto, London, 2003, pp.238-241

> much anecdote at his command; but his extreme
> biliousness made him irritable in a painful
> degree, and impatient of contradiction –
> impatient even of dissent in the most moderate
> shape

This, and his subsequent description of Mendip Lodge, while amusing, was not altogether accurate. For example, he suggests that Thomas Sedgwick imposed himself on Mrs Siddons, when in fact Mrs Siddons acknowledged Thomas as her greatest friend. He also states that Thomas died in a common lodging house in France, when it was in his own chair in his niece Mrs Sullivan's house in La Fléche where he died. Quincey, who was by this time in debt, clearly disliked Whalley's wealth and the way he had used it.

Though all extravagance proceeds from a selfish principle, yet Dr Whalley was uniformly kind and generous towards his relatives and friends. His gifts, though, were excessive: Miss Seward complains of the amount he gave to her servants. He always travelled in a coach drawn by his own four horses with two postillions.[5] At Bath the post-boys fought for the honour of driving him. Hill Wickham reports that he paid his tradesmen's bills with so much grace that it appeared as if they were conferring, rather than receiving, a favour. When his executor, on his way to settle Dr Whalley's affairs, mentioned his death at the well-known Botham's Hotel near Hungerford, where TSW was in the habit of staying on his journeys to the metropolis, the landlady burst into tears and appeared really affected.[6]

Hill Wickham reports that in a letter to his legal adviser in September 1815 Thomas confesses that the late Sir Horace Mann had cost him £300 a year. It seems that Sir Horace's niece Miss Elizabeth Cornwallis was the daughter of the Bishop of Litchfield, the 4th Earl Cornwallis, and an admired friend of

---

5 JCTSW II p.228 (Footnote)
6 ibid I p.40

Thomas Sedgwick and Anna Seward. Elizabeth used to stay with Sir Horace in Bath and became well known in Bath society. Thomas Sedgwick's annual payment saved them both from debt and loss of reputation in the years prior to their deaths.[7] While this act of generosity was not sought, it was not difficult to impose upon Whalley's generosity for he readily believed a person's character to be what he wished it to be, and so he was often deceived. Such disappointments, however, did not sour his temper nor tinge it with misanthropy. Writing to a young relative in 1825 he says,

> In you the silver cord is bright and strong, and the golden bowl is sound and unblemished. In me the former is attenuated to a trembling thread, and the latter is so irreparably damaged as to be threatened with destruction. Sad and long experience of this vain world and its ways – of the hollowness of profession and promises, disappointed in some, deluded by others – deprived by death of various true and valuable friends, and far distant from a few whom I esteem, and by whom I am valued and loved — the still warm affections of my heart are concentrated within a small circle, and burn the more ardently, because, like the sunbeams on a burning-glass, converging to one focus.

According to Hill Wickham, who as a member of the clergy should have known, Dr Whalley's religious creed was founded on the Tomline school, which was considered the respectable divinity of the day, free from the unorthodox tenets which Miss Seward held and from what was considered the "enthusiasm" of the Methodists or the austerity gaining ground and which his brother Richard followed.

---

[7] JCTSW II pp.351-2

This view of Thomas Sedgwick's religious beliefs may not be correct, as it was not until the late 1790s that Pretyman became noted as a theologian. His two-volume work *Elements of Christian Theology*, designed for Anglican ordinands, was not published until 1799, by which time Thomas Sedgwick was in his 50s. More likely, Thomas originally saw himself, like so many who had entered the church at this time, as joining the ruling elite but with a duty to take care of society – the so called "noblesse oblige". These views he only changed after long contact with others, such as Hannah More, and perhaps through the influence of his brother. By the end of his life, he was admitting to his friend and legal adviser Anstey Calvert that he had been 'guilty of too much waste, and too many folies in money matters'[8] and two years before his death, as described above, seems to have decided that salvation was only achieved through faith and prayer.

There is one other, more independent, account of Thomas Sedgwick's early character. Fanny Burney, who was visiting his house for the first time in 1780, described him as

> immensely tall, thin and handsome, but affected delicate and sentimentally pathetic; and his conversation is about "feelings", about amiable motives and about the wind which he said in a tone of dying horror blew in a manner really frightful.[9]

His sensitivity does seem to be borne out in his letters, but this is no more than that expressed by other members of his circle. However, most of these were women, and one can perhaps conclude that such sensitivity was rare among men in those days. A further example is his poem 'The Fatal Kiss' (1781), which relates the seduction and desertion of an impoverished young girl, written from the perspective of the girl herself. The publication carries a subtitle with a manifest threat:

---

8 JCTSW I p.40

9 *The Streatham Years, Part II* 1780-1781 In Early Journals and Letters of Fanny Burney, Volume IV (Rizzo, B., Ed.) Oxford University Press, 2003. p.126

> The singular and melancholy Circumstances of whose Life [the girl] may, perhaps, be one Day offered the Public, to the Confusion and Disgrace of one whose Fortune and Rank would not have Power to shield him from the Censure and Detestation of every one who has true Principles of Honour and Humanity.

Was this an expression of outrage with the intention that the man concerned, so threatened, would make recompense? The story does reflect that of Hannah More, whom was proposed to by William Turner of nearby Tyntesfield. After six years the wedding had still not taken place, and in 1773 Turner broke the engagement off. It seems that, as a consequence, Hannah suffered a nervous breakdown and spent some time recuperating. As a consequence Turner was persuaded by his friends to pay Hannah a £200 annuity for life. However, Thomas Sedgwick did not know Hannah More at this time, so one must conclude that either this was another case where the sensitive Doctor was outraged, or else 'The Fatal Kiss' and the threat its subtitle carried were both works of fiction.

There can be no doubt that, for all his affectations, Thomas Sedgwick was witty, intelligent, and widely knowledgeable and widely read. Had he not been, he would have been ignored by the likes of Hannah More and her bluestocking circle. A number of his long term male friends were intellectual leaders of the day and respected his friendship and judgement. Examples are Bishop Charles Layard, who was a Fellow of St John's, Cambridge, a member of the Society of Antiquaries, a Fellow of the Royal Society and their Foreign Secretary: 'A month has elapsed since I received from you a letter, written in a style, as worthy of your abilities, as its sentiments are of your friendship.'[10] Bishop Beadon, eighth Wrangler and Senior Chancellor's Medallist in his undergraduate years, became among other things Master of Jesus College, Cambridge:

---

[10] JCTSW I p.316

> I am not without hope of your having some time
> or other [to] call towards Gloucester, so as to
> make a visit to the Palace as little inconvenient
> to you as it would be highly gratifying to myself
> and Mrs. Beadon...

The following is from the pen of Bishop Porteous, Fellow of Christ's College, Cambridge:

> Mr Whalley's letters [about the meeting there had
> been at the George Inn Blagdon during the
> Blagdon Controversy] are excellent, and they give
> so minute and circumstantial a detail of the
> alehouse conclave, that I would wish to keep the
> copies you sent me, if you have other copies for
> yourself; or I will send them back to you and beg
> the favour of your sister to get them copied for
> me.[11]

Nor were his long-term friends Mrs Thrale/Piozzi, Hannah More and Anna Seward noted for tolerating fools gladly, and there are many references in their correspondence to others who held Thomas Sedgwick in esteem.

He was good looking and charming, which makes it seem rather odd that almost immediately after he was ordained he appears to have sought out a rich, childless widow to marry. Even before he settled upon the widowed Mrs Sherwood, he seems to have had his eye on another widow in N. Wales. This seems to have been a quite deliberate strategy and is very unusual when a major concern of every 18th-century man was to produce an heir. It cannot be that he disliked children, as he was soon very much involved in the welfare and education of his niece Frances Sage and later his great nephew Hill Wickham. In the case of the former, he seems to have been more adoring than her father. One might believe that perhaps he was unaware as an unmarried young

---

[11] JCTSW II p.169

man how fond he would become of children, yet when his first wife died he seems to have made sure that this second wife was beyond child bearing age. Was it just that he wanted wealth uncluttered by the distractions of family life? Alternatively, he had perhaps been shocked by the suffering his sister had undergone in pregnancy, from which she never really recovered. There is no evidence to support such a suggestion, but his extreme sensitivity, reported by Fanny Burney, makes this plausible. He would also have been fully aware that the Anglican Marriage Service, as laid down by the *Book of Common Prayer*, had for its prime purpose the procreation of children who were to be brought up 'In the fear and nurture of the Lord'. How could he marry and yet avoid putting a woman through the traumatic a risky process of child bearing? The only way would be to marry a lady who was either beyond child bearing age or one who had shown herself to be incapable of producing children, i.e. a childless young widow. He could then still fulfil his Christian duty by devoting himself to bringing up other people's children to be god-fearing Anglicans.

There is another, equally plausible, explanation, which is that Thomas Sedgwick was a homosexual, although a very circumspect one. There seems little doubt that Mrs Piozzi (Mrs Thrale), one of Thomas Sedgwick's closest and lifelong friends, had a great ability to recognise homosexual men. According to Norton, there were a couple whom she liked even though she strongly disapproved of their sex lives.[12] One of these was probably David Garrick, another contributor to Lady Miller's poetical assemblies at Bath, who had great difficulty in extricating himself from the scandal of being associated with Isaac Bickstaff, who was accused by *The Daily Advertiser* on 30 April 1772 of being a sodomite and forced to flee to France as a consequence. Perhaps Marie Antoinette's charming description of Thomas Sedgwick as 'le bel Anglais' carried a hidden meaning?[13]

---

[12] Rictor Norton (Ed.), 'Mrs Piozzi's Reminiscences, 1770s-1790s', in *Homosexuality in Eighteenth-Century England: A Sourcebook,*
<http://rictornorton.co.uk/eighteen/piozzi.htm>. Accessed 20 April 2003

For many years Thomas Sedgwick had William Walter Slade Amans living with him 'at his own table'. Mrs Piozzi describes Amans as a confidential servant.[14] It seems that Thomas took pity on him as a man of good birth brought down by family circumstances.[15] He remained with Thomas until 1814, when he acquired independent means. There is no correspondence with him recorded, but Thomas Sedgwick, aged 68, spoke of him as being 'an unspeakable comfort to me' in that year.

Soon after his second wife died, Thomas rented a house in Baker Street, London and spent much of the time from 1809-1813 living there, where, according to Hill Wickham, he 'entertained sumptuously, was a collector of paintings, and had a weakness for expensive jewellery by which Messrs Rundell and Bridge [the Royal Jewellers] must have considerably profited'.[16] But who did he entertain and who was the jewellery for? It seems unlikely it was for himself: he is not wearing any in his portrait, nor is there any mention of him doing so in any correspondence, nor would it be seen as appropriate for a clergyman to do so. In fact, there is only a single piece of jewellery mentioned in his Will: 'my gold snuff box with a rare and valuable agate on its to go to my respected friend Lady Jane James cousin to my second wife'. So where did the other jewellery go?

His third wife had been married to General Horneck, who was known as the Military Macaroni (see Chapter 12). It seems she was very largely living apart from him, which is perhaps why he left his entire estate to his 'faithful servant Henry Genean'. Major Horneck's earlier marriage in 1773 had been no more successful, as his first wife almost immediately ran off with a fellow officer. After 1772 the Macaronis in the public's mind had become firmly associated with homosexuality:

---

13 JCTSW I p.16
14 TPL V pp.152-153
15 JCTSW II p.389
16 ibid I p.33

> But Macaronies are a sex
> Which do philosophers perplex;
> Tho' all the priests of Venus's rites☐
> Agree they are Hermaphrodites.

('The Vauxhall Affray', from a 1770s pamphlet)[17]

Was this the reason for the failure of Horneck's two marriages? Thomas Sedgwick must have been aware of his history, as, by the time of his marriage to her, he had known Mrs Horneck for thirty years or more. So perhaps neither had any illusions about the other, but he found 'Her habits of Life and turn of Mind are peculiar, and new ones even with bonne Volonte, are not easily adopted, at 58' (see Chapter 12). He does not make it clear whether it was he or she who needed to adapt but was quite prepared to support her and pay her debts and only sought a legal separation after she 'ran off' and accused him of cruelty. Even then he provided her with a house and a generous settlement.

By the last years of his life, Thomas Sedgwick was a wiser and a sadder man; many had taken advantage of his generosity. By this time his religious views had altered. It would seem that Wilberforce's hope in 1815 that he was 'beginning to be serious' came to pass. The Tomline doctrine of a union of faith and good works as the price of salvation was rejected,[18] and he believed that only faith offered true salvation. Writing two years before his own end in reference to the death of a relative, he says,

> O that my last hour may be as calm, and as full of
> a blessed hope (through the stupendous sacrifice
> and infinite mercy of our Divine Redeemer, on
> which the best of human beings can only rely) of
> eternal salvation! With this new and solemn

---

[17] West, S., *The Darly Macaroni Prints and the Politics of "Private Man"*. Eighteenth-Century Life, 2001, 170-182

[18] See Scott, S., *Remarks on the Refutation of Calvinism by George Tomline*, G Macintosh, London, 1817

warning close at hand, I must work at the one thing always most needful, while a little day is still graciously left me, since that last night must ere long come on me when I shall no longer be able to work.

APPENDIX 5

The Will of Thomas Sedgwick Whalley, Written on 25th June 1824, with a Long Codicil Added on 11th August 1828

I Thomas Sedgwick Whalley of Bath in the County of Somerset Doctor in Divinity being feeble in body but sound of mind do hereby revoke all Wills, Codicils and their testamentary dispositions made by me at any time or times heretofore. I hereby nominate constitute and appoint my nephew James Anthony Wickham of North Hill Froome in the County of Somerset Esquire the sole executor of this my Will and I hereby desire and order my said executor to cause the wretched body that has reason to be inhabited and animated by my immortal soul to be buried in the same vault in Burrington Church in the County of Somerset as my first and second excellent wives and it is my positive will and order that my body may be buried with as little useless expense possible and that my coffin my be borne to the aforesaid church by four poor married men of the parish of Churchill in the said County of Somerset and four poor married men of Churchill in the county of Somerset to be chosen by my said Executor and to each of the said eight men chosen as aforesaid I hereby give and bequeath the sum of two Guineas and a complete and new suit of mourning including two pairs of stocking two shirts two neck cloths a pair of shoes a pair of black gloves and I further direct that the wives of the said eight poor men shall be my pall bearers to each of whom I give and bequeath the like sum of two Guineas and a complete and new suit of mourning including a bonnet, two neckerchiefs, two pairs of stockings and an apron an under flannel petticoat a pair of shoes and a pair of black gloves and I direct that such several sums of two Guineas respectively and such suits of mourning as aforesaid be respectively by paid delivered and given to such poor men and women as soon as maybe after my decease and it is my desire that no kind of memorial be erected to my memory.

I give and bequeath the sum of two hundred pounds of lawful money of Great Britain to be for the benefit of the poor of the parish of Burrington aforesaid and the like sum two hundred pounds of the like lawful money be for the benefit of the poor of the parish of Churchill aforesaid in manner following (namely) the said several sums to be respectively laid out and invested in the parliamentary stocks or public funds of Great Britain or at an interest in such securities as may from time to time be thought proper and dividends interest and annual product of such stocks funds and securities to be annually expended in household bread to be distributed to poor and distressed persons of families belonging to the said parishes, but not receiving the parish pay according to the judgement of the respective officiating clergymen and churchwardens for the time being of the said several parishes, every Sunday from the first day of December to the first day of March inclusive in every succeeding year and so on for ever

And I further give and bequeath the sum of three hundred pounds of lawful money to be for the support and benefit of the weekly Sunday schools in the parish of Hagworthingham in the county of Lincoln the same to be laid out and invested from time to time in such of the like stocks and funds and securities as aforesaid and the dividends interest and annual product thereof be for ever after expended for the support and benefit of the said Schools by and according to the direction of the officiating clergyman and churchwardens for the time being of the said parish of Hagworthingham and to each of the three several sums or legacies of two hundred pounds, two hundred pounds and three

Top of Page 2

394

hundred pounds respectively hereinbefore given for such charitable purposes as aforesaid and direct that the same respectively shall be raised and appropriated at the expiration of one year to be ????? from the date of my decease out of such parts of my personal estate as shall not consist of Chattels real and the same shall be a prior charge thereon before and in preference to any of the pecuniary legacies or annuities hereinafter given and each of the said sums respectively when so raised shall be laid out and invested by the said executor of this my will or other[?] the person or persona who may be acting in the execution of my will at his or their direction in the name of the trustees to be chosen or approved of by him or them in such stocks funds or securities aforesaid upon and with such powers in the allocation and variation of the same respectively from time to time and for applying the dividends interest and annual produce thereof respectively for the respective purposes hereinbefore declared thereof and for the appointment of new trustees and upon and with such other trusts and powers in generally in such manner for completing effectuating, facilitating and securing the charitable purposes whereto I have hereby directed the said several sums respectively appropriated as my said executor or other the person or persons so acting in the execution of this my Will as aforesaid shall their his or their discretion think reasonable and proper. And I herby declare that on his of their paying out and investing such sums respectively in the name of the Trustees in the manner aforesaid my said executor or other the person or persons so acting in the execution of this my Will as aforesaid shall be thereupon and thereby discharge and exonerated from all further obligation or liability of seeing to the application of the respective sums so laid out and invested or being otherwise responsible of seeing to the future execution of the trusts and purposes to which the same respectively are hereinbefore directed to be appropriated.And I direct and declare my will and mind to be that so soon as maybe after my decease the whole of my ornamental china (except such ornamental china as belong to or is usually used or enjoyed with my house at Mendip Lodge and also except such as belongs to or is let with my freehold house and all the freehold premises attached to it at Bath to Lady Hocton and likewise except such as is not hereby specifically or otherwise bequeathed or disposed of) shall be divided by my said executor into three parts as nearly equal in value as maybe. And I give and bequeath unto the Reverend Thomas Whalley Rector of Yeovilton near Ilchester in the county of Somerset on third part of my said ornamental china so to be divided as aforesaid together with my fine prints of the Vatican at Rome in handsome gilded frames and glazed together with the frames and glasses thereof and my copy of Humes Quarto History of England with fine engravings [This is perhaps the Smolett edition published in 1758] and also my tea service of Worcester China with landscapes painted at the bottom of each cup and saucer and the head of Laocoon [A Trojan Priest] drawn in chalk by the father of my nephew the said Richard Thomas Whalley. And I give and bequeath unto the Reverend Thomas Wickham Rector of Horsington in the County of Somerset one other third part of my said ornamental china so to be divided as aforesaid as also my three glazed cabinets and all the table and bed linen belonging to me at my decease I direct that my said executor to prevail the same to be used and enjoyed by Maria Anne Wickham

Top of Page 3

the wife of the said James Anthony Wickham during her life and from and immediately after her decease I give and bequeath the said last mentioned third part of my said ornamental china and the said three cabinets and table and bed linen unto and between Mary Agnes Wickham and Caroline Wickham (the two oldest daughters of the said James Anthony Wickham by his said wife) or their respective executors, administrators or assigns in equal shares and if but one of them the said Mary Agnes Wickham and Caroline Wickham shall be living at my decease then the said last mentioned third part of my said ornamental china and the said three cabinets and table and bed linen (subject only to such life interest of her said mother therein as aforesaid) shall belong to that one her executors, administrators and assigns. And I give and bequeath unto Eleanora Lewis the wife of the Reverend Lewis of Gwinfe[?] near Lanhyottork[?] [This would seem to be Gwynfe near Llangadog] in the county of Carmarthen in south Wales my fine diamond ring with the name of her cousin and my first dear and excellent wife Elisabeth Whalley engraved on its reverse and also my silver tea kettle and lamp two of my silver sauce boats with their silver ladles and a dozen of my silver forks and my table service of rolaced[?] old china with round dishes and I give and bequeath unto my faithful servant John Clark if he shall be in my service at the time of my decease all the body linen and wearing apparel belonging to me at my decease and also my two dressing boxes and my writing box with the several articles or things belonging to or ordinarily contained in the said boxes and I give and bequeath unto my old dear and highly respected friend Lady Jane James cousin to my second wife my gold snuff box with a rare and valuable agate on its lid requesting her acceptance of the same as a small memorial and my grateful attachment And I give and bequeath unto Hill Dawe Wickham the third son of the said James Anthony Wickham and his sister Caroline Wickham my collection of gold silver and copper coins to be divided between the said Hill Dawe Wickham and his said sister share and share alike but if only one of the said Hill Dawe Wickham and Caroline Wickham shall be living at my decease then the whole of my collection to that one. And I give and bequeath unto Elizabeth Whalley the wife of the said Richard Thomas Whalley my desert service of china painted with different flowers and embossed border of grapes and gilded. And I give and bequeath unto Mary Wickham the wife of the said Thomas Wickham my set of curious old Chelsea tea china painted with groups of boys etc[?] and bordered with festoons of green and gilded leaves and I give and bequeath unto the said Mary Agnes Wickham my desert set of old Worcester china with pheasants etc together with my beautiful set of tea china painted with peacocks and a circle border sand also all the little trinkets though of trifling value parked up in my India Ivory Tea Caddy and in another small box together with the said Caddy and said box both which are at present in the house of my said Executor at North Hill aforesaid And I give and bequeath unto Catherine Richards of Taunton in the county of Somerset spinster the portrait in crayon of my late dear wife when she was a little girl executed by the late Mr Hoare[?] of Bath and also the miniature pictures of my father and mother in law and Mrs Heathcote painted in enamel by Zinks[?] .And I give and bequeath unto my dear friend Eleanora Lewis the miniature picture of my first excellent wife's father painted in enamel by Zinks[?] and also the miniature picture of my great great uncle Mr Musgrave with a large flowing wig painted in his old age And as to and concerning my eight coal canal shares I direct

Top of Page 4

that my said Executor shall permit William Walter Slade Amans of Connaught Terrace Edgeware Road in the county of Middlesex Esquire and his assigns to receive take and enjoy the dividends increase and other annual or periodical profits in respect of the said eight Coal Canal Shares during the life of the said William Walter Slade Amans and from and immediately after the decease of the said William Walter Slade Amans I give and bequeath the said eight Coal Canal Shares and all my Estate and interest whatsoever therein to the said Mary Agnes Wickham and Caroline Wickham and their Executors Administrators and Assigns share and share alike as tenants in common and if but one of them the said Mary Agnes Wickham and Caroline Wickham shall be living at my decease then the entirety of the said 8 Coal Canal Shares[1]

[1] The Somerset Coal Canal, opened in 1805, gave access from the Somerset coalfield, which at its peak contained 80 collieries, to London via the Kennet and Avon Canal. The Share Capital was £80,000 in £100 shares. Among the original Committee were John Billingsley, James Tooker and Francis Whalley, all of whom were said to be connected with the coal trade. The interest paid on the shares varied greatly but at its peak in 1839 was 7%, . The canal made a good profit until the Radstock and Frome railway opened in 1846. By the time of

(subject only to such life interest of the said William Walter Slade Amans therein as aforesaid) shall belong to that one her Executors Administrators and Assigns. And I give and bequeath unto the said Eleanora Lewis the sum of one thousand one hundred pounds of lawful money of Great Britain and unto Eustatia Shairpe the wife of Major Shairpe now residing at Bouffs[?] in the county of Linlithgow in North Britain the sum of one thousand pounds in like lawful money the said two several sums to be respectively paid and payable to the said Eleanora Lewis and Eustatia Shairpe respectively out of the monies now due and owing or at the time of my decease to be owing to me or my estate from the Right Honourable Lord Ventrys [sic] and the said two several legacies to be respectively payable at the expiration of one whole year next after my decease or as soon after the expiration of the said year as the principal monies owing or to be owing from the said Lord Ventry whereout the same are to be paid as aforesaid shall under or by force of the Bond or other instrument whereon the same may be served at my decease be due and payable and in ruse[?] by virtue of the directions hereinbefore lastly contained the said two said legacies of one thousand one hundred pounds and one thousand pounds respectively shall not be payable until after the expiration of the said year then the said Eleanora Lewis and Eustacia Shairpe shall respectively be entitled to receive interest and the rate of four pounds percent on their said respectively legacies to be paid out of the interest payable on such bond or other security and to commence and be computed from the expiration of the said year and to continue and be payable by half yearly payments until the principal of their said legacies be respectively paid my mind and Will being that neither of the said two several sums of one thousand one hundred pounds and one thousand pounds respectively shall in any event be paid or payable at or shall bear interest from an earlier period than the expiration on one whole year form my decease and if by reason of the said monies so

---

Whalley's death, the Canal was in decline but was nonetheless profitable for another 60 years finally going into liquidation in 1893

owing or to be owing from the said Lord Ventry being wholly or partially paid or discharged in my lifetime or any other cause whatsoever the fund whereout the said legacies of one thousand one hundred pounds and one thousand pounds hereinbefore made payable shall not be in existence at my decease or shall otherwise fail or prove insufficient fully to discharge the said legacies then and in that case I hereby direct and declare that the said legacies shall not nor shall any parts thereof respectively be advanced or otherwise prejudiced by such non existence failure or insufficiency of the said fund as aforesaid but the same or so much thereof respectively as the said fund shall fail to answer shall be payable (together with such interest in

Top of Page 5

such event and at such rate as aforesaid) out of my general personal estate yet so that the said legacies of one thousand one hundred pounds and one thousand pounds respectively shall not in any event be payable before the expiration of one whole year next after my decease and I hereby direct and declare that the said two several sums of one thousand one hundred pounds and one thousand pounds and such interest for the same respectively as aforesaid shall be for the separate use and benefit of the said Eleanora Lewis and Eustacia Shairpe respectively and shall be respectively paid and applied by my executor or other the person or persons arising in the execution of this my will as and when the same shall respectively so become payable as aforesaid to the such person or persons for such ends intents and purposes generally in such manner as the said Eleanora Lewis and Eustacia Shairpe respectively shall by any writing or writings under their respective hands (notwithstanding their present or any future coverture [the position of a married woman considered to be under the protection of her husband] respectively direct and appoint and in default of such direction or appointment and so far as no direction or appointment shall extend into the proper hands of the said Eleanora Lewis and Eustacia Shairpe respectively for their own sole separate and peculiar use and benefit so that the same several sums and interest may not be subject or liable to the debts control or interference or engagements of their respective present or any future husbands and that the respective receipts of the said Eleanora Lewis and Eustacia Shairpe respectively or of the respectively appointees shall (notwithstanding such coverture) be good and sufficient discharges for the same respectively. And give and bequeath unto John Whalley Yeates the oldest son of my late niece Frances Yeates and now clerk to Mr Cunnington solicitor at Braintree in the county of Essex the sum of two hundred pounds of like lawful money but I hereby direct that my said executor shall retain the said sum of two hundred pounds in his hands and shall pay and apply the same or any part thereof and his direction in or towards placing the said John Whalley Yeates in the office of some eminent solicitor in London for the purpose of perfecting his professional education as and when he shall have served and completed his five years clerkship or such portion of his said clerkship as is in similar cases usually served in the county and shall pay the residue and surplus if any of the said legacy of two hundred pounds after answering the purposes aforesaid unto the said John Whalley Yeates at his age of twenty two years and a further direct that from and after the expiration of one whole year next after my decease and until the said legacy of two hundred pounds shall be paid and applied in manner aforesaid the interest for the same or the unpaid or unapplied part thereof at the rate of four pounds per cent per annum shall be paid by my said executor by equal half yearly payments to the said John Whalley Yeates for pocket money and the receipt of the said John Whalley Yeates shall notwithstanding his minority be sufficient discharges for the same. And I give and bequeath the sum of three hundred pounds of the like lawful money to be raised and paid or appropriated one whole year next after my decease unto the said James Anthony Wickham and William Bromley of Grays Inn the county of Middlesex Esquire their executors administrators and assigns upon trust to pay apply and advance the same or any part of parts thereof for the benefit of Luther Yeates the full brother of the said John Whalley Yeates and youngest son of my said niece Frances Yeates in placing him out when he shall be old enough

Top of Page 6

to learn or acquire some trade business or profession as they the same James Anthony Wickham and William Bromley and the survivor of them his executors administrators and assigns or such of them as may be for the time being be acting in the trusts hereby declared shall in their or his direction think proper and most for the said poor boy's advantage and in the mean time invest the same or the unpaid or unapplied part thereof either for the purpose of accumulation or otherwise howsoever as my said trustees or trustee for the time being in their or his direction think fit and to pay the unapplied residue or surplus (if any) of the said legacy of three hundred pounds and the accumulations thereof (if any) unto the said Luther Yeates upon his attaining the age of twenty one years. And I give and bequeath unto Eleanora Lewis the daughter of the Reverend Lewis and Eleanora his wife (hereinbefore mentioned) the sum of one hundred pounds of like lawful money to be paid on the expiration of one whole years next after my decease.And I give and bequeath unto Harriet Davie of Exeter in the County of Devon spinster, (sister of the said Eleanora Lewis the older and of the said Eustacia Shairp) the sum of five hundred pounds of like lawful money to be payable at the expiration of one whole year next after my decease and if not then actually paid to bear interest at the rate of four pounds percent per annum to commence and be computed from the expiration of such year and to continue and be payable by equal half yearly payments until the principal of the said legacy of five hundred pounds shall be paid. And I give and bequeath to Maria Somers spinster the first cousin to Mr Benjamin Somers MD of the parish of Wrington in the county of Somersetshire the sum of one hundred pounds to be payable at the expiration of one whole year next after my decease and also an annuity or clear yearly sums of twenty pounds of like lawful money for her life the first payment of the said annuity to be paid at the expiration on one whole year next after my decease if the said Maria Somers be living at the expiration of such year. And I give and bequeath unto Frances Sayer the wife of [a gap has been left for a first name] Sayer and sister of the said Dr Benjamin Somers the sum of fifty five pounds of like lawful money to be paid at the expiration of six calendar months next after my decease.And I give and bequeath unto Mrs Sarah Siddons of upper Baker Street London widow the sum of one hundred pounds to be paid at the expiration of one whole year next after my decease as a small token of my friendship.And I herby direct that the note of hand of my nephew Hyde Salmon Whalley for securing to me the payment of the sum of two thousand pounds be given up by my said executor to the said Hyde Salmon Whalley as soon as maybe after my decease to be burned destroyed or otherwise cancelled and so that the said Hyde Salmon Whalley may be wholly released and discharged from the payment of all and any principal monies which at the time of my decease may be due or owing upon the said note. And I give and bequeath unto William Elbourne who served me faithfully several years and whose worthy father was my father's butler many years (which said William Elbourne now lives on a farm which he rents[?] of [a gap has been left for first name] Brook Esquire somewhere in Cheshire the sum of one hundred and fifty pounds of like lawful money to be paid at the expiration of one whole year after my decease. And I give and bequeath unto Mary Heathcote spinster now residing in Bath the sum of two hundred and twenty pounds of like lawful money to be payable and the expiration on one whole year next after my decease and if not then actually paid to bear interest at the rate of four ponds per cent per annum to commence and be computed from the expiration of

Top of Page 7

such year and to continue and be payable by equal half yearly payments until the principal of the said legacy of two hundred and twenty pounds shall be paid. And I give and bequeath unto Hilary Simms the wife of [a gap has been left for a first name] Simms now residing in London who served my excellent second wife many years the sum of thirty pounds of like lawful money to be paid at the expiration of six calendar months next after my decease and also an annuity or clear yearly sums of five pounds of like lawful money for life the first payment of the said annuity to be made at the expiration of one hole year next after my decease if the said Mary Simms [then an insert as superscript which could be "dcab"] be living at the expiration of such year. And I give and bequeath unto Hannah Scunton[?] [then an insert as superscript which could be "dcab"] of the City of Bath spinster my late wife's faithful waiting woman the sum of twenty five pounds of like lawful money to be paid at the expiration of one whole year next after my decease and also an annuity or clear yearly sums of five pounds of like lawful money for life the first payment of the said annuity to be made at the expiration of one whole year next after my decease if the said Hannah Scunton[?] be living at the expiration of such year. And I give and bequeath unto Elizabeth Sly now residing in Bath who was my cook many years and who is now too old and infirm for service and annuity or clear yearly sums of ten pounds of like lawful money for her life the first payment of the said annuity to be made at the expiration of six months next after my decease if the said Elizabeth Sly be living at the expiration of the said six months. And I give and bequeath unto my faithful servant John Clarke if he shall be in my service at the time of my decease one year's full wages amounting to fifty guineas and also the further sum of two hundred and twenty pounds of like lawful money the said two several sums of fifty guineas and two hundred and twenty pounds respectively to be made at the expiration of one whole year next after my decease and if not then actually paid the same respectively to bear interest at the rate of four pounds per cent per annum to commence and be computed from the expiration of such year and to continue and be payable by equal half yearly payment until the principal of the said legacies of fifty guineas and two hundred and twenty pounds respectively shall be paid. And I give and bequeath unto Mrs Penelope Pennington wife of William Pennington of Dowry Square Clifton in the County of Somerset the sum of one hundred and ten pounds of like lawful money to be paid at the expiration of one whole year next after my decease I also give and bequeath unto the said Penelope Pennington and said William Pennington and to the survivor of them one annuity or clear yearly sum of fifty pounds of like lawful money for and during the lives of the said William Pennington and his said wife and the life of the survivor the first payment of the said annuity to be made at the expiration of one whole year next after my decease if the` said William Pennington and his said wife or either of them be living at the expiration of such year. And I give and bequeath unto Arthur Anstey Calvert of Park Street in the City of Bath Esquire the sum of two hundred pounds of like lawful money to be paid at the expiration of one whole year next after my decease and I also direct that in addition to the said last mentioned legacy of two hundred pounds the note of hand of the said Arthur Anstey Calvert (which will be found among my papers) for securing to me the payment of certain monies due from him to me amounting together with the interest due thereon above two hundred pounds shall be

Top of Page 8

given up by my said executor to the said Arthur Anstey Calvert as soon as maybe after my decease to be burned destroyed or otherwise cancelled and so that the said Arthur Anstey Calvert may be wholly released and discharged from the payment of all and any principal monies and interest which at the time of my decease may be owing upon the said note. And I give and bequeath unto Diana Calvert the wife of the said Arthur Anstey Calvert the sum of fifty pounds of like lawful money as a small testimony of my friendship and affection the same to be paid at the expiration of one whole year after my decease. And I give and bequeath unto my dear old friend Letitia Sparrow of Bourton in the County of Somerset widow the like sum of fifty pounds of like lawful money as a testimony of my respect and friendship the same to be paid at the expiration of one whole year after my decease. And I give and bequeath unto the said William Slade Walter Amans the sum of three hundred pounds of like lawful money to be paid at the expiration of one whole year next after my decease provided as always and as to and concerning all such of the said charitable and other legacies hereinbefore given as to which I have made no direction for the payment of interest thereon I hereby generally direct and declare that although it is my wish that any said Executor should pay the same respectively at the times several times hereinbefore mentioned for the payment thereof respectively yet the same shall not bear any interest notwithstanding the same may not be paid at such appointed days of payment and I give devise and bequeath unto my said Nephew James Anthony Wickham all that my messuage or tenement estate and premises called Mendip Lodge with all its furniture and pictures together with such ornamental china as belongs to or is usually used or enjoyed with my said house at Mendip Lodge and all and singular my freehold and leasehold messuages lands tenements hereditaments [any kind of property which can be inherited]. and premises in the several parishes of Churchill and Burrington aforesaid and wheresoever otherwise situate with their and every of their appurtenances to hold the same unto and to the use of the said James Anthony Wickham his heirs executors administrators and assigns according to the nature and quality thereof respectively upon and for the trust intents and purposes and with under and subject to the powers provisions and declarations hereinafter expressed of an concerning the same (that is to say) upon Trust that he the said James Anthony Wickham his heirs executors administrators and assigns do and shall as soon as maybe after my decease absolutely sell and dispose of the said messuages or tenement and estate called Mendip Lodge and other the freehold and leasehold estates and premises hereinbefore lastly devised and bequeathed to him in manner aforesaid either together or in parcels by public auction or private contract to any person or persons willing to become the purchaser or purchasers thereof respectively for such price or prices or sum or sums or money as to the said James Anthony Wickham his heirs executors administrators and assigns shall seem reasonable or so and shall complete and fulfil such contracts or agreements (if any) as I may have entered into for the sale of all or any part or parts of the same premises and which may be subsisting at my decease And of promoting and facilitating such sale or sales and the completion of such contracts and agreements (if any) as aforesaid so and shall enter into make or execute all such contracts covenants agreements conveyances assignments assurances acts deeds matters and things which to the said James Anthony Wickham his heirs executors administrators and assigns shall seem meet and do and shall stand possessed of and interested in the purchase or consideration money to arise or come to his or their hand or hands

Top of Page 9

or from or upon such sale or sales or the completion of such contracts and agreements (if any) as aforesaid and which shall remain after full payment and satisfaction of all and any of the costs charges and expenses of such sale or sales or otherwise attending the execution of the aforesaid trusts upon and fir the trusts intents and purposes hereinafter declared and expressed of and concerning the same (that is to say) upon trust that he or they so and shall by with and out of the said monies in the first place pay and satisfy unto Captain John Davie of the Royal Navy of Exeter in the said county of Devon his executors administrators or assigns all and such sum or sums as now are or at the time of my decease shall be owing by me to the said John Davie it being my intention that my general personal estate shall be exonerated from the payment thereof. And so and shall in the next place raise

and pay the several legacies or sums of lawful money of Great
Britain hereinafter mentioned (that is to say) the sum of two
thousand pounds to unto Hyde Salmon Whalley (in addition to
the note of hand so hereinbefore directed .to be given up to him
as aforesaid) the said legacy of two thousand pounds to be paid
to him as soon as maybe after such sale or sales as aforesaid And
the sum of three hundred pounds unto the said Hill Dawe
Wickham to be vested in the said Hill Dawe Wickham as and
when he shall attain his age of twenty one years and payable at
such his age or the expiration of one year after my decease which
shall last happen. And the sum of eight hundred pounds unto the
said James Anthony Wickham and his oldest son Whalley
Wickham of North Hill Aforesaid Esquire their executors
administrators or assigns but the said sum of eight hundred
pounds to be paid by them upon and for the trusts intents and
purposes and with under and subject to the powers provisions
and declarations hereinafter declared expressed or contained of
and concerning the same. And the sum of five hundred pounds
unto Frances Davie of Exeter spinster (the cousin of my first dear
and excellent wife Elizabeth Whalley and sister of the said
Eleanora Lewis the older and Eustacia Sharp and Harriet Davie)
and the sum of three hundred pounds unto Charlotte Debrisay
of Ilfracombe in Devonshire (Widow of the late Lieutenant
Colonel Debrisay and another sister of the said last mentioned
ladies). And the like sum of three hundred pounds to Mary Jones
the wife of Captain Jones of Ireland being also another sister of
the said ladies. And the like sum of three hundred pounds to the
Reverend Charles Davie Rector of Braunton near Barnstaple in
the County of Devon. And the like sum of three hundred pounds
to Captain Peregrine Davie [marginal comment which is
unreadable] now serving in the Madras Army in the East Indies.
And the sum of five hundred pounds unto the said Catherine
Richards. And the sum of five hundred pounds unto her sister
Bridget Richards of Taunton spinsters. And the sum of two
thousand pounds unto the said Catherine Richards and Bridget
Richards but the said sum of two thousand pounds to be held by

them in trust for the benefit of the orphan children of their deaf and dumb brother John Richards late of near Hereford in the County of Hereford deceased in manner hereinafter mentioned. And the sum of two hundred pounds unto Mary Heathcote Spinster now residing in the City of Bath provided always and I hereby direct and declare that all and every of the said sums and legacies hereinbefore directed to be paid out of the purchase monies of my said estates (other than and besides the said several legacies of two thousand pounds to the said Hyde Salmon Whalley and three hundred pounds to the said Hill Dawe Wickham as to the times of payment whereof directions are hereinbefore given) shall if the said Mendip Lodge and other estates hereinbefore directed to be sold shall be sold accordingly within one year after my decease

Top of Page 10

respectively paid and discharged at the expiration of one whole year next after my decease and not before but if such sale shall not take place until after the expiration of such year then the said sums and legacies (other than as aforesaid) shall be respectively paid and discharged so soon as maybe after such sale in which latter case the said several sums or legacies shall respectively bear interest and the rate of four pounds per cent per annum to be paid out of the rent and annual profits of my estates until sold and to commence and be computed from the expiration of one year from my decease and to continue to be payable by equal half yearly portions until the same sums or legacies other than as aforesaid shall in any event be paid or payable at or shall bear interest from an earlier period than the expiration of one whole year next after my decease. And after full payment and satisfaction of the said sums or legacies hereinafter directed to be paid out of the said purchase monies and which said last mentioned legacies I hereby direct shall be a primary charge on the said purchase monies or so and shall by with and out of the said purchase monies or so much thereof as shall remain after satisfying such primary sums and legacies as last aforesaid raise and pay the other legacies or sums of lawful money of Great Britain hereinafter mentioned (that is to say) the sum of three hundred and thirty pounds unto Marianne Somers of spinster (the sister of the said Frances Sayer and Benjamin Somers MD of the parish of Wrington in the county of Somersetshire) and the sum of two hundred pounds to my dear God daughter Cecilia Siddons (the daughter of the said Mrs Sarah Siddons widow) which said last mentioned legacy I intended to have made much larger but severe losses have put it out of my power to do so consistent with my duty and sense of justice to others. And the sum of three hundred pounds unto my dear and highly esteemed friend George Siddons Esquire at present in the service of the Honourable East India Company in Bengal. And the sum of two hundred pounds unto Frances Sullivan widow now residing near the town of La Flèche in the Kingdom of France. And the sum of two hundred and twenty pounds unto Frances Stafford (the wife of Lieutenant Colonel Stafford residing also near La Flèche in France) to be by her paid or applied for or towards the education of her three sons now living or such as may be living at my decease as she me in her discretion think fit. And the receipt of the said France Stafford to be (notwithstanding her coverture) a sufficient discharge for the same. And the sum of three hundred pounds unto the said Reverend Richard Thomas Whalley. And the like sum of three hundred pounds. And the like sum of three hundred pounds unto the said Reverend Thomas Wickham. And the sum of two hundred pounds unto my Great Niece Augusta Edgell of West Allington in Devonshire, spinster. And the sum of one hundred and fifty pounds to the sister of Frances Edgell of West Allington spinster provided always I hereby direct and declare that all and every of the said sums sand legacies hereinbefore lastly directed to be paid out of the said purchase monies shall respectively to be paid and discharged (but without any interest in the meantime in respect thereof) at the expiration of one whole year next after the sale of my said estates so hereinafter directed to be sold as aforesaid. And I hereby declare that if there shall remain any residue or surplus of the said purchase monies after fully paying and answering all and singular the sums and legacies hereinbefore directed to be paid thereout as aforesaid such residue or surplus shall (subject nevertheless and without prejudice to making good any deficiency of my personal estate

Top of Page 11

According to the direction hereinafter in that behalf contained) go remain and belong to the said James Anthony Wickham his executors administrators and assigns for his and their own absolute use and benefit provided always and I hereby desire and recommend that my said nephew James Anthony Wickham his heirs executors or assigns respectively do and shall sell and dispose of Mendip Lodge and other the estates and premises hereinbefore directed to be sold as aforesaid within two years next after my deceases unless such sale or disposition within such period shall in his of their judgement be impracticable or manifestly inexpedient and disadvantageous[2] but so that his present desire or recommendation shall not prejudice and of the trusts or powers hereinbefore or hereinafter contained for or relating to any such sale or disposition nor shall any purchaser or purchasers of the same premises under the said Trust or Powers be bound or concerned to ascertain or enquire in to the necessity propriety or expediency of delaying such sale or disposition until after the said period of two years provided always and as to and concerning as well the said sum of eight hundred pounds hereinbefore bequeathed to the said James Anthony Wickham and Whalley Wickham as also the interest hereinbefore directed to be paid in respect thereof unto the said eight hundred pounds be actually paid or appropriated I hereby direct and declare that the said James Anthony Wickham and Whalley Wickham the executors administrators and assigns shall stand and be of and interested in the same respectively upon and for the trusts intents

---

[2] This seem to have been the provision which allowed his executor James Anthony Wickham to defer the sale of Mendip Lodge

and purposes and with under and subject to the powers provisions and declarations hereinafter declared expressed and contained and concerning the same (that is to say) upon trust that they the said James Anthony Wickham and Whalley Wickham or the survivor of them of the executors administrators or assigns of such survivor or such of them as shall for the time being be acting in the Trusts hereby declared do and shall lay out and invest the said sum of eight hundred pounds in their or his names or name in the parliamentary stocks or public funds of Great Britain or at interest on Government or real securities in England or Wales and do and shall from time to time at their of his direction alter vary or transpose the said trust monies stocks fund sand securities for and into other stocks funds and securities of the like nature and do and shall pay as well the pay the interest to be paid in respect of the said sum of eight hundred pounds until the payment or appropriation thereof as aforesaid as also the dividends and annual produce of the stock funds and securities in or upon which the same when so paid or appropriated shall from time to time be laid out or invested unto or permit the same to be received by the said Frances Sullivan her assigns during her life and from and immediately after her decease do and shall pay the said dividends interest and annual product to such person or persons for such ends intents and purposes and generally in such manner as the said Frances Stafford (the wife of the said Lieutenant Colonel Stafford) shall by any writing or writings under her hand (notwithstanding her present or any future coverture [position of a married woman under the protection of her husband] direct and appoint and in default of such direction or appointment and so far as no such direction or appointment shall extend into the proper hands of the said Frances Stafford for her own sole separate and peculiar use and benefit so that the same may not be subject of liable to the debts control interference or engagements of the present or any future

Top of Page 12

412

husband and I hereby declare that the receipts of the said Frances Stafford or her appointees shall (notwithstanding her coverture) be good and sufficient discharges for the same and subject to such life interests of the said Frances Sullivan and Frances Stafford respective in the said dividends interest and annul produce as aforesaid and I declare that the said sum of eight hundred and the stocks funds securities in or upon which the same shall be laid out or invested and as well the interest to be paid in respect of the said sum of eight hundred pounds until the payment or appropriation thereof as aforesaid as also (after such payment or appropriation) the dividends interest or annual product of the said stock funds and securities shall be in trust for all and every the daughter or daughters now living of the said Lieut Colonel Stafford by the said Frances Stafford his wife who shall be living at my decease and shall attain or have attained the age of twenty one years or shall marry or have married under that age to be divided between and amongst such daughters is more than one in equal shares or if but one then the whole to be in trust for that one daughter provided always and as to and concerning as well the said sum of two thousand pounds hereinbefore given to the said Catherine Richards and Bridget Richards out of the produce of the said Mendip Lodge and other estates hereinbefore directed to be sold in manner aforesaid as also the interest and hereinbefore directed to be paid in respect thereof until the sum be actually paid. I hereby direct and declare that the said Catherine Richards there executors administrators and assigns shall stand and be possessed of and interested in the same respectively upon and for the trusts intents and purposes and with under and subject to the powers provisions and declarations hereinafter declared expressed and contained of and concerning the same (that is to say) upon trust that they the said Catherine Richards and Bridget Richards or the survivor of them or the executors administrators or assigns of such survivor or such of them as shall for the time being be acting in the execution of the trust herby declared do and shall lay out and invest the said sum of two thousand pounds in their or her names or name in the parliamentary stocks or public funds of Great Britain or at interest on Government or real securities in England or Wales and so and shall from time to time at their or her discretion alter vary and transfer the said trust monies stocks funds and securities for and into other stocks funds and securities of the like nature and do and shall stand and be possessed of and interested in the said sum of two thousand pounds and the stocks funds and securities in or upon which the same shall be laid out or invested as well as the interest to be paid in respect in respect of the said sum of two thousand pounds until; payment thereof as aforesaid as also (after such payment) the dividends interest and annul product of the said stocks funds and securities in trust for all and every of the child or children of the said John Richards their brother deceased who shall be living at my decease and being a son or sins shall attain or have attained the age of twenty one years or being a daughter or daughters shall attain or have attained the said age or marry or have married under that age to be divided between or amongst the said children if more than one in equal shares and if but one then the whole to be in trust for that one child provided always and as well in respect of the said last mentioned trust

Top of Page 13

monies stocks funds and securities as likewise in respect of the Trusts monies stocks funds and securities hereinbefore directed to be in trust for the daughters of the said Lieutenant Colonel Stafford and Frances Stafford his wife (subject nevertheless without prejudice to the life interest of the said Frances Sullivan and Frances Stafford in the interest dividends and annual product of the said last mentioned trust monies stock funds securities as aforesaid) I hereby declare that in the meantime and until the vesting of the shares and proportions thereof respectively hereinbefore provided for the Daughters now living of the said Lieutenant Colonel Stafford and Frances Stafford his wife or for the children of the said John Richards respectively the said respective trustees of the said several trust monies stocks funds and securities or such of them respectively as may for the time being be acting in the Trusts hereinbefore declared thereof respectively may at their his or her discretion pay or apply all or any part of the interest dividends and annual product of the share or portion shares or portions to which any such daughter or daughters child or children may be respectively entitled in expectancy for or towards his or her of their maintenance education and benefit and may also at their his her discretion advance any part not exceeding one moiety of such exportant share or proportion or share or proportions of any such daughter or daughters child or children respectively for or towards his her or their advancement or establishment in the world and shall and may accumulate by repeated investments in any of the stocks funds or securities hereinbefore mentioned the surplus or residue of the said interest dividends and annual product which shall respectively remain after such application for maintenance education or otherwise as aforesaid and the respective accumulations so to arise shall respectively belong to and be in trust for the person or persons who shall ultimately become entitled to the respective funds whence the same shall respectively proceeded provided always and I hereby declare that if no daughter of the said Lieutenant Colonel Stafford and Frances Stafford his wife of no child of the said John Richards shall under the several trusts aforesaid become entitled to the several trust monies stocks funds securities and the interest dividends and annual product thereof respectively then in each and either of the said events the said several trust monies stocks funds securities interest dividends and annual product or such of them as shall so fail to become vested as last aforesaid or such part thereof respectively as shall not have been paid or applied for the purposes hereinbefore mentioned and under the powers and authorities hereinbefore contained shall (subject nevertheless and without prejudice to the life interests hereinbefore given to the said Frances Sullivan and Frances Stafford in the manner aforesaid) belong to and be in trust for the said James Anthony

Wickham his executors administrators and assigns for his and their own absolute use and benefit provided always that that if the said Mendip Lodge and other estates hereinbefore directed to be sold as aforesaid or any part of parts thereof shall be sold in my lifetime or if the monies to arise upon any sale or disposition thereof under the trust in [unreadable word] of this my will shall be any reason or means whatsoever fail or prove insufficient to fully answer and satisfy all of the several charges sums and legacies by this will made payable thereout and my personal estate shall prove more than sufficient fully to answer and satisfy all of the several legacies sums and an annuities by this my will made payable thereout or if my personal estate shall by any reason or means whatsoever fail or prove insufficient

Top of Page 14

fully to answer and satisfy all the several legacies sums and annuities so payable thereout as aforesaid and the product from such sale or disposition of the said Mendip Lodge and other estates as aforesaid shall prove more than sufficient fully to answer and satisfy all the several charges sums and legacies so payable there out as aforesaid then and in either of the said cases the several charges sums legacies or annuities whose fund of payment shall so fail or prove insufficient shall not nor shall any part thereof be adeemed [?] or otherwise prejudiced by such failure or insufficiency but the same or so much thereof respectively as the fund so failing or proving insufficient shall fail to answer shall be paid and payable so far as may be by and out of the surplus or residue of the other fund remaining after full payment and satisfaction of the several charges legacies sums or annuities payable out of such last mentioned funds and shall be paid and payable out of such surplus or residue as nearly as may be at such time with such interest (if any) and with such priority (if any) inter se and generally in such manner as the same are hereinbefore directed to be respectively paid and payable out of the fund hereinbefore originally appropriated to their payment and as to all the rest residue and remainder and my real and personal estate whatsoever and wheresoever not hereinbefore specifically or otherwise disposed of I give and devise and bequeath the same unto and to the use of the same James Anthony Wickham his heirs executors administrators and assigns respectively all the estates which at the time of my deceases shall be vested in me upon any trusts or by way of mortgages or security of which I have power to dispose by this my will with their rights members appurtenances to have and to hold the same premises unto the said James Anthony Wickham his heirs executors administrators and assigns respectively according to the nature and quality of the redemption which at the time of my decease shall be subsisting or capable of taking effect therein respectively but the money secured on such mortgages or securities or so much thereof respectively as shall be due and owing to me and my estate to be considered and taken as part of my personal estate and I hereby declare that the receipts in writing of the said James Anthony Wickham his heirs executors or administrators for any sum or sums of money payable to them or him for the purchase of my said estates or any part thereof or otherwise under or by virtue of this my will and generally the receipts of all and every the respective trustees hereinbefore appointed or to be appointed after my decease as hereinbefore mentioned or of such of the said respective trustees as shall for the time being be acting in the trusts hereby in him of them respectively reposed [?] or whereof he or they shall be appointed a trustee or trustees shall be good and effectual releases for the money therein respectively acknowledged to be received and shall to all intents and purposes discharge the person or persons taking any such receipt his her or their heirs executors or administrators from seeing to the application or being accountable or answerable for the misapplication or non application of the same or any part thereof And I herby authorise my said executor to pay any debts owing by me or claimed from me or my real or personal estate upon any evidence he shall think proper and to accept and security real or personal for any debt or debts owing to me or my estate and also to allow such time for the payment thereof as to him shall appear reasonable provided always and I hereby declare my will and mind to be that if the said James Anthony Wickham, Whalley Wickham, William Bromley, Catherine Richards Bridget Richards, or any or either of them or their or any or either of their heirs executors or administrators or the trustees to be appointed as hereinafter is mentioned or any of them or their or any of their heirs executors administrators or assigns shall depart this life or decline of become incapable to act in the trusts hereby reposed in him or them respectively or whereof he or they shall be so respectively appointed a trustee or trustees as hereinafter is mentioned then if the person so dying declining or becoming incapable as aforesaid shall be the said James Anthony Wickham it shall (as to and concerning every or any of the devises, bequests trusts and purposes of any for which he is hereinbefore appointed the sole trustee) be lawful for the said James Anthony Wickham or any other trustee or trustees dying declining of becoming incapable in manner aforesaid it shall be lawful for the surviving or continuing trustee or trustees of the trust estates monies or premises the trustee or trustees whereof shall so depart this life or decline of become incapable to act as aforesaid or the executors or administrators of the last surviving or continuing trustee by any writing or writings under their his or her hands or hand to appoint any person or person to be a trustee or trustees in the event of the trustee or trustees so dying or refusing or becoming incapable to act therein as aforesaid so as in every case to make up and complete the full number of two trustees and that upon every such appointment the said trust estate monies and premises shall be conveyed assigned and transferred so and in such manner that the same may become vested in the new trustee or trustees jointly with the surviving or continuing trustee or trustees or solely as occasion may require and every such new trustee shall have such and the same powers and authorities and discretion to all intents and purposes as if he had been originally nominated a trustee in this my Will provided and I hereby declare that the said several trustees hereby nominated and appointed or to be appointed by virtue of the proviso hereinbefore lastly contained and each and every of them and their and each and every of their heirs executors and administrators and assigns shall be charged and chargeable respectively only for such monies as they shall respectively actually receive by virtue of the trusts hereby in them respectively exposed notwithstanding his of their or any of their giving or signing or joining in giving or signing any receipt or receipts for the sake of conformity and every one or more of them shall not be answerable or accountable for the other or others of them of for acts receipts and neglects[?] or defaults of the other or others of them shall not be answerable or accountable for any Bank or Broker or other person with whom or in whose hands any part of the said Trust monies shall or may be deposited or lodged for the safe custody or otherwise in the execution or the trusts hereinbefore mentioned and that they or any of them shall not be answerable or accountable for

Top of Page 16

the insufficiency or deficiency of any security or securities stocks or funds in or upon which the said trust monies or any part thereof shall be placed out or invested or for or for any other involuntary loss or damage that may happen in the execution of the aforesaid trusts or in relation thereto except the same shall happen by or through their own wilful default respectively And also that it shall be lawful for the trustees hereinbefore named and such future trustee or trustees hereinbefore named and such future trustee or trustees to be appointed as aforesaid and every and any of them their and every of their heirs executors or administrators and assigns by and out of the monies which shall come to their respective hands by virtue of the trusts aforesaid to retain to and reimburse himself and themselves respectively

419

and also to allow to this and their co-trustee and co-trustees all costs charges damages and expenses which they or any of them shall or may suffer sustain expend disburse be at or be put unto in or about the execution of the aforesaid trusts or in relation thereunto In witness whereof I the said testator Thomas Sedgwick Whalley have to the twenty one preceding sheets of this my Will set my hand and seal this twenty fifth day of June in the year of our Lord one thousand eight hundred and twenty four THOMAS SEDGWICK WHALLEY [his signature] signed sealed and declared by the said testator Thomas Sedgwick Whalley as and for his last Will and Testament in the presence of us who at this request in his presence and in the presence of eachother have hereunto set our names as Witness Josephe Lamoureux [his signature] 23, Green Street Grosvenor Square Housekeeper, Wm Bromley Gray's Inn Sq Cha Parsons [his signature] Clk to Messrs Bromley Grays's Inn Sq

THIS IS A CODICIL to the last Will and Testament of me Thomas Sedgwick Whalley of Bath in the County of Somerset Doctor of Divinity which Will rears date the twenty fifth day of June One thousand eight hundred and twenty four. I hereby give and bequeath unto Eleanor the wife of the Reverend Lewis in my said Will named the sum of four hundred pounds of lawful money of Great Britain in addition to and by way of augmentation of the legacy of one thousand one hundred pounds give to her by my said will Also I hereby give and bequeath unto Eleanora the Daughter of the said Reverend [space left for forename] Lewis and now the wife of [space left for name] Bishop of Llandillo in the County of Carmarthenshire the sum of two hundred pounds of like lawful money in addition to and by way of augmentation to the legacy of five hundred pounds given to her by my said Will Also I hereby give and bequeath unto Maria Somers in my said will named the sum of fifty pounds in addition to and by way of augmentation to the legacy of one hundred pounds given to her

Top of Page 17

420

by my said will Also I hereby give and bequeath unto Frances Sayer the sum of five pounds in addition to and by way of augmentation of the legacy of fifty pounds given to her by way of my said Will Also I herby give and bequeath unto me servant John Clarke if he shall be in my service at the time of my decease the sum of ninety five pounds in addition to and by way of augmentation of the legacy of two hundred and twenty pounds given to him by my said Will and also an annuity or clear yearly sum of twenty pounds of like lawful money for his life the first payment of the said annuity to commence six months after my decease Also I hereby give and bequeath unto Diana Anstey Calvert in my said Will names the sum of Sixty pounds of like lawful money in addition to and by way of augmentation of the legacy of fifty pounds given to her by my said Will Also I hereby give and bequeath unto Frances Davie also named in my said Will the sum of one hundred and fifty pounds of like lawful money in addition to and by way of augmentation of the legacy of five hundred pounds given to her by my said Will Also I hereby give and bequeath unto George Siddons also named in my said Will the sum of one hundred pounds of like lawful money in addition and by way of augmentation of the legacy of three hundred pounds thereby given to him by my said Will. Also I hereby give and bequeath unto my niece Frances Sullivan widow also named in my said Will the sum of two thousand pounds of like lawful money in addition to and by way of augmentation to the legacy of two hundred pounds thereby given to her. And I hereby declare that the said increased legacy of two thousand two hundred pounds shall be for her sole and separate use and benefit so that the same may not be subject or liable to the control debts interference or engagements of any future husband of the said Frances Sullivan and that her receipt shall notwithstanding any coverture be a good and sufficient discharge for the same Also I hereby give and bequeath unto the Reverend Richard Thomas Whalley also named in the said Will the sum of twenty pounds of like lawful money in addition to and by way of augmentation of the legacy of three hundred pounds thereby given to him and the sum of twenty pounds to the Reverend Thomas Wickham also therein named in addition to and by way of augmentation of the legacy of three hundred pounds hereby given to him And I hereby revoke and make void the legacy of one hundred pounds given by my said will to Mrs Sarah Siddons widow and I hereby give and bequeath unto her the said Sarah Siddons in[?] view thereof the sum of fifty pounds only And I hereby also revoke and make void the legacy of two hundred and twenty pounds given by my said Will to Mary Heathcote Spinster and I also revoke and make void the legacy of two thousand pounds given by my said will to Hyde Salmon Whalley therein named in addition to the note of hand therein before directed to be given up to him and which direction I hereby confirm. And I hereby also revoke and make void the legacy of two hundred pounds given by my said Will to my God daughter Cecilia Siddons and I hereby give and bequeath unto the said Cecilia Siddons in lieu thereof the sum of fifty pounds only. Also I give and bequeath unot Hill Dawe Wickham named in my said Will the sum of two hundred pounds of like lawful money in addition to and by way of augmentation of the legacy of three hundred pounds thereby given to him and I hereby give and bequeath unto Thomas Lewis of Gwinfe in the County of

Top of Page 18

Carmarthen aforesaid the sum of one hundred and fifty pounds of like lawful money and to Lewis Lewis [sic] of Gwinfe aforesaid his brother the sum of one hundred pounds of like lawful money. And I give and bequeath unto Miss Iles of Chalford near Stroud in Gloucestershire the sum of three hundred pounds of like lawful money And I hereby give and bequeath unto my dear god daughter Mrs Louisa Ffisher late Miss Sparrow of Bourton in the County of Somerset the sum of fifty pounds of like lawful money And I hereby also give and bequeath unto Miss Sarah Sparrow of Bourton in the County of Somerset the sum of twenty pounds of like lawful money for a ring And I give and bequeath unto the

422

said Frances Sullivan all the silver articles which I have reserved for my own use as well as all the furniture of my house on Windsor Terrace Clifton with the three cabinets bequeathed in my said will to Mary Agnes Wickham now Mary Agnes Ffawcet (and which bequest I hereby revoke except the pictures of all kinds) And I hereby give and bequeath unto Whalley Wickham the eldest son of my executor James Anthony Wickham the sum of two hundred pounds of like lawful money and also my state trials [? perhaps the Howells State Trials] And I hereby declare that since the date of my said Will I have given unto the said Mary Agnes Ffawcet all my books (pictures China and Glass then in my said house at Clifton except such as are hereinafter mentioned) And I have also given And I have also given away all my household linen since the date of my said Will also all my plate except the few articles reserved for my own use and herby given to the said Frances Sullivan And I have likewise given away all my coins to the said Hill Wickham and I hereby declare that my mind and Will is that the said Frances Sullivan should be joint residuary devisor and legatee of my real and personal estate together with the said James Anthony Wickham who is appointed such residuary Deviser and Legatee in my said Will and therefore I hereby revoke and make void the devise and bequest of such residue as well as the ultimate residue of the purchase monies of my real Estate in my said Will made to the said James Anthony Wickham and hereby give and devise and bequeath all the reside and remainder of my real and personal estate not disposed of by my said Will or by this codicil thereto unto and to the use of the said James Anthony Wickham and Frances Sullivan their heirs executors and assigns for ever for their own absolute use and benefit as tenants in common and not as joint tenants but in case [obscured or erase words] either of my said residuary devisees and legatees shall happen to depart this life before my decease then as to one moiety or half part of the share of him or her so dying I give devise and bequeath the same unit the said Hill Dawe Wickham his heirs executors and assigns for ever for his own absolute use and benefit And as to the other moiety or half part thereof I give devise and bequeath the same unto Suzanna Whalley and Caroline Whalley the daughters of the said Hyde Salmon Whalley share and share alike as tenants in common and not as joint tenants to be vested in them at my decease but to be paid and transferred when and as soon as the shall respectively attain the age of twenty one years or marry and I herby direct that in the mean time the interest rents and annual produce of such share of my said residue shall be paid to [left blank] the wife of the said Hyde Salmon Wickham to be applied by her for and towards the maintenance education and bringing up of the said Suzanna Whalley and Caroline Whalley respectively And I herby declare that the receipt alone notwithstanding her

Top of Page 19

Present or any future coverture shall be a sufficient discharge for the same Nevertheless I hereby declare that the above revocation of the devise and bequest of the residue of my real and personal estate made to the said James Anthony Wickham by my said Will does not extend to the devise of all Estates vested in me by way of trust or mortgage but I herby confirm the devise of such estates made to the said James Anthony Wickham by my said Will And I hereby direct and declare that the Annuity or [?] yearly sum of twenty pounds hereby given to the said John Clarke shall be raised and paid out of the same fund as the said legacy given to him by my said Will is directed to be paid And my mind and will is that all such Legacies as are decreased or augmented by this codicil shall be payable out of the same fund and at the same time and enjoyed in the same manner and subject to the same contingencies as the original legacies would have been under the directions of my said Will it being my desire that the only alteration in the said legacies should be in the amounts of them respectively subject nevertheless to the further directions and provisions hereinafter mentioned that is top say and I herby direct and declare that all and every the pecuniary legacies not including those by way of annuity) (*NB no left bracket*) in and by my said Will and this present

424

codicil or either of them given and bequeathed and which shall be payable after my decease whether for charitable purposes otherwise and upon or out of whatsoever fund or part of my property or the produce thereof the same may be chargeable or payable (*other than and except the several legacies or sums of two guineas each in and by my said Will respectively given and bequeathed to the poor men who shall bear my coffin and their respective wives as in my said Will mentioned and which said several hereby excepted legacies I intend shall be paid at the several times and in the manner in and by my said Will mentioned and directed in that behalf*) shall not nor shall any of them be raised or paid to the several legatees to whom the same are respectively mentioned and limited (that is to say all such of the said pecuniary legacies as shall severally and respectively independently of interest) exceed in amount the sum of one hundred and fifty pounds and shall be primarily charged upon and be paid out of any part of my property or produce thereof other than out of the monies to arise by the sale of the Mendip Lodge estate and others the estates and premises in and by my said Will thereby devised and bequeathed in trust for sale as therein mentioned) shall not be raised or paid until after the expiration of four years to be computed from the fifteenth day of January one thousand eight hundred and twenty six and all such of the said pecuniary legacies as shall severally and respectively (independently of interest) exceed in amount the sum of one hundred and fifty pounds and shall be primarily charged upon or payable out of the monies to arise out of the sale of the Mendip Lodge estate and other the estates and premises in and by my said Will therein mentioned shall not be raised or paid until the expiration of three years to be computed from the time of such sale being made And all such of the said primary legacies out of whatsoever funds or part pf my property of the produce there of the same way be payable as shall not (independently of interest) exceed in amount

Top of Page 20

425

the sum of one hundred and fifty pounds shall not be raised or paid until after the expiration of fifteen calendar months from and after my decease provided always and I hereby declare my Will to be that although certain of the said pecuniary legacies the payment whereof is in hereinbefore postponed as aforesaid are or may be in and by my said Will and this Codicil or out of them directed or mentioned to bear interest as from a particular time until payment thereof respectively nevertheless the same respectively shall not carry interest until the expiration of those periods for which the payment of the same is so respectively postponed as aforesaid or until such respective times after the expiration of the said respective periods of postponement during which the payment or commencement whereof is hereinbefore postponed in manner aforesaid (other than and except the legacy of two hundred and twenty pounds by my said Will bequeathed to Mrs Frances Stafford therein named for the purpose of being applied towards the education of her sons as in my said Will mentioned and the two several sums of eight hundred pounds and two thousand pounds respectively thereby bequeathed the former to the said James Anthony Wickham and his son Whalley Wickham and the latter to the said Catherine Richards and Bridget Richards upon and for the several trusts and purposes therein declared and contained thereof respectively) shall be vested interests until the expiration of the several periods during which the payment or commencement thereof respectively is hereinbefore postponed as aforesaid And in the event of the several persons to whom the same pecuniary legacies so postponed as aforesaid (other than the said three several Trusts legacies hereinbefore excepted) respectively dying before the expiration of such several periods of postponement his or her Legacy shall lapse and become void And I hereby further direct and declare that during the several periods for which the payment of such legacies is hereinbefore postponed in manner aforesaid the respective funds or parts of any property or the produce thereof upon or out of which the same several legacies may be respectively primarily charged or payable shall be respectively accumulated in the way of compound interest in manner hereinafter mentioned And for that purpose I direct and declare that my nephew the said James Anthony Wickham (the sole executor and trustee of my said Will named and the joint residuary devisee sand legatee in this Codicil to my said Will named) with the said Frances Sullivan) [sic] or other the person or persons who may be acting in the execution of may said Will and this Codicil do and shall call in receive compel payment of and recover the monies which at or after my decease may be or become owing from Lord Ventry or his trustees to me or my Estate and the several instalments thereof and as and when the same shall from time to time become payable under or in pursuance of the security or trust created for the liquidation of such Debt and do and shall lay out and invest the monies so to be received or recovered as aforesaid in his or their name or names in or upon the parliamentary stocks of public funds of Great Britain or as interest on Government or real securities in England or Wales to be from time to time transferred altered and varied as my said Executor of other the person or persons so

Top of Page 21

acting as aforesaid shall in his or her if their discretion think proper And do and shall with all convenient speed after my decease call in collect sell dispose of and convert into money all and singular (other the personal estate and effects whatsoever other that leasehold estates which are in and by my said Will already made saleable) of or to which I may be possessed or entitled at the time of my decease and not in and by my said Will or this Codicil specifically disposed of and so and shall by with and out of the monies to arise from such calling in collection sale disposition and conversion as last aforesaid pay satisfy and discharge my financial and testamentary expenses and debts without prejudice nevertheless to my general personal Estate being exonerated by my real and leasehold Estates from any debt or debts which under or by virtue of my said Will and this Codicil or either of them may be charged on my said real and Leasehold estates or any part thereof respectively in exoneration of my said general personal estate) And do and shall out of the same last mentioned monies set apart and appropriate such a sum of money as together with the accumulations to be made thereof under the direction on this Codicil will in his or their opinion be competent and sufficient to answer the [unreadable word in superscript] several charitable legacies in and by my said Will respectively given and bequeathed the first to or for the benefit of the poor of the parish of Burrington in the County of Somerset the second to or for the benefit of the parish of Churchill and the third for the benefit of the weekly Sunday Schools for the poor in the parish of Hagworthingham in the County of Lincoln as and when the same three special legacies shall from time to time under the direction of my said Will and this Codicil or of either of them become payable and do and shall lay out and invest the sum so to be set apart and appropriated as last aforesaid in his of their name or names in or upon the parliamentary Stocks or public funds of Great Britain or at Interest on such securities as my said executor or other the person or persons so acting as aforesaid may think fit and to be from time to time transposed altered and varied as he of they shall in his or their discretion feel proper And as to all such surplus or residue of the monies to arise from such calling in collection sale disposition and conversion as aforesaid as shall remain after payment and satisfaction of my funeral and testamentary expenses and debts (without prejudice as aforesaid) and after setting apart and appropriating such sum for the said Charitable Legacies as last aforesaid do and shall layout and invest the same in his or their name or names in or upon the parliamentary stocks or public finds of Great Britain at interest on Government or real securities in England or Wales to be from time to time transposed altered and varied as he or they shall in his or their discretion think proper and as to and concerning as well the purchase or consideration monies to arise or come to the hands of the said James Anthony Wickham his heirs executors administrators or assigns by from and upon the sale or sales of

my house and estates called Mendip Lodge and other the estates
and premises in by my said Will thereby devised and bequeathed
In Trust for sale as therein mentioned or from or upon the
completion of such contracts and agreements (if any) for sale of
the same

Top of Page 22

premises or any part or parts thereof as in my said Will particularly
mentioned as likewise the rents and profits of the same estates
and premises in the meantime and until such sale or sales or the
completion of such contracts or agreements (subject nevertheless
and without prejudice to the jointure of five hundred pounds per
annum charges thereon or on some part thereof in favour of my
present wife) I direct and declare that the said James Anthony
Wickham his heirs executors administrators and assigns so and
shall lay out and invest such purchase or consideration monies
and rents and profits respectively (or so much thereof respectively
as shall remain after payment and satisfaction of the costs charges
and expenses payable thereout in his or their name or names in
or upon the parliamentary stocks or public funds of Great Britain
or at interest on Government or real securities in England or
Wales to be from time to time transposed altered and varied as
the said James Anthony Wickham his executors administrators
and assigns may in his or their discretion think proper And as to
and concerning all and singular the several monies and premises
hereinbefore directed to be respectively laid out and invested in
manner aforesaid I direct and declare that he the said James
Anthony Wickham his executors administrators and assigns or
other the person or persons acting in the execution of my said
Will or this Codicil from time to time as the same shall become
respectively due and payable receive the interest dividends and
annual produce of the said several monies and premises and of
the several stocks funds and securities in or upon which the same
may be respectively laid out or invested and layout and invest the
same in his or their name or names in or upon such of the like

stocks funds or securities as are hereinbefore mentioned and directed with reference to the particular monies or funds from which such interest dividends and annual produce may have respectively proceeded to be from time to time transposed altered and varied at his or their discretion and do and shall receive the interest dividends and annual produce of the said several last mentioned stocks funds and securities and lay out and invest the same respectively in his or their name or names upon the like stocks and funds or securities and so and by repeated layings out and investments from time to time in order and so that the same and the resulting income and produce thereof may respectively during the several periods for which the payment of the legacies and commencement of the annuities thereon respectively charged are postponed in manner aforesaid accumulate in the way of compound interest and that the said several dividends interest and annual produce stocks and funds and securities and the several accumulations thereof respectively shall be respectively added and become part of the several funds from which the same accumulations may have respectively proceeded And do and shall upon the expiration of such respective periods of accumulation or from time to time when and as the said several legacies chargeable upon or payable out of the said several monies stocks funds securities and premises and the several accumulations thereof shall respectively become payable to commence and take effect by with and out of the same several monies stocks funds and securities accumulations and premises pay appropriate discharge and satisfy or otherwise only provide for the same legacies

Top of Page 23

so respectively charged thereon or payable thereout as aforesaid and I hereby further direct and declare my will to be that (subject to the payment and satisfaction of the several legacies and annuities out of the several legacies and annuities out of the several funds and generally in the manner in and by my said Will

430

and this Codicil mentioned and directed and to such and the like provision and direction for applying the surplus of any of the said funds towards making up the deficiency of any other or others of them as in my said Will in that behalf contained and mentioned) those accumulations of the said several funds shall go and belong to the said James Anthony Wickham and Frances Sullivan under or by virtue of the residuary devise and bequest in my said Will and this Codicil contained in such or the like manner as if such several, accumulations were respectively part of the several funds from or in respect of which the same may have respectively arisen or proceeded And I hereby further direct and declare that as between the several legatees or annuitants whose pecuniary legatees or annuities are under or by virtue of my said Will and this Codicil or either of them primarily charged upon or payable out of one and the same funds or part of my Estate and property or of the produce thereof such of the said legatees or annuitants as are relations of my first and second wives shall be preferred to my own relatives and to all other legatees or annuitants claiming out of the same fund and shall have their several legacies and annuities respectively paid and satisfied or otherwise only provided for before the several legacies or annuities given to my own relations or to any of the other legatees or annuitants claiming out of the same funds shall be paid satisfied or provided for provided always and I hereby direct and declare my Will to be that it shall be lawful for the said James Anthony Wickham his heirs administrators and assigns respectively (according to the nature and quality of the same estates and premises) from time to time after my decease until and sale of the estates and premises in and by my said Will devised and bequeathed to him in trust for sale as aforesaid to demise[?] or lease the house and premises on Windsor Terrace Clifton in the county of Gloucester (lately taken by me for a term of seven years) with the appurtenances to any person or persons for all or any part of the term or interest which I may have therein at my decease And likewise from time to time until such sale to demise or lease the other estates and premises devised and bequeathed In trust for sale as aforesaid or any part or parts thereof respectively with the appurtenances to any person or persons for any term of year not exceeding twenty one years so that any and every such demise or lease of any said house and premises at Clifton aforesaid or of any said other estates and premises or any part thereof as aforesaid be made to take effect in possession and at rack rent [i.e extortionate rent] but otherwise on such terms and conditions as he or they may in their discretion think proper. And I hereby given and bequeath unto the said Frances Sullivan all the rent which the said house at Clifton may let for over above that which is payable to Mr Isaac Cook solicitor under my lease of the same And as to all and singular other my paintings drawings engravings which shall belong to me at the time of my decease (other than and except the portrait in crayon of my said dear wife and the several miniature pictures in my by my said Will respectively given and bequeathed to Catherine

Top of Page 24

Richards therein named and also the miniature pictures in and by my said Will given and bequeathed to the said Eleanor Lewis and which several bequest of the said excepted portrait and miniature pictures in and by my said Will given and bequeathed to the said Eleanor Lewis and which several bequests of the said excepted portrait and miniature pictures in my said Will contained as last aforesaid I do hereby confirm) I give and bequeath the same unto and among the said James Anthony Wickham and Richard Thomas Whalley and Hyde Whalley of Midsomer Norton Esquire to be divided between them in equal third parts as tenants in common And I give and bequeath unto the infant and only daughter of the said Captain John Davie deceased the sum of three hundred pounds of like lawful money to become an interest vested in her at the age of eight years but to be paid and payable to the said daughter of the said Captain John Davie deceased out of my general personal estate on her attaining twenty one years of age with the dividends and interest thereon to accumulate in the mean time And as to and concerning the bequest directions and disposition in my said Will contained of or respecting my eight Coal Canal Shares and my estate and interest thereon and the dividends income and other annul or periodical profits arising in respect thereof to or in favour of the said William Walter Slade Amans for his life and after his decease to or in favour of my great nieces Agnes Wickham and Caroline Wickham in manner therein particularly mentioned I do hereby revoke and make void all and every the said bequest directions and dispositions of an concerning the same to all intent and purposes whatsoever the said shares having been given away by me to some time since to my niece Agnes Wickham And I hereby ratify and confirm my said Will save and so far as the same is not revoked or altered by this present Codicil It witness thereof I the said Thomas Sedgwick Whalley the testator have to this Codicil to my last Will and Testament contained in twelve sheets of paper set my hand and to this twelfth and last sheet thereof my hand and seal this fourteenth day of July in the year of our Lord one thousand eight hundred and twenty eight   THOMAS S WHALLEY Signed sealed published declared by the said Thomas Sedgwick Whalley the testator as and for a Codicil to his last Will and Testament in the presence of us who in his presence at his request and in the presence of each other have thereunto subscribed out names as witnesses S.A Notcutt Junr   C.W.Rolfe CP Parsons Clerk to Messrs Bromley Gray's Inn

[Then, on what appears to be the same sheet, which means that it was added as a translation from the version written in French one month later and, as it appears to be in the same hand (and as a continuation of the same sheet as the Codicil above), copied in Messrts Bromley's Gray's in office]

I Thomas Sedgwick Whalley DD do hereby acknowledge to you the Executor of my last Will and Testament that I owe my niece Mrs Frances Elizabeth Sullivan otherwise Sage widow of the late Revr. Boyle Sullivan residing at La

Flèche Department of the Sarthe In France the sum of one thousand and fifty two pounds sterling which she lent to me and which I am bound to repay her as follows Viz four hundred and fifty two pounds sterling on the twenty fifth day of December one thousand eight hundred and twenty eight and six hundred pounds sterling on the twenty fifth day of June one thousand eight hundred and twenty nine I order you the Executor of my last Will and testament in case my death should take place before the payment of the abovementioned Debt to pay my niece Mrs Frances Elizabeth Sullivan the aforesaid sum of One thousand and fifty two pounds sterling out of my property before any Legacy or other sum of money whatsoever that may be claimed upon my property I approv'd entirely by me with the erasure of certain words as above four hundred and fifty two pounds sterling being to be paid to my niece Mrs Sullivan by my nephew and executor James Anthony Wickham Esq of North Hill in Somersetshire in England on the twenty fifth day of December one thousand eight hundred and twenty eight the larger sum of six hundred pounds on the twenty fifth day of June one thousand eight hundred and twenty nine both the above sums to be paid as soon as possible after my decease Dated the 11th day of August at La Flèche in France sign'd with my own hand in the year of our Lord 1828 Thomas S Whalley [signature]

APPENDIX 6
The Jane Austen Connection

It seems highly likely that Jane (1775-1817) and her family knew
of Thomas Sedgwick Whalley by reputation even if they did not
know him personally. Many names of people Thomas Sedgwick
knew appear in Jane's correspondence.[1]

Jane's father, George Austen, and his sisters had the
misfortune of losing both parents when they were very young.
George was lucky to have been brought up by an aunt and sent
to Tonbridge School. His sister Phila was not so fortunate. After
training as a milliner she made her way to India to find a rich
husband and a way out of her poverty, as many good looking
ladies did. A companion on the boat was Margaret Maskelyne,
sister of the Reverend Dr Nevil Maskelyne, the fifth Astronomer
Royal. Margaret would become a good friend and went on to
marry Robert Clive Governor of Bengal. At about the same time
Phila married Tysoe Hancock, through whom she met Warren
Hastings, who would become the first Governor General of India.
Hastings knew Isaac Sage and had recommended him for the
Governorship of Patna.[2] To supplement his income, the Rev
George Austen took in students, turning the Steventon parsonage
into a private boarding school. These young men included the
son of Warren Hastings. In 1761 Phila gave birth to her only
child, Elizabeth; Warren Hastings was reputedly the father, and
he certainly supported the child very generously. The experiences

---

[1] *Jane Austen's Letters* LeFaye, D., (Ed). Oxford University Press, 3rd Ed.,
Oxford, 1995.
[2] JCTSW I p.309

of Phila and her daughter would later become woven into Jane's novels.

The Rev George Austen (1731-1805) was married at Walcot in Bath in 1764 and from 1773 onward took a series of well connected boys as pupils to supplement the family income at the Steventon village rectory. Jane's mother, Cassandra (née Leigh; 1739-1827), was a contemporary of Thomas Sedgwick Whalley and spent her youth in Bath and so knew it well. Jane Austen's aunt, her mother's elder sister, Jane Leigh, and her husband Revd Dr Edward Cooper lived in Royal Crescent and Bennett Street Bath (1771-1783), although this was before Thomas Sedgwick and his wife bought their house there. The Reverend Cooper, like Thomas Sedgwick, was a Prebend of Wells Cathedral, though senior to him, and both became Doctors of Divinity, yet there is no mention of either the Leigh or Cooper families in Hill Wickham's two volumes.

Jane Austen's uncle, her mother's elder brother, James Leigh Perrot (1735-1812) and his wife, Jane Cholmeley (1744-1836), were a wealthy couple who were always referred to in Jane's letters as 'my uncle and my aunt'. The Leigh Perrots soon developed the habit of spending half the year on their estate in Berkshire and the other half in Bath at No 1 Paragon Buildings. This is precisely what the Whalley's were accustomed to doing, alternating between Mendip Lodge in Upper Langford and Royal Crescent in Bath.

Jane probably knew Fanny Burney personally, as Jane's godfather Samuel Cook was a close friend of Burney. Jane admired Fanny Burney's first novel *Evelina* and was one of the subscribers to her third novel *Camilla*, published in 1796. Fanny Burney had been a guest of the Whalleys in Bath in 1780, and a number of his friends were also subscribers (Hannah More, Humphrey Repton, Rev William Mason, Mrs Porteus). Mrs Piozzi and her daughters subscribed to twelve copies between them; Thomas Sedgwick himself did not subscribe, but at the time his niece Frances was going through her divorce and perhaps he had no desire to read such things.

Jane Austen's first novel, *Lady Susan*, copied the epistolary style of Fanny Burney's *Evelina*. It was probably written in 1793-4, though the only known manuscript is a copy dated 1805.[3] The locations of 'Langford' and 'Churchill' as the addresses of the two main characters, Lady Susan and Mrs Vernon, are intriguing. By this time Thomas Sedgwick Whalley had completed the building of his Cottage at Langford, later to become known as Mendip Lodge, and was entertaining the great and good there during the summer months. He was still the owner of Langford Court, although this was let in 1794 to his good friend Henry Bosanquet, who had married Christopher Anstey's daughter Caroline in 1790.[4]

There are no surviving letters of Jane Austen from before 1796, and the date of her first visit to Bath was in November/December 1797, when the 22 year old stayed with the Leigh Perrots in Paragon Buildings. The Whalleys were certainly in Bath at this time.[5] Jane and her family were again in Bath from 17th May 1799 until June 22nd 1799, when they rented 13 Queen Square. Thomas, though, was in London, awaiting the production of his play *The Castle of Montval* at Drury Lane.

Alethea Bigg was a long-standing friend from Austen's childhood at Steventon. Jane had attended the Biggs Manydown Ball, where Cath Bigg was her favourite partner when men were in short supply.[6] This is not surprising, as there were six daughters of Lovelace Withers Bigg living there at the time.[7] Another Elizabeth Bigg married the Reverend William Heathcote (1772-1802), a Prebendary of Winchester who was a relative of Thomas Sedgwick's second wife, Augusta Heathcote of Devizes. Elizabeth Heathcote's name appears in many of Jane's letters, but there is no evidence that the Austens ever had any connection with the Devizes branch of the Heathcote family. William Heathcote died

3 Southam BC., *Jane Austen's Literary Manuscripts,* Clarendon Press, Oxford, 1964

4 *Bath Chronicle and Weekly Gazette,* Tuesday 6th May, 1790

5 JCTSW I p.108

6 Byrne P. *The real Jane Austen.* Harper Press, London, 2013 p.94

7 Bigg Wither, R.F., *A history of the Withers family.* Wykeham Press, Winchester, 1907, p.53

shortly before Augusta, in 1802, whereupon Elizabeth returned to Manydown to become a neighbour of Jane; she had copies of all Jane's books. It is quite certain that Thomas Sedgwick knew the Reverend Gilbert Heathcote, MA Oxon (1765-1829).[8] Gilbert was later Archdeacon of Winchester and eventually became Treasurer of Wells in 1814, under the patronage of Bishop Richard Beadon, who was Thomas Sedgwick's relative. The Reverend Gilbert married Maria Lyell, but it is not clear if she was related to the Lyells mentioned in Jane's correspondence.

It is in *Northanger Abbey*, written in 1798/9 but not published until after Jane's death in 1817, that the Master of Ceremonies of the Lower Rooms, James King, introduces Catherine to the book's hero, Henry Tilney. James King was the Master of the Ceremonies of the Lower Rooms at the time of Jane's visit in 1797 and is one of the few living people to be mentioned in her novels. One wonders if it was his daughter 'Miss King' to whom Miss Weston refers as leading Frances Sage astray in May 1789.[9]

---

[8] No less than 32 Heathcotes graduated from Oxford and 16 of these held holy orders.

[9] JCTSW II p.33

INDEX

NOTES

NOTES

NOTES

NOTES

NOTES